DRESSING FOR THE CULTURE WARS

DRESSING FOR THE CULTURE WARS

STYLE AND THE POLITICS OF SELF-PRESENTATION IN THE 1960s AND 1970s

BETTY LUTHER HILLMAN

UNIVERSITY OF NEBRASKA PRESS | LINCOLN & LONDON

Publication of this volume was assisted by the
Virginia Faulkner Fund, established in memory of
Virginia Faulkner, editor in chief of the University
of Nebraska Press.

Library of Congress Cataloging-in-Publication Data

Luther Hillman, Betty.
Dressing for the culture wars:
style and the politics of self-presentation
in the 1960s and 1970s / Betty Luther Hillman.
pages cm
Includes bibliographical references and index.
ISBN 978-0-8032-6975-0 (cloth: alk. paper)
ISBN 978-0-8032-8444-9 (epub)
ISBN 978-0-8032-8445-6 (mobi)
ISBN 978-0-8032-8446-3 (pdf)
1. Clothing and dress—Sex differences—United
States. 2. Clothing and dress—Social aspects—United
States. 3. Fashion—Social aspects—United States. 4.
Fashion—United States. 5. Feminism—United States. 6.
Sex—United States. 7. Sex role—United States. I. Title.
GT605.H57 2015
391.00973—dc23
2015017201

Set in Sabon Next by M. Scheer.

CONTENTS

ILLUSTRATIONS

ACKNOWLEDGMENTS

This book began as a dissertation during my years in graduate school at Yale University, and both projects have benefited enormously from the guidance and support of my adviser, Joanne Meyerowitz. She has been a wonderful mentor, and I'm grateful to have worked with her. I'm also thankful to Matthew Jacobson, George Chauncey, and Robert Gordon, for their astute comments and suggestions, and to Joanne Freeman, Steve Pitti, John Mack Faragher, and Mary Lui, for their scholarly feedback and support. I am grateful for the invaluable input from Nancy Cott, Nancy Hewitt, Susan Ware, and anonymous readers at a number of scholarly journals. Nancy Hewitt's workshop group at the 2008 Schlesinger Library Summer Seminar on Gender History provided crucial feedback early in my research. Many other friends and colleagues also helped to shape my thoughts on this topic, especially Adam Arenson, Anne Blaschke, Ryan Brasseaux, Debbie Dinner, Brian Distelberg, Kate Kokontis, Ana Minian, Katherine Mooney, Lauren Pearlman, Aaron Potenza, Tim Retzloff, Timothy Stewart-Winter, and Miti von Weissenberg. I'd like to offer special thanks to Stephanie Kenen and Amy Dru Stanley, my mentors at Harvard and the University of Chicago. In particular, I never would have made it through graduate school without Katie Turk. No matter where our paths will lead, I hope we'll continue to be on panels together discussing all that the world needs to know about gender history.

I am thankful to the archivists and librarians who helped me to find critical sources in my research, in particular, Tim Wilson at the San Francisco Public Library, Rebekah Kim at the GLBT Historical Society of Northern California, and Kevin Pacelli and Gregory Eow in the microfilms division at Yale's Sterling Memorial Library. I would like to thank the Woodrow Wilson Foundation, the University of Chicago, and Yale University for their financial support, and Edward Barnaby, Pamela Schirmeister, and especially Marcy Kaufman for their administrative support during my time at Yale.

Alicia Christensen believed in this project and lent her support and advice as I was writing this book. I am grateful for comments from Gael Graham as well as an anonymous reviewer, both of whom seemed to understand what my project was "about" and offered suggestions that helped to strengthen it. Thanks also to Daley El Dorado, Maggie Boyles, and the publication and marketing teams at the University of Nebraska Press. Judy Wu believed in my work and published my article in *Frontiers*, which is what connected Alicia Christensen to me in the first place. She has been a generous mentor, and I'm grateful for her support.

In my quest to find engaging images for this book, I am thankful for the time and generosity of Tricia Gesner, Rosemary Morrow, Nichole Calero, Karen Hagberg, Susan Carter, Jeanne Cordova, Tim Wilson, Jim Baldocchi, Christina Moretta, Merrideth Miller, Meredith Eliassen, Michael Denneny, Marjorie Bryer, Cheryll Fong, Bernard and Howard Gotfryd, and the "wrong" Rita Goldberg.

For three summers during graduate school, I taught history courses at the Center for Talented Youth at Johns Hopkins University, which was always the highlight of my year. I'm particularly indebted to the students in my summer 2009 course, American Studies: The

Sixties, whose insights about cultural and political conflicts in the 1960s helped to shape this project in crucial ways. I'm also grateful to Galen White and many others at CTY for fun times. Teaching at CTY inspired me to return to a career in secondary school teaching, and I'm lucky to have landed at Phillips Exeter Academy, with wonderful students and colleagues. I'm thankful for the support of Meg Foley and Bill Jordan, the previous and current history department chairs, as well as to each of my history colleagues, for their enthusiasm and dedication to the study of history.

Portions of material in chapters 2, 3, and 5 have appeared in an article entitled "'The Clothes I Wear Help Me to Know My Own Power': The Politics of Gender Presentation in the Era of Women's Liberation," published in *Frontiers*. Portions of materials in chapter 4 have appeared in an article entitled "'The Most Profoundly Revolutionary Act a Homosexual Can Engage In': Drag and the Politics of Gender Presentation in the San Francisco Gay Liberation Movement, 1964–1972," published in the *Journal of the History of Sexuality*. My thanks to the editors of those journals for their support of my scholarship.

I am grateful to my family for their love and support. Starting with our weekend-long car trip from Minneapolis to move me into my apartment in Chicago, my father, Mark Luther, has been consistently enthusiastic about my pursuit of education in history, and I know he is very excited to add this book to his long reading list. My mom, Carolyn Ameli, has been continually supportive of me and has also been a huge help in the editing process. I'm lucky to count my twin sister, Beverly Luther, among my fans. I'm also thankful to my grandparents, Shirley and Earl Hill, for their encouragement throughout my life. I am grateful, too, for the support of Phyllis Siracusa, Tamar Siracusa, Robi and John Richards, Carol and Charles Tropp, Jennifer and Howard Sneider, and Laura and Michael Grabowski. Special thanks to Laura for her academic publishing advice and to Charlie for doing the index!

My most important word of thanks goes to my spouse, partner, and best friend, Benjamin Siracusa Hillman. He has provided me so much guidance, encouragement, support, and love throughout this process. From DC to Chicago, New Haven to San Francisco, Brooklyn to New Hampshire and beyond, I'm lucky to have found a partner with whom to share life's adventures. Our biggest adventure so far has been in raising our daughter, Johanna. Tied with Ben, she is my favorite, and I love her more than words can say.

INTRODUCTION

*The Significance of Style in
American Culture and Politics*

The dress and hairstyles of campaign volunteers
are rarely considered significant to politics; but in the 1968 presidential election, hair and dress mattered to the Eugene McCarthy
campaign. McCarthy positioned himself as the anti–Vietnam War
candidate, and hoped to garner the support of youth activists and
college students who had helped to make the war a central political
issue of the election. However, McCarthy also wished to distance himself from the tactics of so-called hippie youths, who irritated political moderates. Therefore, McCarthy's campaign adviser instituted a
strict dress and grooming code for volunteers. Men had to cut their
hair, shave their beards, and wear coats and ties. Women were forbidden from wearing pants or miniskirts. Students who failed to follow
the dress code were turned away, or were moved to the basement of
campaign headquarters to file papers, out of the sight of the public.

FIG. 1. A McCarthy campaign volunteer shaves his beard to get himself "Clean for Gene." Special Collections, University of Minnesota Libraries.

"Clean for Gene" became a slogan of the McCarthy campaign, portraying a "clean-cut," respectable, and gender-normative image for the Democratic candidate.[1]

The "Clean for Gene" campaign slogan is rarely recounted among the significant events of the tumultuous year that was 1968; the assassinations of Martin Luther King and Robert F. Kennedy, the violence at the Democratic National Convention in Chicago, and Richard Nixon's ultimate victory in the presidential election are most often cited as major turning points in the year that allegedly marked the demise of 1960s radicalism and the rise of the New Right political coalition. McCarthy's campaign, however, was not the only time that year that styles of self-presentation became the topics of public debate. Newspapers discussed the wide marketing of unisex fashions

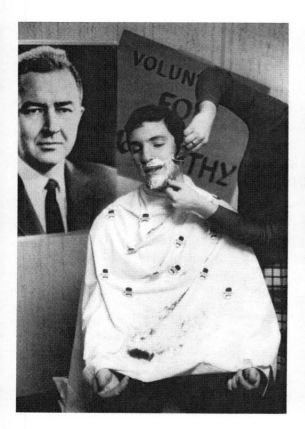

that blurred gender distinctions in clothes and dress; presidential candidate George Wallace derided the long hair and short skirts of student protestors; and women's liberationists demonstrated at the Miss America pageant by throwing cosmetics, girdles, and bras into a "Freedom Trash Can," protesting mainstream fashion and beauty culture as oppressive and objectifying of women.[2]

At the outset, these events might appear to be tangentially related at best, symbols of the restlessness and dissent that characterized the 1960s. However, the examples above illustrate how debates over dress, hair, and self-presentation were deeply implicated in the larger cultural and political struggles of the 1960s and the decades that followed. Bell-bottom jeans, miniskirts, love beads, and long, flowing hairstyles on both men and women are ubiquitous in images of the

1960s. While many scholars have discussed hair and dress styles as part of the history of the 1960s, no scholarship thus far has integrated these fashion styles into the larger story of the conflicts of the era, nor have scholars fully explored how dress and hairstyles impacted the political activism and polarizations that defined the decade.

This book explores how changing styles of self-presentation shaped the culture, politics, and social movements of the 1960s and 1970s, illustrating how culture and dress contributed to the tumultuousness and conflict of these decades. It shows how numerous social movements, such as the hippie counterculture, Black Power, the New Left, women's liberation, and gay liberation, adopted and adapted popular hair and dress styles as cultural tools for their political activism. Long hair, beards, "strange" and "colorful" dress styles, blue jeans, and other styles of self-fashioning became symbols of social activists' fights against American racism, sexism, imperialism, materialism, and conformism. A closer exploration of the politicization of dress and hairstyles illustrates how these cultural tactics united many of these disparate social movements as they fought for various, and sometimes opposing, goals.

But particular styles of self-presentation also carried implications that became a point of contention for both the activists themselves and for their observers. Broader changes in fashions among men and women in the 1960s fueled cultural anxieties about gender, race, class, and norms of traditional American respectability. Conflicts over the implications of these self-presentation tactics divided activists of the era and often fostered political backlash against them. This book thus illustrates how dress and hairstyles operated as symbols of the divides in American culture—what some have called the "culture wars"—that have come to define American society in the decades following the 1960s.

Scholars have increasingly recognized the importance of fashion as a political and cultural statement. Contemporary fashion theorists have described a "language" or communicative aspect of fashion. Clothing and dress signify racial, class, and gender identities, and social norms are both constructed and challenged by individual choices of dress. As fashion theorist Elizabeth Wilson has noted, "Everywhere dress and adornment play symbolic, communicative, and aesthetic roles."[3] Fashion and style thus contain meanings that stretch far beyond the actual clothes or styles on one's body; rather, fashion and style can take on political, cultural, and societal meanings, signifying messages about the individual wearer and creating a nonverbal discourse on the messages contained in individual choices of style.[4]

The 1960s were certainly not the first time that styles of self-fashioning became imbued with political meanings. Nor did Americans adopt new styles of hair and dress in the 1960s solely for political reasons. American consumption increased in the decades after World War II, and the rise of baby-boom youth culture in the 1960s provided a large and profitable market for new fashion trends.[5] Moreover, the rise of visual culture through the media and television played a large role in increasing knowledge of and attention to these trends, in some cases making changes in style appear more widespread than they actually were.[6] Television also helped to increase the emphasis on personal appearance as part of one's politicization. The chant "the whole world is watching" by protestors at the Chicago Democratic National Convention in 1968 signaled their awareness that television and the media were instrumental in visually broadcasting their message to the outside world. Knowing that the eyes of the world were upon them helps to explain why some activists used dress and hairstyles as visual cues to signify their political goals.

Indeed, many social movement activists adopted nonnormative dress and hairstyles as symbols of the ideological messages imbedded in their political activism. While the social movements of the 1960s are best known for their political accomplishments—the end of Jim Crow laws in the South, the passage of civil rights legislation, legal battles against racial and gender discrimination in the workplace, and protests of the Vietnam War—underlying the political activism of each set of activists was a broader critique that each group offered of American culture. Martin Luther King Jr., in his famous letter from a Birmingham jail in 1963, explained that racial injustice was not merely the product of racist laws, but of an American culture that denied to African Americans the "self respect and a sense of 'somebodiness'" that was afforded to whites. Similarly, the Port Huron Statement, written by members of Students for a Democratic Society (SDS) in 1962, was less a criticism of specific American policies than it was a treatise on the state of American culture in the postwar era. Racism, the threat of atomic warfare, and the typical middle-class lifestyle revealed to its authors the "complicated and disturbing paradoxes in our surrounding America." Unjust American policies could be easily linked to the "hypocrisy of American ideals" that SDS lambasted. It was America's "twin needs for richness and righteousness" that ultimately caused the war in Vietnam, according to SDS president Carl Oglesby in a 1965 speech; American materialism was thus considered to be the underlying cause of anticommunist policies that the New Left criticized. Feminists and gay liberationists also attacked American culture for the gender stereotypes and roles that rested on notions of female and homosexual inferiority. While activists disputed American policies at home and abroad, it was American culture itself that was to blame for creating a society that supported these policies.[7]

Self-presentation techniques provided a rich tool for activists to visually display their disagreement with and alienation from American culture. By growing their hair long and donning beards, activist men protested middle-class standards of respectability they saw as conformist and artificial. "Hippie" men and women adopted "strange" dress styles as part of their disagreement with American materialism and aesthetic competition. Some antiwar protestors connected men's long hair to their critiques of militarism that they argued promoted needless warfare abroad. African American men and women wore "natural" hairstyles and Afro garb to challenge white, Euro-American cultural standards of beauty as racially biased and disrespectful to their African heritage. Feminists and gay liberationists used hair and dress styles to visually dispute fallacies of gender difference and stereotypes of masculinity and femininity. And teenagers fighting for the right to dress and wear their hair as they wished pointed to the hypocrisies of parents and schools attempting to restrict their attire, wondering why the American creed of "freedom" did not seem to apply to them. Self-presentation through dress and hairstyles was thus a cultural tool for activists to display their disagreement with and alienation from an American culture they abhorred as hypocritical, discriminatory, and misguided. Self-presentation styles also symbolized the freedom of expression guaranteed by the American creed, and the right of social activists to express their opinions no matter how unpopular or radical their ideas might seem.

However, many others disagreed with these activists' interpretations of American culture. Groups that found comfort and privilege in the old social order felt threatened by these movements for racial and gender equality and against traditional middle-class values. Scholars have linked these groups to the New Right political coalition that emerged in the 1960s and 1970s.[8] On nearly every count, this new coalition of conservatives disagreed with the views of leftist activists. Policies that social movement activists described as discriminatory and imperialist were to social conservatives the bulwarks of an American culture that they adored. Anticommunism was not an imperialist ploy to feed American corporations, but a necessary set of policies to protect America from a dangerous economic and political system that would destroy economic freedoms, outlaw democracy, and place the world at risk for nuclear war. Conservatives perceived battles for racial integration as causing restrictions on their freedom of association, destruction of the property values of the homes they had worked so hard to purchase, and degradation of the school systems for which their tax money paid. The "sexual revolution" emerging in the 1960s was further proof of the erosion of Judeo-Christian values upon which American society had been built. And increasing numbers of women working outside of the home, young men dodging the draft and speaking out against warfare, and the rise of feminism among young women, all signaled that so-called radical activists were out to destroy the gender roles and family structures that were central to traditional visions of American social order. The hairstyles and modes of dress adopted by some youths and activists were thus interpreted and portrayed as symbols of their fundamental threats to traditional American society. To opponents, these styles came to symbolize rebellion, dirtiness, overt sexuality, gender-role confusion, and lack of middle-class "respectability," mirroring the fundamental threats that other changes in America seemed to hold for the traditional social order that they prized.

Scholars often position the 1960s as the beginning of the "culture wars" that would come to shape American politics in the decades to come.[9] Religious conservatives in the 1960s and 1970s focused on Supreme Court decisions involving birth control, prayer in schools, and abortion to illustrate how American culture was straying from the traditional Judeo-Christian values upon which they claimed America was based. At the same time, the civil rights, Black Power, feminist, gay liberationist, New Left, and student movements mounted challenges to cultural conceptions and social hierarchies of race, class, age, and gender. This book suggests another point of origin for these culture wars: not just religious or political differences in philosophy, but also differing interpretations of the messages conveyed in changing styles of self-presentation. What some Americans saw as stylistic freedom or political protest, others saw as signs of the demise of the gender, sexual, racial, and middle-class traditions of "respectability" they held dear. While these latter concerns would fade into the 1970s as social activism waned, they would never cease entirely, remaining embedded in American cultural discourse as a warning of what might happen if certain fashion styles were taken too far.

The following six chapters present a chronological and thematic exploration of changing styles of self-presentation and their political implications from the mid-1960s through the mid-1970s. Utilizing newspaper and magazine articles and advertisements, the grassroots periodicals and papers of social movement organizations, court cases, photographs, and memoirs, this book charts shifting styles of self-presentation as part of American fashion trends and illustrates the significant roles that these styles played in the political landscape of the 1960s and 1970s. It shows how social movement activists adopted and politicized these trends, and how cultural anxieties over changing styles became intertwined with political anxieties over gender and sexual mores, racial and class tensions, increased feminist activism, and the state of American youth. While popular culture promoted acceptance of these styles by the 1970s, cultural battles over styles of self-presentation continue in some cases to the present day. Hairstyles, dress, and self-presentation therefore remained potential signs of political and cultural conflict into the 1970s.

Chapter 1 discusses the media's focus on cultural changes in dress and hairstyles among white, middle-class American youths in the 1960s. Starting with the Beatles, who popularized the "mop" hairstyle among male teenagers in 1964, this chapter explores how hair and clothing trends in the second half of the 1960s blurred gender, sexual, and class boundaries and garnered scrutiny from various social commentators. Opponents of the new styles criticized their disruption of gender and sexual norms and their challenges to middle-class respectability. In response, teenagers and liberal adults argued that one's choice in hair and dress styles was an extension of the freedom of expression guaranteed to American citizens, and they forged legal battles against school officials who attempted to suspend students for their unconventional styles. Dress and hairstyles in the 1960s, this chapter shows, were never merely cultural phenomena or simple matters of style; rather, they were intertwined with generational conflicts and political debates over American ideals and social norms.

Chapter 2 analyzes how styles of self-fashioning became political tools for social movements of the 1960s. Black Power activists were among the first to politicize dress and self-presentation by adopting natural hairstyles and "African heritage" clothing. New Left and hippie countercultural activists built on this politics of appearance, promoting long hair as a protest against the image of "crew-cut masculinity," which they associated with the Vietnam War. The unconventional dress and hairstyles of both men and women in these movements also contributed to their critiques of American conformity and capitalist materialism. However, opponents of these movements interpreted their self-fashioning styles as a threat to norms of gender, sexuality, and respectability, intertwining with the larger threats of the sexual revolution and the Cold War that troubled many Americans in the 1960s. As opponents of these social movements grew more adamant, dress and self-presentation became a point of contention among activists themselves, disagreeing as to whether or not self-presentation tactics ought to be used as part of their political protest. As conservative politicians targeted the dress and hairstyles of antiwar protestors in garnering support for the burgeoning New Right political coalition, the leaders of some New Left organizations and liberal political campaigns pushed their student members to adopt more traditional styles of dress. This chapter therefore argues that the self-fashioning styles of leftist social activists advanced their political goals but also helped to inspire conservative backlash against them.

Chapters 3 and 4 focus on self-presentation in the feminist and gay liberation movements. Unlike earlier social movement activists who did not explicitly protest gender norms, women's and gay liberationists were the first to connect gender-bending dress and hairstyles to an explicit politics of gender that challenged broader conceptions of sex roles, masculinity, and femininity. Some women's liberationists and lesbian feminists cut their hair, rejected traditional feminine clothing styles and makeup, and donned men's jeans and work boots to protest fashions that they claimed sexually objectified and demeaned women. Similarly, some male gay liberationists wore "political drag," which mixed countercultural long hair and beards with women's dresses and makeup, to symbolize their disagreement with norms of heterosexual masculinity. These groups of activists used dress and hairstyles to challenge the naturalness of gender distinctions between males and females, which they believed were socially constructed to be a source of their oppression as women and homosexuals. These self-presentation tactics, however, exacerbated the fears of outside observers that feminists and gay liberationists aimed to destroy all distinctions between the sexes, rejecting masculine and feminine differences entirely. Dress and self-presentation tactics thus exacerbated the backlash experienced by these movements and created dissent from within the movements about the appropriate modes of feminist and gay liberationist self-presentation. Some feminists, such as

Betty Friedan, rejected the politicized self-presentation of women's liberationists as damaging to the image of feminism. Moreover, some women's liberationists argued that politicized styles of self-fashioning exacerbated class and racial divisions among women and failed to allow women the essential choice to dress as they wished. Gay and lesbian activists criticized drag styles for confusing homosexuals with transsexuals and perpetuating harmful stereotypes of homosexuals and women. The politics of self-presentation thus became fraught for activists who wished to challenge gender norms in their political activism, but also hoped not to alienate mainstream Americans from their cause.

Chapter 5 explores the growing ubiquity of unisex styles in the 1970s and changing media reactions to them. On the one hand, as styles from the 1960s became popularized and commercialized, the media found them harder to oppose and promoted acceptance of these styles through newspaper articles, movies, television shows, and Broadway musicals. On the other hand, the media helped to strip these styles of their political meanings, portraying long hair on men, pants on women, miniskirts, and Afro hair as styles among an array of choices in hair and dress. These styles, the media began to claim, were not necessarily political, nor were they disruptive to traditional conceptions of gender, class, or respectability. As the social activism of the 1960s faded, acceptance of these styles became more palpable as their political messages faded into the background.

However, chapter 6 explores continued anxieties over self-presentation as reflected in court cases challenging workplace restrictions on dress and grooming styles. Utilizing the guarantee of freedom of expression in the First Amendment and Title VII of the 1964 Civil Rights Act, which outlawed discrimination based on race and sex in the workplace, men and women began to challenge workplace restrictions on long hair, facial hair, Afros, miniskirts and pantsuits. These legal cases forced the courts to grapple with standards of dress at a particular historical moment when norms of self-presentation were changing rapidly. The opinions of judges provide insight into how changes in dress and self-presentation were perceived in courts of law, as well as how cultural norms of gender shaped court decisions surrounding the legality of restrictions on dress. Some judges acknowledged that changing styles—long hair on men, pants on women, and unisex clothing—made old regulations outdated. But other judges were hesitant to rule against regulations of gendered self-presentations, choosing to recognize the fears of both private employers and of American society more broadly when men and women crossed certain boundaries in their fashion choices. These court decisions reflected continued conflicts over changing dress and hairstyles into the 1970s despite their ubiquitous spread in popular culture.

Dress and hairstyles were more than just cultural phenomena of the 1960s and 1970s; they held connotations that grew to symbolize the broader political challenges of these decades. Some social activists used dress and hairstyles to fight for a new vision of America: a society without "machismo" warfare and gender stereotypes and with equality, justice, and freedom for all. But opponents of these movements defended their own vision of America: a society with clear distinctions and rules governing gender, sexuality, respectability, and social order. It was this polarization on the meaning of cultural changes in dress and self-presentation that helped to define the broader conflicts of the era. Nothing less than the direction of America itself was at stake.

DRESSING FOR THE CULTURE WARS

1

"YOU CAN'T TELL THE GIRLS FROM THE BOYS"

Changing Styles among American Youths, 1964–1968

In January 1968, fifty-three boys were suspended from Brien McMahon High School in Norwalk, Connecticut, because of the length of their hair. The school, fed up with new fashions and hairstyles among their teenage students, began to enforce their dress code more rigorously, also sending home female students wearing "thigh-high miniskirts." "We aren't anxious to see boys' hair becoming as long as girls," a school official explained. "We are simply holding the line." Rather than cut their hair, the students fought back. Enlisting the help of the American Civil Liberties Union, the students picketed the school, carrying signs reading "Does Society Hang by a Hair?" "Is Hair Unfair?" and "Unconstitutional Harassment." In court, the lawyer for some of the suspended students quoted the Magna Carta and the U.S. Constitution in arguing that the school regulations were a violation of fundamental liberties that had nothing to do with the purpose of public education. While the students lost the case—the judge ruled that it would be unfair to overturn the rule when some of the suspended boys had already cut their hair, avoiding the constitutional issues at hand—they still made their point that restrictions on hair and dress contradicted fundamental American values of democracy, liberty, and freedom of expression.[1]

This incident was just one example of the many conflicts that arose across the country in the 1960s over new styles of self-presentation among American youths. Longer hairstyles on men, miniskirts and pants on women, "Peacock" clothing styles for men, and unisex styles for both males and females became significant sources of social concern and debate. This chapter traces changes in self-presentation styles among white, middle-class American youths in the 1960s as they were discussed in newspapers and other forms of media of the era. These new styles of personal presentation stoked unrest among the adults, social commentators, and authorities who struggled to reconcile them with their own understandings of social norms of self-presentation. In particular, these ascendant styles rejected the stark gender divide that limited males to "masculine" styles and women to accentuated female styles. Media coverage of these tensions sparked a national conversation, often sensationalizing these changes while also reflecting broader national discussions on the meanings of these new styles of fashion.

Clashes over the meaning of stylistic changes exposed the deep and widening fault lines that separated the ascendant youth culture from their parents. The "baby boom" generation, born in the years following World War II, was reaching adolescence in the 1960s, and producers of television, movies, music, and goods marketed products specifically toward baby boomers for consumption.[2] But teenagers of the baby-boom generation also created and popularized their own cultural styles and senses of social mores, both of which often irked older generations for their alleged loudness, uncleanliness, and rebelliousness. Despite the controversies they evoked, these styles proved popular and eventually reshaped

FIG. 2. Students protesting the suspension of fifty-three boys from Brien McMahon High School in 1968. AP photo courtesy of the *Greenwich Times*.

mainstream style conventions. Indeed, as they gained media and marketing attention, older men and women began to adopt the styles as well.

Concerns about new styles of dress also channeled deeper concerns that many Americans felt about the revolution in sexual mores that was simultaneously taking place in the 1960s. The advent of the birth control pill in 1960 increased avenues for women to explore their sexuality without fear of becoming pregnant; challenges to college curfews and dorm rules exploded on university campuses in the 1960s; and by 1968, a *New York Times* report on male and female college students "living together" off-campus sparked national controversy.[3] Some of the new dress styles, miniskirts for women most notably, exacerbated concerns that the sexual mores of the younger generation were rapidly expanding outside of the bounds of respectability. Similarly, burgeoning feminist activism in the 1960s increased social concerns about the role of women in American society. Growing numbers of women working jobs outside of the home fostered social anxieties that women would abandon their "traditional" roles as wives and mothers for professions and lifestyles previously designated for men. Changes in self-presentation for women fueled these concerns, with social commentators worrying that women dressing in new styles, and men dressing in styles similar to those previously reserved for women, could further erode traditional gender roles.

Analyzing tensions over changing fashion styles during the 1960s reveals how mainstream American notions of gender, sexuality, and class were challenged and remade in those years. In rejecting the highly gendered style of their parents' generation, teenagers and young adults began experimenting with personal presentation. Men's hair grew longer, women's hair grew shorter, and unisex styles became increasingly popular. When some social commentators attacked these trends as tearing at the fabric of traditional American culture, the young people fought back, framing the issue as profound and political. They defended Americans' right to dress and wear their hair as they pleased—rights, they noted, that were part of the concept of freedom of expression at the heart of American ideals. Hair and dress styles thus became battlegrounds, not only for differences of age and class, but also for concepts of American values and liberties. Dress and hairstyles were never merely frivolous accouterments of the 1960s; rather, they held serious implications for underlying conflicts in American culture over gender, respectability, and the meaning of American identity.

Long before the sixties, various styles of personal presentation challenged cultural norms of gender and respectability. Hair had always been a particular flashpoint for these debates, with Elvis's "greaser" hairstyle reviled as a symbol of his challenge to conventional propriety.[4] The Beatles, however, took concerns about hair to a new level. The British rockers first arrived in the United States in February 1964 and were greeted at airports, hotels, and theaters by thousands of screaming fans (mostly young women), eager to get a glimpse of the four young men. The Beatles became a music and media sensation, playing on the *Ed Sullivan Show* for a television audience of seventy-four million people, nearly half of the American population at the time.[5] The television performance exposed many Americans to the Beatles for the first time, introducing them not only to their music but also to their hairstyles. A *Chicago Tribune* columnist described their hair the day after the live performance: "Their bowl haircuts flop over their eyes in sheepdog fashion. Their haircuts, or lack of them, are somewhere between the styles of Julius Caesar and Daniel Webster. Their hair is long, but their pants are tight."[6] The reporter's reliance on figures from Ancient Rome and nineteenth-century U.S. history to describe their hairstyles indicates just how unusual they were for the time.

Although their styles, just slightly longer than the standard crew cut of the 1950s, would look tame in just a few years, the hairstyles of the Beatles attracted as much media attention as their music. And most media commentators, whether journalists or individuals writing letters to the editor, focused predominantly on the gender implications of the Beatles' "mop" hairstyles. "Now come the Beatles, the bushy-haired boys whose sex is not immediately apparent," wrote one reporter in the *Hartford Courant*. The author postulated that the gender ambiguity of the Beatles helped them to attract so many teenage girl fans, who "seize on the boy-girl type of crooner who, while undoubtedly masculine, has much of the same appearance as the adolescent girl."[7] A later column further explained why adolescent women were attracted to these "boy-girl" styles on men: "The boy-girl is not a girl. Neither is he a masculine man. His hair distribution . . . is typically feminine . . . . The boy-girl makes it possible for the timid adolescent girl to make a tentative step toward the opposite sex without too much danger."[8]

Whether or not the Beatles' hairstyles were merely a marketing ploy to attract teenage girls through unusual gender cues, commentators tended to agree that there was something about the Beatles' "long" hairstyles that was gender bending, if not gender ambiguous. Whichever it was, many adults did not like it. "The Beatles are a curse to humanity," wrote one reader in a letter to the editor in the *Chicago Tribune*. "They have no talent. They cannot sing. . . . They . . . have queer hair-dos. . . . The world is fast disintegrating into a bedlam of chaos."[9] "I want to tell girls from boys," wrote another reader in the *Christian Science Monitor*. "I think the Beatles are sissies!"[10] The editor in chief of the *Christian Science Monitor* wrote numerous columns deriding the hairstyles of the Beatles as effeminate and therefore improper for young men. "This isn't the Middle Ages. Isn't it rather pleasant for boys' hair to be distinguishable from girls' hair?" he asked in one column.[11] "I like to tell boys and girls apart just by looking at their heads," he wrote in another column. "So I'm hoping that the longs and shorts of fashion will run their course speedily, and we'll go on as before."[12]

But to these onlookers' horror, the mop style quickly spread as a fashion trend among American youths. Whether they were aspiring to the Beatles' celebrity success, or perhaps hoping to attract female admirers of the Beatles, teenage boys began wearing their hair in the mop cut, which became known as the "Beatle" style.[13] For youths who didn't want the permanence of a haircut, or because their parents forbade it, wigs imitating the Beatles' hairstyle became widely available.[14] The *New York Times* declared that these hairstyle trends were the latest evidence that "Beatlemania" was taking over: "Teen-agers who once considered the G.I. crew-cut the height of adolescent fashion are letting their locks curl down their necks and over ears and across foreheads. Twenty thousand beatle wigs have been sold."[15] In 1964 the Beatles had sparked a revolution in teenage hair, even as the enduring impact of their music remained an open question.

Other male performers adopted similarly unkempt hairstyles. Perhaps attempting to imitate the Beatles' massive success, other British bands began growing their hair even longer, flaunting their locks during their American tours. The Rolling Stones appeared on the American music scene in the summer of 1964, with "hair ... twice as long as the Beatles' and they never comb it," according to the *Washington Post*.[16] The Dave Clark Five was another British group that imitated the Beatles' mop-hair look, although the *New York Times* explained that "they swirl their hair around their foreheads instead of wearing it in a beefeater bob."[17] Before long, American musicians adopted these styles as well. By 1967, at the Monterey Pop music festival in Northern California, numerous musicians wore longer hairstyles, including the members of Jefferson Airplane, the Mamas and the Papas, the Who, and Country Joe and the Fish. Male young adults in the audience also wore hairstyles of various lengths, ranging from the Beatles' mop style to the shoulder-length styles sported by many of these musicians.[18] Indeed, by 1967, some of the Beatles members themselves had grown their hair down to their shoulders.[19] Mick Jagger, the lead singer of the Rolling Stones, spoke about the vast attention given to his band members' hair: "[Commentators] seem to have a sort of personal anxiety because we are getting away with something they never dared to do. . . . They've always been taught that being masculine means looking clean, cropped and ugly."[20] Jagger was thus explicit about the ways that these styles challenged traditional standards of self-presentation that were expected of white, middle-class Americans and mirrored many of the concerns that consternating adults raised about the new hairstyles.

One often-expressed concern over long hair was the issue of cleanliness. Commentators often assumed that longer hairstyles were more difficult to wash and that boys wouldn't take the time to do so properly. But even the look of longer hair signified dirtiness to some individuals. "It doesn't look good at all—it is sloppy," said one person. "It makes them look . . . as if they came from rotten homes." Another person decried the styles: "I think long hair looks disgusting. . . . It makes them look sort of cheap and dirty."[21] Others complained that long hairstyles on boys violated gender norms. Adults claimed that boys with longer locks could easily be mistaken for girls with short hair.[22] "This will go down in many family histories as the year of the great haircut wars—or the summer you could no longer tell for sure at more than 10 paces which of Junior's friends is male and which is female," reported the *Chicago Tribune* in 1965.[23] One Cleveland gym teacher told the longhaired boys in his class that they would have to wear pink hair nets, a subtle reference to the alleged feminine quality of their hairstyles.[24] A 1965 Gallup poll on the issue of hair length found "overwhelming opposition to the long hair styles" among its respondents. "If my son wore his hair like that, I'd make him wear a skirt until he got it cut," said one individual. Replied another: "There are enough 'queers' around and letting boys look like girls won't help to identify the deviates."[25]

Negative comments about long hair on teenage men revealed a number of concerns. One was the concept that men were supposed to look different from women and that males adopting a longer hairstyle closer to that of females were deviating from masculinity by implicitly calling into question this supposedly inherent gender difference. As one newspaper columnist put it, "Long hair is a violation of what people are used to; our culture has distinct notions of an obvious separation between the sexes. Long hair tends to confuse that separation. And because we tend to place a higher value on the male than the female, long hair may debase the supposed prize of masculinity."[26] The gym teacher who threatened to force his male students to wear pink hairnets, or the parent who said he would make his longhaired son wear a skirt, underscored this idea that boys with long hair were, in some way, less masculine. Second, statements that long hair was "queer" or "deviate" suggested that these critics feared a latent homosexuality among the wearers of these styles, or that longer hair could be a step toward a homosexual lifestyle. Stereotypes of homosexual men as "effeminate" bolstered this concern, with critics contending that long hair on men was a sign of male effeminacy.[27] Finally, concerns about cleanliness underscored norms of middle-class, clean-cut respectability that these styles seemed to violate. "We associate short hair," one commentator noted, "with the middle-class tradition of the good guy."[28] Fears of gender, sexual, and middle-class respectability thus became combined in the minds of social commentators who feared the implications of long hair on teenage men.

Underscoring these concerns was the problem of the perceived rebelliousness of longhaired male youths. In the 1950s, fears of juvenile delinquency made teenage rebellion seem particularly problematic; parents in the suburbs feared that their children would squander the opportunities of middle-class life by engaging in crime.[29] While concerns about juvenile delinquency had decreased from their fever pitch in the 1950s, many parents and adults believed that longer hairstyles symbolized a rejection of middle-class values and signaled the potential for more serious forms of rebellion that teenagers could commit. One psychiatrist interviewed in the *Los Angeles Times* explained, "Hair not only threatens the authority of parents but it hangs out there for the rest of the world to see, advertising the willingness to rebel."[30] Long hair itself was thus seen as a form of rebellion against the ideas and authority of the older generation. Another father of a longhaired teen noted, "If our young people don't have anything to rebel against, they rebel by letting their hair grow."[31] Some teenagers played up the rebellious aspects of their longhaired appearance. "You don't like my long hair, do you?" said one teenager interviewed in the *New York Times*. "It really gets you, doesn't it? You're annoyed? You hate it? Good!"[32] As another teenage commentator put it, "It is a much-talked-about subject among the older generation and this only makes the style more acceptable to the already rebellious teen."[33] Long hairstyles, as well as the growth of facial hair on some male teenagers, were thus seen as symbols of rebellion from authority that some adults found to be inherently threatening to their sense of propriety and social order.

Many teenagers and young adults, however, spoke up to defend their longer hairstyles. Lots of famous men in the past wore their hair longer, wrote one adolescent in the *Chicago Tribune:* "Take Schubert, for instance. He looks like he just took his curlers off. Beethoven's hair doesn't look any better.... These guys' music can't even compare with that of the Beatles," the author concluded.[34] Additional examples that teenagers cited of longhaired figures in history included Samson, Christopher Columbus, and George Washington.[35] Other youths denied that longer hairstyles on men were effeminate. "Long hair shows masculinity," explained another longhaired male. "Look at Sampson; look at Jesus Christ."[36] Others disputed the notion that long hair was unclean: "As long as they are clean physically and morally I see no reason" for deriding the style, claimed one writer in a letter to the editor.[37] Some teenagers complained that long hair wasn't the real issue; parents and adults were simply trying to assert authority over them. "Grown-ups don't like our long hair because it shows disrespect to them," one individual explained.[38] And one youth proclaimed to the adult complainers, "You're just jealous about their hair. You're probably bald!"[39]

Defenders of longer hairstyles thus disputed their opponents on a number of levels. Teenagers challenged adults' authority to regulate their hairstyles, suggesting that superiority in age was not a compelling reason to leave this decision to the grown-ups. They debated the notions that long hair violated norms of class and gender, arguing that these norms were somewhat arbitrary in the first place. Most importantly, teenagers and their adult defenders claimed the right to wear their hair as they wished. "A man's right to wear his hair as he wants to is one of the glories of a free society," wrote one letter writer in the *New York Times*.[40] "Part of our American way is the free expression of individuality," another person wrote in a letter to the *Chicago Tribune*. "Along with free speech . . . we males enjoy also the privilege to wear long hair if we so desire. The idea of forcing a boy to get an alleged 'all-American haircut' . . . is most reactionary and un-American."[41] "The issue is not how long or how silly his hair may be, but whether the personal appearance of . . . any human being . . . ought to be prescribed," wrote another in the *Los Angeles Times*. Unacceptance of long hairstyles, he concluded, "reveals a sad tendency on the part of many Americans to indulge in fuzzy thinking and unwitting bigotry."[42] These defenders of long hair explicitly acknowledged the value of freedom inherent in choosing one's personal appearance. As an editorialist in *Rolling Stone* magazine put it, "The right to be different is at stake."[43] Thus, to many longhaired young men, their hairstyles represented fundamental autonomy and protected self-expression, as well as a rejection of their parents' social norms.

These debates over long hairstyles came to a head as schools across the country attempted to restrict these new styles. The first cases were reported in 1964, as teenage boys began to adopt the Beatles' mop hairstyle; some school officials decided that the hairstyles were not allowed and suspended the students until they got a haircut.[44] These battles continued in schools throughout the decade, as many students challenged restrictions against long hairstyles by bringing lawsuits to court. As Gael Graham has documented, "Over one hundred hair cases were appealed to the U.S. Circuit Courts of Appeals; nine appealed all the way to the U.S. Supreme Court."[45] These court cases were part of broader struggles in the 1960s for legal recognition of the rights of high school students. It would not be until 1969, in *Tinker v. Des Moines*, that the Supreme Court would rule that high school students did retain some of their civil liberties within their high schools, although the opinion did not include freedom from hair and dress regulations as part of its ruling.[46] Beyond the legal question of the civil liberties of minors in a public school setting, these court cases, and the media discussion of high school grooming codes, reflected the broader debates over males' long hairstyles, pitting the maintenance of social order against ideals of freedom of expression.

Defenders of school regulations preached the necessity of maintaining order in a school setting. The *Hartford Courant* argued that schools were "preserving a framework of order and decorum within which teaching and learning may proceed. . . . It is a tough enough job now to get a couple of dozen adolescents to pay strict attention to class work. When a distraction is added, such as a [long] haircut, it creates an atmosphere in which concentration is impossible."[47]

"Distraction" was an often-claimed rationale for the restrictions, arguing that long hairstyles were not "conductive to a good educational atmosphere."[48] The "blurred gender lines" promoted by long hairstyles were also part of the disorder that school officials sought to prevent. Particularly, longhaired boys might be able to more easily "sneak into girls' restrooms," a recipe for both gender and sexual disaster, as far as school officials were concerned.[49] School officials believed that the enforcement of social norms was part of their role as educators. "The school should be a stabilizing force," one principal explained.[50]

Opponents of the regulations argued that these grooming rules were a violation of personal freedoms. They viewed the repression of longer hairstyles for men as a harbinger of more sinister forms of social control. "What has happened to our freedom?" asked one letter writer in a student newspaper. "Where is the line drawn? If they dictate to us the type of dress we should wear, how long our hair should be, what comes next? Will they dictate what books to read, what to believe?" While school officials were worried about disorder and decorum, this student worried about restrictions to freedom of choice and personal expression. "We don't understand this kind of 'democracy,'" he concluded.[51] This sentiment implied that ideals of freedom and choice were more central to American beliefs than traditional notions of order and adherence to social standards. Restrictions of hairstyles, as one commentator put it, "actually violate the most inherent principles of America—democracy and self-expression, and in the one place where these principles must never be violated—our schools."[52] Commentators thus argued that schools, rather than promoting social norms and rules, ought to teach respect for freedom and support individuality: "Schools should be less concerned with unorthodox hair lengths and more concerned with why they are turning out so many orthodox minds willing to submit to the corporate haircut."[53]

Opponents of school regulations were not ignorant of the gender issues implicated in this fight. Here, too, high school students protested the regulation of gender norms. "Why do people criticize men and boys for having long hair like girls when no one criticizes girls and women for having short hair like men?" asked one student. "In the '20s short hair for women was part of emancipation of women. Could long hair for men be a type of emancipation from conformity for men?"[54] Gender norms, this student argued, were yet another way that society attempted to instill conformity in its citizens. Picket signs at Brien McMahon High School noted that Jesus, Shakespeare, and George Washington all had long hair, implying that restrictions on long hair in the 1960s were arbitrary given the hair lengths of men in the past.[55] These high school students thus stressed the arbitrary nature of gender-based dress and grooming codes, implicitly noting the historically changing nature of norms of self-presentation.

In the end, no clear consensus emerged, either in the courts or among the American public, as to whether or not restrictions on hairstyles were valid. As Graham notes, "The opinions of the courts reflected the conflicted views of the nation as a whole. Americans could not agree on what long hair meant, how much it mattered, or if it mattered (although paradoxically some of them expended considerable energy and passion on a matter they proclaimed trivial)."[56] But clearly, hair mattered, as young men with long locks faced continual harassment throughout the decade. By 1968 groups across the country had sponsored billboards in their communities that pictured a longhaired youth and a simple message: "Beautify America: Get a Haircut." Over two thousand billboards appeared in towns across the United States.[57] Workplaces often restricted the hair length of male employees, firing longhaired men from their jobs.[58] At schools, longhaired teenagers were harassed by other students. Kevin Compton, a student in the 1960s, remembered the constant challenges he faced due to his long hair: "I had . . . experienced a lot of prejudice because of [my hair], having the greasers or jocks back at the high school or in town pick on you or try to start fights, just because you had long hair. They'd say things like, 'Are you a boy or a girl?' It got to the point where [I would think], 'God, can't you guys think of anything else?' And this was not just kids, but adults in authority. I remember I got pulled over [by police] a lot of times. . . . Even my physical education teacher threatened me physically, pushed me up against a locker, and said, 'You'd better get a haircut.'"[59]

As Compton's account suggests, a longhaired appearance sometimes provoked violence. In 1966 the student-body president of Stanford University was kidnapped by a group of fraternity brothers and taken to an empty parking lot, where they proceeded to shave off his long hair.[60] In another case, a fifteen-year-old boy was hospitalized after two men assaulted him and "scalped" a patch of skin from his longhaired head.[61] Males with long hair met similar violence in schools and communities across the country.

Debates over men's long hair were symbolic of larger cultural battles of the era over the social mores of youth, middle-class respectability, and authority. Long hairstyles on men also caused controversy due to their implications for gender norms of masculinity. To many, long hair represented a slippery slope. If they refused to conform to traditional masculine styles, what other harbingers of traditional manhood would they attempt to evade? What many teenagers saw as their personal freedom to choose their own hairstyles, some adults and social authorities saw as an implicit threat to norms of middle-class masculinity and respectability.

MINISKIRTS, PANTS, AND CHANGES IN FEMALE FASHION

While long hair on males stood out for the intense debates the style inspired in the second half of the 1960s, changes in women's fashions were equally discussed in the American media. The most famous change, of course, was the introduction of the miniskirt. Miniskirts, which rose to various lengths above the kneecap depending on the whims of the designer, were first introduced in Britain and France in the early 1960s. After much publicity in Europe, by 1966 miniskirts were making waves across the Atlantic.[62] Despite much consternation in the media, the miniskirt became an immediate hit among American youths, "a sweeping success" at stores across the country, and even inspiring above-the-knee hemlines for wedding gowns.[63]

Miniskirt styles were as controversial as they were successful. A 1967 opinion poll found that 95 percent of Americans had "heard or read about the 'miniskirt.'" The poll noted with some irony that "at the same time less than half the populace say they have followed recent discussions over the foreign aid program and far fewer than half are able to identify many national political figures," illustrating the major attention received by the style. The poll found that the majority of adults disapproved of the fashion, with 70 percent responding affirmatively to the question, "Would you object to a daughter of yours wearing a miniskirt?"[64] Like long hair on teenage men, short skirts on teenage women raised concerns of respectability, propriety, and norms of gender and sexuality, in addition to fostering generational divisions among teenage youth and their female elders.

One obvious criticism of the miniskirt was its sexualized nature. One newspaper noted that the phenomenon of women wearing miniskirts in public "causes men to stop and stare on crowded streets or creates disconcerting situations in the subways or draws curious groups when miniskirted women board taxis."[65] The overtly sexual nature of the miniskirt, of course, was seen as a benefit for many of its wearers and admirers. Many men vocally approved of the style, and women from the 1960s remembered the whistles they received from men when they wore miniskirts in public.[66] Other commentators, however, decried the sexualized image of women that the style presented. "Today's immodest fashions—disgusting, ugly, degrading, and deliberately suggestive," one letter writer to the *Washington Post* lamented. "The British fashion designer who introduced the miniskirt says that the purpose of fashion is "sex."[67] Another journalist noted that the short skirts "tend[ed] to make the wearer look promiscuous," and another individual complained, "Women might as well go naked."[68]

Miniskirts were certainly not the first foray of young American women into sexualized styles of dress; the flappers of the 1920s, for example, were equally controversial in their time. But short skirts took on new meaning in the context of the "sexual revolution" of the era. Female sexuality in the 1950s was often repressed and idealized as passive and demur; while "bombshell" pinup models and movie stars were popular, sexual psychologists argued that "normal" women expressed their sexuality solely in the context of heterosexual marriage. Although Alfred Kinsey's 1953 study called into question the notion of female sexual passivity, most public discussion on sexuality centered on marriage and women's role in the home. Jane Gerhard writes that "marriage experts ... felt profound unease at the specter of unconstrained female sexual desire" and therefore depicted female sexuality as "tightly associated ... with motherhood, sexual dependency, and men ... help[ing] to articulate the bounds of normal and implicitly white and middle-class femininity."[69] Women's sexuality was thus "contained and domesticated," according to historian Elaine Tyler May, to stress the maternal and passive nature of female sexual expression.[70]

The "sexual revolution" of the 1960s, along with miniskirts, challenged this view of passive female sexuality. Miniskirts, like the Pill, were imagined to be a sign of women's newfound independence and a symbol "of the new feminine drive for full freedom and equality," as one journalist claimed.[71] Particularly in the realm of sexuality, miniskirts demonstrated women's freedom from previous social mores of modesty. "The miniskirt, of course, is only the latest and most obvious sign of this revolution in mode, manners, mores, and (no doubt) morals," one journalist wrote.[72] Some wearers of the miniskirt embraced the sexual freedom that the style connoted: "It's my independence flag ... and besides I look good in it," one teenage woman remarked.[73] But other commentators found this symbolism to be threatening to traditional norms of womanhood. "This is equality of the sexes gone mad," one journalist remarked.[74]

The popularity of the miniskirt style, particularly among teenagers, also implicated generational divides that shaped youth-elder conflicts of the era. One of the chief complaints about the miniskirt was that many women, particularly of the older generation, did not look attractive in it. One newspaper article noted that some older women were interested in shorter skirt styles, "but recognize that wearing the pure miniskirt requires a strong dash of courage, not to mention good legs and a good figure."[75] Women who did not have the "good figure" of the slender teenage silhouette found themselves left out of the miniskirt craze. "Knees that are protruding or bumpy are not attractive," wrote one commentator in the *Los Angeles Times*.[76] "The miniskirt does look ridiculous on older women," remarked one young woman in the *New York Times*.[77] The publicity of miniskirt styles as a fashion for younger females perhaps exacerbated generational divides that were already causing conflict in the 1960s.

Older women, however, were often quick to deride miniskirt styles as unflattering and unfeminine. "[Men] like ... full skirts that come to a lady-like length just below the knees," one woman wrote in a letter. "They'd like to see more modesty and femininity, not grotesque caricatures. Am I right?"[78] This woman, using the terms "femininity" and "lady-like," implied that miniskirt styles challenged traditional conceptions of "modesty" in femininity, in contrast to the image of female dress that had been common in the suburban 1950s. Another woman, in a letter expressing anger over an airline's decision to allow flight attendants to wear mini-dresses, wrote, "Does the airline ... believe that a young woman is more feminine, womanly, graceful, poised, dignified and efficient when clothed in a mini-dress? Is not the task of a stewardess one demanding a responsible, emotionally mature, gracious personality? Will she best present this image when dressed in a ridiculous little-girl costume? Or is the role of a stewardess becoming so unimportant that her position is now on par with the night-club cigarette girl?"[79] This letter suggested that some commentators saw the sexualized version of womanhood presented by the miniskirt to be at odds with a more traditional vision of female respectability. Another woman expressed the sentiment more politely: "I think teen-agers look cute with short skirts, but after 40 a woman should have a little more dignity about her."[80] These comments suggested that, to some observers, the miniskirt disrupted traditional visions of "dignified" womanhood: an ideal that exuded modesty rather than overt sexuality. Indeed, it was precisely these concerns about modesty that led many high schools and places of employment to restrict the styles, despite the protests of teenage women.[81]

Other fashion changes exacerbated these concerns about traditional norms of womanhood. The emergence of jeans and pants as everyday fashions for women in the 1960s presented a clearer challenge to women's traditional modes of dress. Previously, pants had been considered women's "sportswear," to be worn for casual occasions or the outdoors. But Paris designers hoped to make women's pants an "elegant" alternative to dresses and skirts, appropriate for professional or fancy occasions.[82] Designers hoped to market pantsuits as an elegant alternative to dresses. Coco Chanel, for example, "gussie[d] up" her styles with "glamorous fabrics, jeweled chain belts and pearl and jeweled earrings" to make them "look even more female," and other designers styled the pants so they could be easily disguised as dresses and skirts, sometimes making the bottoms "loose and wide . . . like a sailor's trousers" to give them a more "floppy" look.[83] Known as "bell-bottoms," these styles quickly caught on with younger American women. Teenage and college girls flocked to army-navy stores to outfit themselves in bell-bottom pants and blue jeans.[84] Bell-bottom pants even made their debut in place of a bridal gown for one "far-out wedding."[85] While younger women were somewhat quicker to don bell-bottom pants and jeans, some older women, too, began to adopt the styles, thrilled with what they deemed to be a more comfortable alternative to tight, short skirts.[86]

The American public instantly became divided on the acceptability of these new pants styles for women. Debates ensued as to whether women's pantsuits should be allowed at fancy restaurants or elegant social events. Some workplaces forbade the style, and many restaurants at first refused to allow women wearing pants to be seated, forcing some female patrons to scramble to find a makeshift skirt in order to be admitted.[87] Some restaurants relented on their policies, so long as women still "look[ed] like ladies" in their pantsuits. As one owner explained, "Ladies should be dressed as ladies and gentlemen as gentlemen."[88] As this statement suggests, much of the controversy surrounding pants for women was the concern that pants were simply not feminine enough for women to wear as common attire. Indeed, commentators who discouraged the style, many of whom were women, often claimed that pants were inherently masculine. "It's too mannish [to wear pants]," explained one woman. "After all, we're still women."[89] "Horrible and unfeminine," was how another woman described the style.[90] "Far too masculine," said another female, and yet another woman agreed: "Men like women to be feminine and few women can remain feminine in pants."[91] "If you're really a woman, you don't hanker to look like a boy," explained another. "There's something so pretty about the swirl of a skirt I wouldn't give up."[92]

To some extent, the concerns about the "unfemininity" of pants reflected a generational divide between younger and older women. Similar to the miniskirt, some feared that older women would not look as attractive in pants styles, lacking the slim silhouette of younger women. "It's a darned difficult fashion to wear—hard enough for men who are approaching the paunchy stage let alone women whose curves often run rampant after age 19," one columnist noted.[93] One college woman admitted that pants were "not for everybody": "I'm pretty skinny," she said, "but I don't know about older women. If they made the jackets long enough to cover the bulges, I suppose they would be all right."[94] Another female commentator was more blunt: "Women who own pants should also own rear-view mirrors," she said.[95] Pants and jeans styles thus implicated a generational divide among younger adopters of these styles and older women who found them to be physically unflattering.

But comments that pants were "unfeminine" underscored a deeper concern that these styles disrupted a vision of femininity that had also been challenged by the miniskirt. Indeed, journalists often wrote about miniskirts and pants styles in the same articles, implying that these fashion trends were two sides of the same coin. It was notable, for instance, that the same French pop singer who "helped popularize the miniskirt" later "showed up at a gala Paris opera performance dressed in a man's tuxedo, complete with black tie."[96] Both styles, in different ways, challenged previous conceptions of feminine dress and seemed to symbolize deeper changes in societal definitions of womanhood. Broader shifts in women's lives were often discussed alongside media conversations about pants and miniskirts. One journalist wrote that "the steamroller of Female Emancipation" was reflected in these styles.[97] Another commentator explained, "Women have seen their traditional roles as wives and mothers become less all-embracing in the years since the legal emancipation of the female was followed by The Pill, which has emancipated her in still another way. . . . Increasing numbers of women are pursuing careers after marriage and children."[98] Changing styles of dress for women thus reflected other changes in women's roles that were controversial in the 1960s, thus adding to anxieties over the new styles. "Sure, equal rights . . . but not identical dressing!" one columnist exclaimed.[99] For some, new styles of female self-presentation represented a new frontier for womanhood that they believed should not be crossed, even as they acknowledged other positive elements of this era of personal emancipation for women.

As women's pantsuits gained popularity, however, advocates of the style argued that gender bending was unnecessary. Pants could be just as feminine as skirts and dresses, they argued: "The trouser-wearing girl," *Vogue* explained, was not necessarily one "whose femininity has crossed . . . wires."[100] Women just needed to pay attention to other aspects of their appearance in order to emphasize their femininity: "Now that women are wearing the pants . . . they've simply got to be more female," explained one article in *Cosmo*.[101] "A woman in pants with a man's haircut, man's shoes, shirt and tie, and no make-up is . . . quite different from a feminine woman in slacks carefully tailored to her proportions," wrote fashion columnist Amy Vanderbilt. "This woman will have her nails manicured, wear makeup and some kind of fashionable coiffure even though it may be quite short. In other words, she will be a feminine pants wearer."[102] Women's magazines thus stressed that pants on women could still be feminine as long as women paid attention to other aspects of their appearance, such as hairstyles and makeup.

Defenders of the new fashions, moreover, argued that pants were not necessarily related to political agitation for women's rights; rather, they were simply a comfortable fashion for women. "Pants are comfortable, warm and convenient," wrote one woman. "Women have not donned blue jeans in an organized attack on men's 'sexual superiority.' We'd just like to be as warm in freezing weather as you are. We'd simply like to be able to relax and move, and sit naturally as you do." Fears that women and men were becoming more alike, she argued, were nonsense: "To those men who complain that they can't tell the boys from the girls when both are wearing pants, I suggest that they should concentrate more on improving their familiarity with the subject than on dictating what women should or should not wear."[103]

Finally, advocates of pants also adopted arguments about the importance of freedom of choice in one's dress. Pants, one journalist explained, were the "new symbol of feminine emancipation," promising women "new freedom" from restraining and conforming fashions.[104] "The women who are flocking to the racks holding pants in stores' sportswear, coat, and suit departments give fairly pragmatic reasons: comfort and freedom. They're remarkably similar reasons for getting into miniskirts," explained another journalist.[105] These supporters of women's pantsuits argued that women deserved the freedom of choice to dress as they wished. "We don't have a right to dictate to women," one restaurant owner explained. "If this is what today is, let it be."[106] Teenagers who protested restrictions on skirt lengths at high schools used similar arguments about their right to choose their mode of dress. "They just want us to conform," said one girl who was sent home from school for wearing a miniskirt, "and why should we?"[107] Proponents of women's new styles thus interpreted female emancipation as a positive development, with pants symbolizing the importance of increased choices offered to women.

Miniskirts, pants, and bell-bottom styles for women seemed to signify broader changes in gender roles and sexual mores in the 1960s that had called into question traditional norms of womanhood. Some commentators feared that women were embracing these changes a bit too readily, criticizing the sexualized nature of the fashions that rejected an older vision of traditional "dignified" womanhood. For younger women, however, these styles symbolized fashion, fun, and freedom—a freedom they embraced despite the consternation of adults.

"There's an asexual attitude towards clothes developing," one sales clerk at an army-navy surplus store noted in 1966. "It's getting so you can't tell the girls from the boys."[108] Miniskirts, pants, and jeans on young women and longhaired styles on young men converged in a new form of unisex style that brought both delight and dismay to various factions of the American public. Initially described as "Mod" fashions (short for "modern"), American youths were quick to adopt the styles that had first appeared in England.[109] Young women as well as young men began to imitate the mop hairstyles of the Beatles, with women cutting their hair short to match the style. Hair stylist Vidal Sassoon promoted a "boyishly short" style for women, and when actress Mia Farrow cut her formerly "long, blond hair" into a "crew cut," females of all ages began imitating the style.[110] Similarly, bell-bottom-styled pants, originally introduced to give women's pants a "floppier" look, were quickly adopted in fashions for men. "Remind you a little of that wide-legged outfit on feminique's cover?" asked a caption in the *Chicago Tribune* below a sketch of men's bell-bottom pants.[111] As male and female fashion trends began to converge, the media labeled the fashions "Uni-sex—a peculiar new class of teen-age androgyny."[112]

Fashion commentators also noted how these styles were marketed to men of all ages, rather than solely to youth. Long hair, for example, did not remain restricted to teenage boys; in 1967 both the *New York Times* and *Time* magazine reported that longer hairstyles were becoming a new trend for some middle-aged men as well. "After several years of excoriating . . . their own teenage-sons for hirsuteness, city men of middle-age are letting their hair grow. Such traditional squares as stockbrokers, physicians, and corporation executives are relinquishing the crew cuts to which they have clung since they returned from service in World War II."[113] For men who wanted to keep their hair short for professional reasons but also wanted to look groovy on the weekends, stores began marketing fake hair products to men—beards, sideburns, and mustaches—so they could easily change their look from day to day.[114] While it is unclear just how many men adopted these new hairstyles, the publicity they garnered made some Americans fear that the styles would soon become ubiquitous.

Long hair was only one aspect of broader trends in men's styles that challenged previous conceptions of masculine respectability in personal presentation. The "Peacock Revolution" in men's clothing, analogizing from the male peacock's colorful plumage that attracted female mates, promoted brightly colored clothing styles for men, as opposed to the gray, brown, and black hues that defined menswear in the 1950s.[115] Peacock styles also included the introduction of ruffled shirts, necklaces, medallions, handbags, perfumes, and creams marketed specifically to men.[116] The Nehru jacket, for example, allowed men to forgo collared shirts and ties in dress wear (a jacket, notably, that some women also bought as a dress).[117] Designers also began to show turtlenecks under collarless jackets for men, accented with a necklace-like medallion, which was "necessitated," they claimed, because the outfit lacked a tie.[118]

Despite the bright colors, necklace-like medallions, and ruffles of these "peacock" fashions, designers denied that there was anything "effeminate" about them.[119] Indeed, some claimed that these fashions signaled "an assertion of masculinity" because, "in the animal kingdom . . . it is the male that is resplendent in order to attract his mate."[120] Colorful and intricate fashions for men, thus, might have been imagined as a return to a more "natural" masculinity symbolized by the plumage of male animals in the wild. Clever marketing also made it possible for men to purchase these products without feeling they were risking their masculinity. The *Hartford Courant* noted that "sex, youth, [and] masculinity were the powerful and pervasive messages" in advertisements for these new products.[121] "It is the man who wears colorful, even flamboyant clothing, not the one in grey drab, who is high-spirited, adventurous, courageous, and victorious," one journalist wrote.[122]

Despite the claims of designers and advertisers that these new styles for men were not effeminate, many commentators were still uncomfortable with them. *Newsweek* suggested that the peacock look was "psychologically unsettling to many men" because such fashions might be seen as a "homosexual conspiracy."[123] According to one anti-homosexual pamphlet published in 1964, "a taste for unconventional clothing," "attraction to bright colors," and "special hairstyles and artful combing" were all considered potential signs of homosexuality.[124] "There is something almost feminine about the look of these boys," novelist Tom Wolfe commented on the new Mod styles.[125] Concerns about gender transgression and (homo)sexuality were thus in the forefront of the minds of critics of these male fashions.

As men adopted bell-bottom pants, colorful clothing, and longer hairstyles and women donned pants and short hairstyles, many journalists pronounced that a new era of "unisex" fashion had arrived. "If a Fashion's Good Enough for Her, It's Good Enough for Him," declared the *New York Times* in 1968, announcing the newfound popularity of unisex fashions.[126] *Life* magazine explained the trend as follows: "With-it young couples, no longer inhibited by what looks masculine and what looks feminine, are finding that looking alike is good fashion as well as good fun."[127] While teenage consumers might have led the way in popularizing these look-alike trends, young adults and middle-aged couples joined in as well, and mainstream department and specialty stores began to carry unisex clothing lines, although many stores expressed uncertainty as to whether to place the clothes in the men's or women's department.[128] While unisex styles were sometimes imagined as a way for heterosexual couples to bond, the term itself, and the confusion over which department should carry the clothes, implied that the sexes were moving closer together than ever before in their choice of fashion styles.

Of course, not every fashion trend of the Mods suggested a blurring of the sexes; the facial hair adopted by some men was certainly no harbinger of femininity, nor did men adopt miniskirts as a male fashion, although some journalists wondered if they would.[129] However, some commentators focused on fashions that seemed particularly gender bending, arguing that these styles were evidence of the erosion of traditional gender roles. In 1965 psychiatrist Robert P.

FIG. 3. A designer and his girlfriend model unisex pantsuits. Bettmann/Corbis /AP Images.

Odenwald wrote in his book *The Disappearing Sexes*, "We are raising a race of less masculine men and less feminine women, and we are in danger, if this trend continues, of developing a population of neutrals with virtually nothing to distinguish them but the shape and size of their breasts and genitals." While Odenwald primarily blamed women's work outside of the home and changing sexual mores for the disappearance of gender distinctions, changes in clothing styles were also at fault. "More and more teen-age boys and girls are having their hair cut in identical ways, so that it is increasingly difficult, if not impossible, to tell which sex is which," he explained. "Mommy works in the factory on the night shift and the children see visible proof that she wears the pants," he argued, implicitly connecting the trend of pantsuits on women to their increased employment outside of the home. The result of this gender confusion, Odenwald argued, would be homosexuality.[130] In 1968 sociologist Charles Winick came to a similar conclusion. In his book *The New People*, he argued that unisex dress and hairstyle trends would lead to such confusion in sexual identities that the human race would fail to sexually reproduce. Winick also blamed women's increased work outside of the home and increased sexual permissiveness for the gender confusion in American society, which he argued was symbolized by changing mores of self-presentation. Unisex fashions and hairstyles, Winick argued, were part and parcel of broader changes in masculinity and femininity that threatened the very divisions between males and females that made biological reproduction possible.[131]

More often than not, these theories were derided in the media.[132] "His ideas of social morality seem quite rigid . . . and his forecasts of doom a trifle overwrought," one reviewer of Winick's book wrote diplomatically.[133] "The Cassandras among us are crying out dire warnings about the increasing blurring of distinctions between the male and the female of the human race," wrote one tongue-in-cheek editorial in the *Hartford Courant*. "We are becoming an androgynous world, they mourn. We are being depolarized, they wail."[134] Proponents of unisex fashions argued that the styles represented freedom and individuality to their wearers, who wished to escape from traditional, so-called Establishment styles. Others commended the symbolism of unisex for "mark[ing] the beginning of the end of the ancient battle of the sexes," as one commentator put it. Unisex fashions "symbolize[d] greater freedom of communication between" men and women, the author argued. "It heralds a conjugal era of equality, sharing and togetherness."[135] Proponents of unisex styles argued that the clothing symbolized freedom of choice in one's dress, unconstrained by conventional norms of gender, and allowed men and women to express their individuality and understanding in their relationships. "If young people today are not worrying about sex roles but are just trying to see each other as people, they are going to create a much healthier climate," one journalist concluded.[136]

As unsympathetic as the media was toward criticism of unisex fashions, it was impossible to deny that anxieties existed in some pockets of American culture. Various retailers across the country refused to carry the styles in their stores despite their growing popularity, and others refused to use the term "unisex" in marketing the clothes. "They do not want to appear to encourage a cross-over of the sexes," the *New York Times* explained, and one fashion director noted, "Many don't like the use of the word 'unisex.' It represents a connotation that they would like to avoid."[137] At the very least, both proponents and opponents of the fashions pondered the implications, with journalists interviewing fashion designers, scholars, and shoppers on their thoughts about the trends. "What is happening to the two sexes?" one article pondered. "Do 'male' and 'female' mean anything today?"[138] While the media certainly helped to sensationalize the issue in raising these questions, there was no denying that "sex traditions [were] rapidly changing" in the 1960s, and unisex clothing styles provided yet another sign of these societal trends.[139] In publicizing the issue, the media may have tapped into preexisting social concerns over changing gender roles and norms that the styles seemed to symbolize.

STYLE AND TWO VISIONS OF AMERICAN IDEALS

In January 1970, *Life* magazine published the results of an opinion poll on controversial issues from the 1960s. Hair and dress styles were among the areas of concern, and public opinion was sharply divided. While 54 percent of those surveyed believed that "new styles of hair and dress are signs of moral decay," the results showed that the answers to this question varied greatly based on age, with 65 percent of adults over fifty agreeing with the statement but 64 percent of respondents between the ages of sixteen and twenty disagreeing.[140] While younger Americans seemed to accept new styles more readily than the older generation, the opinion poll suggested that Americans were deeply divided.

This chapter has shown that conflicts over dress and hairstyles ran deeper than mere generational divisions between baby-boomer youths and their elders. Rather, in the context of the sexual revolution and changing women's roles, concerns about dress and hair-styles reflected deeper anxieties about traditional sexual and gender order in America. Miniskirts, unisex clothing, and long hair on men threatened traditional notions of sexual propriety, whether expressed as keeping men from sneaking into women's bathrooms or keeping women from asserting themselves as sexual beings in public. Long hair and "peacock" fashions on men inspired fears of homosexuality, either by suggesting that the wearers of these fashions were gay, or by undermining gender differences that some believed were the basis of heterosexual attraction. Moreover, pants and miniskirts challenged traditional notions of modesty in female respectability, while long hair, bright colors, and ruffles on men seemed to indicate a decline in masculinity. Social commentators concerned about changing styles of self-presentation thus defended their own vision of the American ideal: a society with clear distinctions and rules governing gender, sexuality, and respectability. As one high school principal explained, longer hairstyles on men were "un-American" and "reflects a symbol that we feel is trying to disrupt everything we are trying to build up" in America—a society governed by norms of middle-class respectability for both men and women.[141]

For others, however, battles for freedom in dress and self-presentation focused on the rhetoric of rights, liberty, and freedom of expression. Teenagers argued that restrictions on their hairstyles and dress were arbitrary violations of their personal freedom. Concerns about gender norms, they believed, were merely ploys to enforce conformity and traditional gender and sexual propriety, while ideas of freedom and self-expression at the core of the American creed were overlooked. Proponents of new styles advocated for freedom in fashion choices and the emancipatory nature of these styles from outdated conventions of conformity.

Through the media, each side sparked a national conversation on these dual visions of American culture. Adults and youth who approved of (or tolerated) new styles of self-presentation fought for the liberty and freedom of expression they believed were guaranteed by American ideals. Parents, school authorities, and social commentators who opposed these styles fought for their own set of American values, which safeguarded middle-class respectability through traditional conceptions of masculinity, femininity, morality, and the family. Societal battles over dress, hairstyles, and self-presentation thus revealed larger cultural divisions over the meaning of American values and identity in the 1960s—divisions that reemerged in reaction to the social movements that defined the era.

2

"WHAT TO WEAR TO THE REVOLUTION"

Self-Presentation Politics in Social Movement Activism

On May 8, 1970, a group of New York City college students held an anti–Vietnam War protest on Wall Street. Since the mid-1960s, numerous student protests against the war had taken place in various locations across the country; but the New York City protest quickly turned violent, when a group of middle-aged male construction workers and Wall Street businessmen converged at the protest and attacked the students. According to the front-page article in the *New York Times* the next day, the attackers smashed windows, tore down banners, and beat students with their fists and with their hardhats. The counter-protestors also stormed the steps of City Hall and forced up the American flag, which had been flying at half-staff to commemorate the deaths at the antiwar protests at Kent State a few days earlier, and sang the "Star-Spangled Banner."[1]

This attack, later called the "hardhat riot" due to the number of construction workers involved, epitomized the broader conflicts over student protests and anti–Vietnam War activism that had embroiled the nation during the previous years. Class differences were one root of these conflicts; working-class Americans were angry at the scorn that privileged college students seemed to demonstrate against the American government and its policies, while the sons of the working class were at war fighting against the same Vietnamese communists that the student protestors seemed to support.[2] The hardhat riot also demonstrated deep divides between the protestors and their attackers on the meaning of American identity. Raising the flag at City Hall in spite of the deaths at Kent State symbolized the workers' belief that the Vietnam War was a fight for American values and ideals. To them, the student protestors flouted the American identity that they should have cherished.[3] But Joshua B. Freeman has demonstrated how conflicts over gender also fostered the hardhat riot. Feeling their role as masculine breadwinners threatened by social changes of the 1960s, the construction workers lashed out against "new notions of manhood" represented by the student protestors, who not only shirked their ultimate masculine duty to the state by opposing the war and refusing to fight in it, but also, with their long hair, failed to even *look* like proper men. Indeed, the press at the time noted that the construction workers chose men with long hair for the most brutal attacks.[4]

The cultural changes in self-presentation discussed in the previous chapter shaped the social movements that defined the 1960s. Many of the individuals who participated in social movements and student activism were among the baby-boom teenagers and young adults who first popularized these new trends. But social movement activists imbued these styles with new political meanings, connecting their self-presentation to their political activism. Black Power activists politicized their personal presentation by adopting natural "Afro" hairstyles and African-inspired clothing. These trends also constituted a distinctive black unisex style; both men and women sported Afros, blurring distinctions between mascu-

FIG. 4. A construction worker attacks a longhaired antiwar protestor during the "hardhat riot" on May 8, 1970. Neal Boenzi/*New York Times*/Redux.

line and feminine hairstyles. New Left and hippie countercultural activists built upon this politics of appearance, promoting long hair as a protest against the image of militaristic masculinity promulgated by the Vietnam War and against American conformity and materialism more broadly. Social movement activists of the 1960s thus distinctly politicized their self-presentation, appropriating cultural trends to make ideological statements that supported their political views.

However, opponents of these movements interpreted activists' self-fashioning styles as threats to norms of gender, sexuality, and respectability, intertwining with larger concerns about the sexual revolution and the Cold War that troubled many Americans in the 1960s. Cultural fears about communism became intertwined with concerns about the gender-ambiguous and sexualized styles of student protestors. Self-presentation styles became further proof, along with their open dissent against the Vietnam War and the American government, that student protestors were radicals hoping to sabotage both American national security and the norms of American culture. The self-fashioning styles of leftist activists thus became a point of contention for their opponents, providing symbols, they believed, of activists' threats to American political and social order.

As opponents of these social movements grew more adamant in the late 1960s, self-presentation became a point of contention among activists themselves. As conservative politicians targeted the dress and hairstyles of antiwar protestors in garnering support for the burgeoning political New Right, the leaders of some New Left organizations and liberal political campaigns pushed their student members to adopt more traditional styles of dress and grooming. As police officers attacked student protestors with gendered and sexualized slurs, and voters interviewed by the press decried the long hair of activists, it became clear that politicized styles of self-presentation were just as much a part of the national conversation on the social movements of the 1960s as were their actual political goals.

BLACK POWER, AFRO HAIR, AND GENDER BOUNDARIES

The Black Power movement that emerged in the mid- to late 1960s involved a cultural recognition of black pride that manifested itself in art, music, and literature as well as dress and hairstyles.[5] The Black Power era was not the first time that some black Americans adopted natural hairstyles. Robin D. G. Kelley has illustrated how bohemian female intellectuals in the 1950s and female folk singers in the 1960s, including Odetta, Nina Simone, Abbey Lincoln, and Margaret Burroughs, wore their hair natural instead of following the hair-straightening regime that was most common among black women at the time.[6] Many of these singers and intellectuals implicitly recognized the political ramifications of their hairstyle choices, echoing the ideas of black freedom in their songs and writings.[7] But the self-presentation of civil rights activists in the 1950s and early 1960s was generally defined by traditional respectability and conformity. Suits and close-cropped hair on men, dresses and straightened hair on women, and well-groomed clothing and shoes visually illustrated that African Americans were "respectable" and therefore deserving of equal treatment and integration with whites.[8]

As younger individuals joined the civil rights movement in the 1960s, changes in styles of self-presentation began to spread among a small but significant number of activists. While the first student sit-ins at restaurants in the South enforced the "respectable" dress code of early activists, by 1963 some members of the Student Nonviolent Coordinating Committee (SNCC) began to adopt natural hairstyles and casual forms of dress such as blue jeans.[9] These styles allowed SNCC workers to blend in with the rural, working-class populations they were organizing in the South.[10] Some volunteers also connected these styles to a sense of racial pride. Many female SNCC volunteers, for example, stopped straightening their hair as a symbol of their involvement in the movement and as a sign of their budding impulse to free themselves from the painful, expensive, and time-consuming process that straightening one's hair entailed.[11]

Even before natural hairstyles became popular among SNCC volunteers, some black activists identified natural hairstyles as part of the larger political project of black liberation. Eldridge Cleaver, who would become a leader of the Black Panther Party, became politicized around cultural issues of race while in prison in the early 1960s. In an essay he wrote in jail that was published in the *Negro History Bulletin* in 1962, Cleaver drew attention to the ways in which Caucasians defined cultural standards of beauty to exclude blacks. In films, novels, television, and magazines, blacks were confronted with images of beauty that included "creamy white skin, sparkling blue eyes, and long flowing blonde tresses"; small wonder, Cleaver argued, that Negroes spent their money on "hair-straighteners, wigs, and skin-bleaches." Negro women with naturally short hair, because their "crinkly" hair failed to grow quickly, were "looked upon as an especial abomination." Cleaver argued that legal gains would never be enough to combat the "feelings of inferiority" about African Americans' physical appearance: "It would be facetious of us to campaign for a law to ban the Caucasian standard of beauty," he wrote. Cleaver therefore called upon blacks to take pride in their skin color, hair, and physical features, recognizing that their feelings of shame were "culturally conditioned" and were just as oppressive as were discriminatory laws.[12]

The Nation of Islam, the largest black nationalist organization in the United States at the end of the 1950s, also called for the rejection of white standards of beauty.[13] The organization's magazine, *Muhammad Speaks*, featured photographs of black Muslim women, with captions proclaiming them "The Most Beautiful [Women] in the World." Although many of the women wore their hair covered in accordance with Muslim religious tradition, some of the women were pictured with natural hair. Articles in *Muhammad Speaks* implored men not to straighten their hair, and two articles in 1963 celebrated black women with natural hair.[14] But the Nation of Islam was not always consistent in its calls for "natural" female beauty, sometimes including profiles of women with straightened hair in the "Natural Beauties" section of its magazine.[15] While the organization wanted its women to take pride in their African heritage, it also wanted them to look "feminine," mandating that women wear "feminine" skirts to avoid the "masculine" image of pants that was allegedly displeasing to men.[16]

Malcolm X, a former Nation of Islam minister who became an inspiration to Black Power leaders in the second half of the 1960s, also made hair an explicit part of his politics. In his autobiography, Malcolm X wrote of the pain he experienced while "conking" his hair as a young adult, trying to achieve the straight hair of white men. "This was my first really big step towards self-degradation," he wrote, "when I endured all of that pain, literally burning my flesh with lye, in order to conk my natural hair until it was limp, to have it look like a white man's hair. I had joined that multitude of Negro men and women in America who are brainwashed into believing that the black people are 'inferior'—and white people 'superior'— that they will even violate and mutilate their God-created bodies to try to look 'pretty' by white standards."[17] Malcolm X thus chastised African Americans who straightened their hair for wasting their money on painful chemical treatments and contributing to broader cultural conceptions of black inferiority. In a 1965 speech shortly before his assassination, he explained, "When you teach a man to hate ... the lips that God gave him, the shape of the nose that God gave him, the texture of the hair that God gave him, the color of the skin that God gave him, you've committed the worst crime that a race of people can commit."[18]

In the context of continued violence against civil rights activists in the South and new eruptions of violence in urban ghettos in the North, African Americans began to turn to the words of Malcolm X and the concept of "Black Power" in their calls for black activism. While the Black Power movement is most famous for its promotion of self-defense over nonviolent action, its leaders also advocated a reclaiming of African American cultural pride, including the rejection of white standards of beauty. Stokely Carmichael, chairman of SNCC in 1966, became the unofficial leader of the Black Power movement after Malcolm X's assassination. In speeches and writings, he continued to preach about the importance of black cultural pride. In a 1967 interview, he explained, "We must see ourselves as beautiful people. We keep thinking the only thing that is beautiful is white, a chick with long blonde hair. We've got to understand that we have thick lips and flat noses and curly hair and we're black and beautiful. And we're not going to imitate the white man anymore."[19] The idea of "black is beautiful" recurred in many of Carmichael's speeches and became a slogan among African Americans by the end of the decade.

Inspired by the words of Malcolm X and Carmichael, some black men and women began to wear their hair natural, growing their hair into large Afros to demonstrate that they were not "ashamed" of their "nappy hair" and that they refused to cut it short in order to hide its curls.[20] African American magazines and newspapers began to feature the style, explicitly connecting it to the Black Power movement. One article in *Ebony*, in 1966, profiled a "relatively small" but "outspoken" number of black women who had adopted the "natural" style. Many of the women featured in the article were involved in civil rights activism, and they echoed the statements of Carmichael on the politics of black beauty. "We, as black women, must realize that there is beauty in what we are, without having to make ourselves into something we aren't," explained a twenty-three-year-old Southern Christian Leadership Conference field worker.[21] Similar articles on African American males adopting "natural" or Afro styles connected their hair to a growing cultural politics of racial pride. "[Afros] are part of the debrainwashing of a lot of our people," explained one Afro wearer.[22]

African-inspired dress styles were another trend that symbolized the cultural pride of some Black Power advocates. Maulanga Karenga, the founder of the black nationalist US Organization in 1965, was one of the first individuals to promote the adoption of African language, names, and clothing to restore the "cultural identity" of the African American people.[23] Black nationalists in the 1960s were often visually identified by long, multicolored robes, loose-fitting shirts called "dashikis," Afro-inspired jewelry, and natural hair.[24] The visual distinctiveness of these self-fashioning styles coincided with the overall political ideology of the Black Power movement; rather than advocate integration and "sameness" with whites, as did the ideologies of the early civil rights movement, black nationalists and Black Power advocates argued that integration was impossible, and that separation and independence from white society ought to be the goals of African Americans. Afro hair and dress styles thus served as visual symbols of Black Power ideologies that promoted cultural separation and independence from whites.[25]

While many of the political ideologies of Black Power never were fully accepted by most African Americans—the vast majority rejected calls for separatism and still believed in the goal of integration—hair and dress styles were one of the cultural manifestations of Black Power that gained a significant following among African Americans by the end of the decade.[26] At the beginning of 1969, the *Baltimore Afro-American* reported on the growing popularity of natural hairstyles: "Only the most militant would dare let their hair go natural at the beginning of 1968," the article claimed, "but as the year dies the style is included in some of the most chick [*sic*] fashion salons."[27] The Afro-American beauty industry began marketing products for natural hairstyles, advertising creams and styling sprays that claimed to enhance the Afro's "natural beauty." For those who could not grow their hair in the large Afro style, some businesses sold Afro wigs.[28] Clothing boutiques in black neighborhoods also began selling African-inspired fashions.[29] Many news articles claimed that the adoption of these styles had "nothing to do with the economic and political wars of the Black Power movement," but certainly the messages of "psychological liberation . . . from an anti-black, anti-kink conditioning" were drawn from the ideologies of Black Power activists.[30]

Afro styles, however, were not without their critics. Some feared that individuals wearing Afros would implicitly align themselves with the controversial tactics of the Black Power movement, of which many African Americans vocally disapproved.[31] Other activists objected to Afros for their unkempt appearance; short hair was considered to be more "presentable."[32] As one woman bluntly put it, men with Afros looked like "shaggy dogs."[33] Some black activists worried that Afro styles would stymie progress for racial equality. "Do you know . . . an employer who will offer you a job with a future because you're wearing an Afro?" asked Joe Black, vice president of the Greyhound Corporation, in an advertisement that appeared in numerous black publications in 1970. "Chanting slogans, spewing hate and changing your physical appearance won't stop hunger pains, or get you a solid job with a future. . . . Remember it for yourself, for your future and self respect, and for the dignity of black people everywhere."[34] In this advertisement, Black was concerned about more than employment prospects for African Americans; he also worried about the "respectability" of an African American community besieged by Afro haircuts. Concerns about "dignity" underscored fears that the Afro style defied conceptions of "respectable" self-presentation for African Americans and could undo the gains of the civil rights movement. A letter to the editor in the *Los Angeles Sentinel* perhaps put it best: "Negro men, please improve your image. . . . Trim your hair. . . . You are setting race relations back 100 years."[35]

Other African Americans questioned the gender implications of Afro hairstyles. Some claimed that men with Afros were more masculine because they "seem to be a little more sure of themselves" with natural hair.[36] Others disagreed: "Long hair doesn't make a man look more masculine, but more savage," wrote one woman.[37] Particularly for women, the Afro presented an uncomfortable challenge to normative definitions of feminine self-presentation. *Ebony*'s 1966 article on the increasing popularity of Afros among activist women made this concern clear: "Like all women, those who wear naturals . . . recognize that short hair might detract from their femininity."[38] In 1968 the *Washington Post* discussed the problem of African American women attempting to wear their hair "natural" but still wanting to look "feminine": "No reason [for adopting the Afro] was usually deep enough to prevent the shock of the rather masculine new image in the barber's mirror," the article lamented. Women with natural hair, it claimed, needed to wear large earrings and makeup, and avoid wearing pants, in order not to be confused with men.[39] For some, Afro hairstyles seemed to blur the lines between masculine and feminine self-presentation. Commenting on the natural hairstyles featured in the 1966 issue of *Ebony*, one reader wrote to the editor, "When I got my June, 1966 EBONY and saw the picture on the cover, I thought it was a man. When I found out it was a woman and looked inside and saw all those kinky heads, I just tore the cover off my book. I could not look at it."[40]

Some black activists, in contrast, used the Afro to redefine what natural beauty and femininity ought to mean for African American women.[41] "Today the black woman is seeing the beauty that lies within herself," wrote one woman in *Black Panther*, the organization's periodical. "The natural beauty of her mind, hair, and body. It is as though a seed has been planted and is in the first stages of growth."[42] The magazine of the Black Panthers featured photographs of black women with large Afros, with the captions "Black and Beautiful" proclaiming their beauty and implicitly, their femininity.[43] Some black female activists like Kathleen Cleaver and Angela Davis became famous for their extremely large Afros, which were often displayed in media photographs.[44]

But for a number of black women, Afro hairstyles were rejected as a threat to feminine beauty. "I think it's time the black woman started

FIG. 5. Angela Davis, a Black Power female activist, was famous for her large Afro hairstyle. Bernard Gotfryd. Courtesy of the Library of Congress.

pressing her hair again and even buying an assortment of wigs to keep her looking sweet, delicious, desirable and feminine," wrote one woman in *Ebony*. "Disagree all you want, but think. The men look great and masculine in their Afro hair styles—our women look great and masculine, too."[45] Advertisements for hair-straightening products persisted in black magazines, and many women continued to straighten their hair, perhaps because they feared the gender implications of the natural hairstyle.[46] As one woman explained upon giving up her Afro in 1975, "It just doesn't look feminine."[47]

Even at the height of the Afro's alleged popularity, a *Newsweek* poll in 1969 found that less than half of African Americans approved of natural hairstyles, and even fewer expressed support for African-inspired clothing.[48] While advancing significant political goals for the black freedom movement, Afro hairstyles and African-inspired dress styles also triggered a number of fears—their association with the militant politics and alleged violence of Black Power organizations, their defiance of "respectability" in self-fashioning, and their blurring of gender boundaries. While some African Americans adopted these styles with pride, others rejected them for their challenges to traditional norms of respectable presentation. For significant numbers of African Americans, Afro dress and hairstyles were a liability, no matter how important they might have been for the broader political project of African American cultural pride.

POLITICIZED SELF-PRESENTATION IN THE COUNTERCULTURE AND THE NEW LEFT

At the same time that Black Power activists explicitly politicized their styles of self-presentation, white middle-class youths also began to consider the deeper implications of their choices of hairstyles and fashion. While battles over "Beatle" haircuts and miniskirts raged in schools, students and young adults across the country became involved in a number of social activist causes: the civil rights movement, the Free Speech Movement at Berkeley, and protests of the Vietnam War. Other youths and young adults did not join any specific organizations, but considered themselves to be members of the "hippie counterculture" that emerged in urban areas in the late 1960s.[49] Although involvement in social movement organizations and social protest was often fluid and amorphous for many of the individuals involved, there was no denying the increased political awareness of many youths in the second half of the 1960s. And in a proliferation of writings in underground magazines and newsletters, social activists, self-proclaimed "hippies," and politically minded young adults expressed their views.

As discussed in the previous chapter, students protesting attempts to restrict their hairstyles or modes of dress also began to recognize the deeper political meanings and implications of these styles. Some young activists were inspired by the "beatniks" of the previous decade who adopted alternative styles of dress as politicized statements.[50] One activist remembered her "high school nonconformity" in adopting a beatnik style and was inspired when she arrived at Berkeley for college to meet a group of leftist intellectuals with "beards . . . blue work shirts and lots of baggy corduroys."[51] For others, battles with schools, parents, and the public over hair and dress styles became a gateway for engagement in broader political activism. "As more and more long-haired teenagers found themselves insulted, beaten, jailed, searched, and similarly harassed by the defenders of status quo, it was no time before the lessons of recent political movements became clear to these kids," explained one member of Students for a Democratic Society (SDS), one of the largest organizations of the growing New Left in the 1960s.[52] Indeed, activist publications editorialized on student battles against dress and grooming codes in high schools, encouraging students to stand up for their rights and perhaps also attracting young adults to join their cause.[53]

As young Americans began to join social movement organizations and political activism, they brought their new styles of fashion with them. In the early years of SDS, which formed in 1960, members followed a dress and grooming code similar to that of early civil rights activists: short hair, jackets, and ties for men; blouses and skirts for women.[54] But by the mid-1960s, styles of self-presentation began to change among SDS members. Todd Gitlin, a former president of the organization, recalled that some of the changes began during trips to join civil rights activism in the South; to blend in with the local, rural culture, SNCC and SDS volunteers began to adopt the "back-country look of Georgia and Mississippi: denim jackets, blue work shirts, bib overalls."[55] Returning to Northern campuses in the mid-1960s, older members noticed that "the new generation . . . dressed and acted more casually than their predecessors" and were "shaggy in appearance."[56]

Indeed, some members of SDS argued that hair and dress styles were critical components of their politicization. Carl Davidson, the national vice president of SDS in 1965–66, was inspired by Stokely Carmichael's speeches on black beauty and realized that one's physical appearance could be just as political as one's ideas: If "you were representative of the dominant culture [in your appearance], even if you had revolutionary values, people would still look at you a certain way," he explained.[57] Students at the University of Kansas recalled the solidarity they felt with those who adopted their same unconventional dress and hairstyles.[58] As changing styles took hold, older members of SDS soon began to don the "new styles" promoted by younger members.[59]

Some SDS members also began to argue that hair and dress styles could be symbolic of their broader protests against American values. Dress and grooming codes in high schools were "symptomatic of one of the most serious problems in American society," one SDS member wrote—cultural conformity to middle-class "respectable" standards of dress. "People are too afraid . . . to deviate from the standards of their middle-class community," the member complained. "They have adopted an uncompromising view of the way people should look and dress. They hold that students should be clean-cut, well-scrubbed, and properly tailored. They assert that boys should look like middle-class boys; and girls, like middle-class girls."[60] Critiques of middle-class standards of respectability and conformity were common in writings of social activists of the era. The 1950s was a decade of mass prosperity and growth for the white middle class, as suburbs grew, consumer spending increased, and more individuals than ever before attained college and graduate degrees.[61] Many members of the older generation, having grown up during the lean years of the Great Depression and World War II, welcomed these developments; their children often found them to be stifling. Todd Gitlin called the middle-class culture of the 1950s "a seedbed as well as a cemetery," and the affluence and prosperity of the 1950s also created expectations of consumption and capitalist materialism against which the student and youth activists of the 1960s would rebel.[62]

The Port Huron Statement, one of the founding documents of SDS, vocally decried the values of the middle-class lifestyle: "The majority of Americans are living in relative comfort—although their nagging incentive to 'keep up' makes them continually dissatisfied with their possessions."[63]

Young activists often connected their dress and hairstyles to a broader rejection of middle-class values. Some self-identified hippies, for example, derided the conformity of the normative middle-class lifestyle, which mandated not only certain types of jobs and standards of living, but also certain modes of self-presentation. In a 1967 essay, "What Is a Hippie?," one individual explained the connections between countercultural dress and middle-class values: "The hippies dress strangely. They dress this way because they have thrown a lot of middle-class notions out the window and with them the most sensitive middle-class dogma: the neutral appearance." A "neutral appearance," according to the author, was one that blended in, showing one's tacit acceptance of middle-class values. The appearance of the hippies, in contrast, symbolized their rejection of the middle-class "rat race" of employment, money, and consumerism: "He [the hippie] has escaped from a culture where the machine is god, and men judge each other by mechanical standards of efficiency and usefulness. He sees a madness in the constant fight to sell more washing machines, cars, toilet paper, girdles, and gadgets than the other fellow. He is equally horrified at the grim ruthlessness of the men who participate in that fight."[64] The culture of middle-class consumption, this individual argued, created a lifestyle of greed and conformity that the hippies allegedly rejected. Another self-identified hippie mocked the consumerist routines of middle-class families: "Then comes Sunday, when we all dress up in our best, go out to our shiny new car. . . . We sit in our shiny automobile, nobody can see the potbelly sitting in our legs, no one knows that the wife is wearing a Maidenform outfit two sizes too small and can't move."[65] The hippies decried the shiny automobile, the too-tight dresses and clothes, and the general expectations of middle-class life as materialist, shallow, and conformist.

In contrast, many hippies and youth activists promoted their modes of self-presentation as more "natural" forms of self-styling. Hair and dress styles (or nondress, in the case of public displays of nudity) provided a means for individuals to replace the conformity and consumerism of middle-class America with what they considered to be a more natural lifestyle. As one "wild-haired" hippie explained, "We are hip to all the mistakes society has made and is making. . . . We are hip to the fact that Nature is everything. Nature is ageless."[66] Long hair on men was imagined to signify a more natural form of masculinity. As Jerry Rubin, a self-proclaimed spokesperson for the counterculture, explained, "Man was born to let his hair grow long and to smell like a man. We are descended from the apes, and we're proud of our ancestry."[67] Another longhaired hippie said even more simply, "I wear long hair because I think that's the way God meant me to look."[68] Long hair, as well as love beads and other styles of dress, were considered to be symbols of Native American cultures, who were imagined to be closer to nature and therefore more authentic in their masculinity (and who were also the victims of American imperialism).[69] Facial hair on men was also sometimes considered a facet of this natural ideal. Some activist men grew long beards in addition to their long hair, returning to what men looked like in "nature," without razors or scissors.[70] For women, rejecting brassieres, makeup, girdles, and not setting their hair or shaving their legs, constituted a more natural form of femininity, free from the trappings of middle-class consumerism (although some countercultural women did wear miniskirts, perhaps contradicting this anticonsumerist ideology).[71] As one activist woman who participated in the Free Speech Movement at Berkeley recalled, "Of the many lessons I learned for the revolution ... not the least of them was what to wear to the revolution: Wear cotton. Wear open shoes. They breathe. We might even say, they breathe freely. Which was, after all, what the FSM was all about."[72]

Hippies and youth activists also saw their choices in hairstyles and dress as emblematic of the freedoms that were promised by American culture but were rarely realized. Echoing the cries of high school students and defenders of long hair, hippies used their self-presentation to critique American culture more generally, which obscured true freedom of expression, they claimed, by instituting arbitrary restrictions on "acceptable" dress and hairstyles (as well as equally arbitrary restrictions on drug use and sexual behavior). When hippies were harassed or arrested for their appearance, they defended themselves by citing concepts of individual rights and the constitutional guarantees of freedom of thought and expression. As one hippie explained, everyone had an "American right" to dress how they wished, but "American rights are largely disregarded by the municipal courts here. The one who dares to defy the mores (not the laws) here is bound to have a legal bill to pay. All this is done in the name of 'order.'"[73] As this author pointed out, while legal channels might have guaranteed individual freedoms, social mores seemed to trump freedom in practice. Hippies implored America to live up to its ideals of freedom and liberty for all, including the freedom to choose one's personal appearance. "There are no exceptions in this document . . . regarding age or length of hair," explained one hippie as he pointed to a copy of the Bill of Rights.[74]

Student and youth activists also used their hair and dress styles to make connections to other topics of political activism during the decade. Influenced by the cultural politics of Black Power, some activists argued that their self-presentation turned them into minorities and outsiders. Jerry Rubin made these connections between black and hippie oppression explicit: "Long hair is our black skin. Long hair turns white middle-class youth into niggers. Amerika is a different country when you have long hair. We're outcasts. We, the children of the white middle class, feel like Indians, blacks, Vietnamese, the outsiders in Amerikan history."[75] By equating hippies with other minority groups, Rubin argued that long hair allowed white youths to express solidarity with those who were oppressed because they looked "different" from "normal" (i.e., white) Americans. Hippies, they contended, also faced harassment due to their outward appearance. As Abbie Hoffman explained in 1968, "You want to get a glimpse of what it feels like to be a nigger? Let your hair grow long. Longhairs, that new minority, are getting the crap kicked out of them by . . . police harassment previously reserved only for blacks."[76] Hippies thus claimed to attain experiential solidarity with racial and ethnic minorities. As one hippie in Atlanta explained, after his cooperative store was fire-bombed, "We've got a new nigger in our society, and the way to tell him is by his hair and his beard."[77] While surely some members of minority groups found this reasoning to be offensive—white men and women could *choose* to look different, whereas many members of racial minorities could not—these arguments did signal a feeling of solidarity with minorities that white activists wished to express.

Styles of self-presentation not only made activists identifiable by others for harassment, but also were believed to build solidarity as members of a growing community with similar political and ideo-logical views. As Jerry Rubin wrote, "Long hair is communication. We are a new minority group, a nationwide community of longhairs, a new identity, new loyalties. We longhairs recognize each other as brothers in the street." While Rubin's use of the term "brothers" might have made female members of this "community" feel ignored, he elu-cidated the idea that long hair could symbolize a particular set of ideological or political commitments: "Wherever we go, long hair tells people where we stand on Vietnam, Wallace, campus disruption, dope. We're living TV commercials for the revolution. We're walk-ing picket signs," Rubin concluded.[78] Another individual explained, "When I show up anyplace, I don't need to tell my brothers and sis-ters, or my enemies, 'Hey look, I'm against the Vietnam War, racism, poverty and pollution. I dig grass, black power and revolution.' They look at me and they know. . . . My hair tells the story."[79] Long hair and nonconformist dress thus provided a symbol, at least in theory, to identify like-minded dissenters and activists. One student activist recalled looking around at the 1967 antiwar protest in Washington DC, "and as far as the eye can see in any direction are people with protest signs, kids with hair that's getting longer, and banners, and it's like you just have a sense of solidarity."[80]

Indeed, long hairstyles on men became particularly poignant as a symbol of protest against the Vietnam War. American involvement in the war escalated in the second half of the 1960s after Congress authorized President Lyndon B. Johnson to use military force in fighting the North Vietnamese, and Johnson reinstated the draft to increase the amount of American troops in South Vietnam. While in reality, working-class and minority men were drafted most often (as many middle- and upper-class men obtained educational deferments or were otherwise excused from service), all men ages eighteen through twenty-six were technically subject to the draft, and as deaths of American soldiers in South Vietnam mounted, so too did the fears of the men of the baby-boom generation who were coming of age in the 1960s.[81]

The escalation of the Vietnam War coincided with the growing disillusionment of many younger Americans with the government's Cold War policies. SDS identified atomic weaponry as the source of the terror that many young Americans had experienced surrounding the tensions with the USSR: "The enclosing fact of the Cold War, symbolized by the presence of the Bomb, brought awareness that we ourselves, and our friends, and millions of abstract 'others' we knew more directly because of our common peril, might die at any time," they wrote in the Port Huron Statement.[82] Some young Americans began to wonder if the fight against communism was necessary or worthwhile. "The proclaimed peaceful intentions of the United States contradicted its economic and military investments in the Cold War status quo," SDS wrote.[83] Investment in the military, weaponry, and the "Cold War status quo" were linked in the minds of some young Americans with the misguided values of American culture: "We've watched them run into so many dead ends while they're playing with all their toys like the bomb," one hippie wrote.[84] Dissent against the values of American culture—namely, materialism and capitalism—thus fueled the ideologies expressed in anti–Vietnam War protest and fit well with the alternative styles of self-presentation of some activists.

Long hair, in particular, also became a symbol of protest against militarism itself. Previous generations had considered service in the army to be an honorable obligation to one's country, as well as a critical component of masculinity. Nearly all of the men who came of age in the 1930s and 1940s had fought in World War II, making the war a significant coming-of-age experience for American men of all races and ethnicities in the 1940s.[85] But many men coming of age in the 1960s feared their lives would be cut short by death in the war. Moreover, some saw the war in Vietnam as yet another aspect of American hypocrisy in which freedom was denied to citizens of other countries who did not agree with America's capitalist values. As Barbara Ehrenreich has explained, the Vietnam War became too brutal and too costly to be justified by the notion of masculine obligation. Moreover, the horrifying images of war—the "gratuitous brutality of American fighting men, as shown in full color on television and in the pages of *Life*"—illustrated the pitfalls of aggressive, warmongering masculinity.[86]

Long hair thus symbolized for some activists their criticism of the forms of masculinity promulgated by a culture of militarism and warfare. "They say the army makes a man out of you," one individual explained. "By now you know better. The army just tries to make a robot out of you. . . . There isn't a damn thing about killing that is 'manly.' A man's job is to make babies, not kill them."[87] "This country was built on MACHISMO," another activist explained. "Lovely longhairs—they aren't afraid to say To Hell With Machismo."[88] For some, long hair was a criticism of the "mental indoctrination" of the army itself, reflected in the short haircuts required of all soldiers.[89] Some Vietnam War veterans grew their hair long when they returned from service, symbolizing their protest against the war and against the American military.[90] However, other activists recognized that this "army culture" of crew cuts and warfare actually held deeper roots in the culture of Cold War America. One author in a 1967 anthology of hippie writings decried his past as a "crew-cutted Seattle boy" who was ignorant of the "poisoning and blighting" of Vietnamese men and women in warfare.[91] In expressing dissent against the war and discarding his past identity, the author implicitly rejected the masculinity of the 1950s—a masculinity defined not only by crew cuts, suits, and ties, but also by masculine service in the war as an obligation of citizenship. Through their long hair, antiwar activists implicitly rejected an army culture that seemed to infuse American society, promoting warfare and aggression as part of societal expectations of masculinity.

The writings of self-proclaimed hippies and activists thus illustrate how many individuals politicized their styles of self-presentation on a number of levels. Countercultural or nontraditional hair and dress styles came to symbolize a rejection of the middle-class "lifestyle," solidarity with other radicals and racial minorities, dissent against a culture of warfare and militarism promoted by the Cold War, and the freedom and independence of the American creed that activists hoped to realize. Self-presentation became an obvious cultural tool through which activist youths displayed their political messages. However, self-presentation also became a cultural tool for opponents of these social movements to symbolize the threats these movements seemed to promulgate against traditional American values.

CULTURAL ANXIETIES AND BACKLASH
OVER POLITICIZED STYLES

While the political messages of certain styles carried deep meaning for many activists, they also created consternation within and outside of the movement. The media, for example, was certainly focused on these styles and played a large role in highlighting or even exaggerating the stylistic aspects of student activism. Media photographs of sds, Todd Gitlin claimed, often purposely focused on members with long hair or untraditional appearance. One issue of the *New York Times Magazine* put a "long-haired, droopy-mustached" member of sds on its cover, while "photos of five other, less hairy staff members appeared safely inside" the magazine, which "superimposed a frame of hairy deviance" on the organization.[92] Similarly, media photographers focused on hippie youths with particularly long hair or outlandish clothes in their photos.[93]

The Federal Bureau of Investigation (FBI) aided the media in portraying a "deviant" image of sds members. Starting in 1964, the FBI began to monitor the activities and meetings of sds, convinced that the organization was connected to the Communist Party and infiltrated with Soviet spies.[94] While the FBI never found concrete evidence to support these claims, its research helped to portray the organization as a threat. The FBI built upon common themes in anticommunist propaganda that alleged deviant sexuality and nontraditional gender roles as characteristics of communists.[95] In their memorandum on the 1965 SDS national convention, the FBI reported that "sexual promiscuity" was "prevalent" among SDS members, that students slept in co-ed sleeping arrangements and shared bathrooms regardless of gender, and that attendees were "beatnik types who wear sandals, long hair, and dress in bizarre clothes."[96] The FBI thus conflated sexual "deviance" with "bizarre" styles to hype the nonconformist nature of activists. Sometimes the FBI leaked these memoranda to the press. One was sent to a Columbus, Ohio, newspaper, and warned of the upcoming SDS national meeting in Yellow Springs, Ohio, which would bring "more pairs of worn leather sandals, dirty tennis shoes, smelly sweatshirts, and soiled T-shirts and slacks than ever before in the community's history." The memorandum highlighted the dirtiness, sexual promiscuity, and drug use of the activists along with their styles, emphasizing the "shoulder-length hairstyles among both males and females ... that will stir memories of the pirate-infested days of the West Indies." The memo also emphasized that the attendees would include "swarms of young subversives and near-subversives, including Communist Party members."[97] Another leaked memorandum identified the "wildly nonconformist style ... which sometimes defies the outward visual determination of the sex of the person involved." The report concluded: "Ultimately, [their] hope is to tear our society apart."[98] When similar statements appeared in newspaper articles, it was clear from whom the media had obtained its information.[99]

Perhaps in response to this media coverage, some members of SDS began to fret about the organization's image in the public eye. At their 1965 national convention, concerns about styles of self-presentation came to the surface when attendees discussed a proposal to hold a protest at the White House against the Vietnam War. During the discussion, some delegates suggested that only "clean-cut, 'girl-next-door-type' students" should be allowed in the protest, and that "beatnik-type students" should be excluded.[100] This discussion signaled that not all SDS members were comfortable with changing self-presentation styles, believing that their outward appearance was crucial to the organization's public image. The organization also attempted to highlight leaders who displayed a more "clean-cut" style of appearance. Paul Booth, who was described by the *Harvard Crimson* as an "unlikely-looking revolutionary," was featured on CBS in 1965 wearing a suit and tie, "confounding the stereotype of the radical agitator."[101] By trying to maintain a traditional, "respectable" appearance, these SDS leaders hoped that the organization would avoid the controversies surrounding changing styles of personal presentation.

But opponents of hippies and antiwar leftist activism were quick to channel their frustrations with these movements into criticisms of their hair and dress styles. Leaders of the organization Young Americans for Freedom (YAF), a conservative student organization that often pitted itself against SDS and anti–Vietnam War protestors, often called attention to the hair and dress styles of New Left activists as further proof of their threat to American society. Nate Gordon, a spokesman for YAF, explained that "most of the people who were demonstrating [against the American government] were the beatnik type of person," and that this beatnik style was a sign of their "sick personality."[102] Articles in *New Guard*, the monthly magazine of YAF, derided the hair and dress of left-leaning activists, and cartoons in the magazine portrayed leftist protestors as longhaired beatniks.[103] Perhaps as a counterpoint to the image of longhaired leftist protestors, photographs of clean-cut, short-haired YAF male leaders were regularly featured in the organization's magazine, implicitly portraying the middle-class respectability of its members.[104] This traditionalist image of YAF members was not necessarily accurate. A number of YAF members wrote letters of complaint to the magazine, arguing that they, too, wore long hair and unconventional clothes. "If conservatism is truly individualism, then don't ridicule individualists!" one letter proclaimed.[105] But YAF still implied that the alleged normative self-presentation of their membership was evidence of the virtue and Americanism of the organization.

Some politicians also focused on the self-presentation—and particularly the long hair—of leftist student protestors. George Wallace, the former governor of Alabama who gained significant popular support as a conservative third-party presidential candidate in 1964 and 1968, often decried the "long hairs and short skirts" of student protestors in his campaign speeches and would threaten to "grab some of those college students by their long hair and teach them a thing or two."[106] When leftist activists protested at his rallies, Wallace wasn't afraid to deride them to their faces. At one speech in Orange County, California, when a longhaired man yelled at the stage, Wallace replied, "And let me, ma'am, say this to you," explicitly calling into question the gender of the protestor.[107] Not all of Wallace's hecklers had long hair or wore "hippie" styles, of course; but Wallace emphasized and exaggerated these traits to exploit their self-presentation for his own political gain.[108] Indeed, crowds at Wallace rallies were occasionally incited by his rhetoric. At one rally in San Francisco, some listeners chanted "kill the hippies," and one woman hit a bearded, hippie-looking youth with an umbrella.[109]

Historians documenting the unexpected success of George Wallace's presidential campaigns have mainly focused on his views on race and segregation, which garnered support from whites across the country who were growing wary of the African American civil rights movement in the wake of urban riots, the growth of Black Power, and challenges to segregated schools and housing in the North.[110] But Wallace also gained support from Americans who were outraged by the "unruliness" of student protestors who not only seemed to support anti-American communist forces in Vietnam, but also allegedly refused to listen to authorities and obey the law. As historian Dan Carter explains, "Wallace wove the specter of civil disorder, street crime, the growing assertiveness of minorities, and Communist-inspired pro-Vietcong street demonstrations into an angry tapestry."[111] Wallace's specific attacks on long hair and miniskirts suggest that self-presentation styles signified the rebelliousness and "civil disorder" that these activists seemed to represent to their opponents. Interviews with Wallace voters emphasized not only their disagreement with liberal public policies, but also their hatred of long hair on men, miniskirts on women, and changing sexual mores among youths. "If any of my sons came home with long hair ... I'd cripple him for life," one Wallace supporter in Birmingham proclaimed.[112] In contrast to their portrayals of student protestors, newspaper articles emphasized the "clean" and "decent" styles of Wallace supporters. "No miniskirts to speak of, but plenty of matrons with heavy makeup and floppy hats and hairstyles," was how one journalist described the Wallace crowd. "They were all decent looking people . . . the men wearing slacks and short-sleeved sport shirts and the women cotton frocks," wrote another.[113] These descriptions of self-presentation styles contrasted with images of "disorderly" and "rebellious" social activists to symbolize the ideological differences between the two groups. To opponents of the social movements of the 1960s, the hair and dress styles of activists symbolized their anti-Americanism, demonstrated by their antiwar activism and their alleged contempt for social order.

George Wallace was not the only politician to criticize the self-presentation styles of student activists. Ronald Reagan, the Republican governor of California, famously described a hippie as someone "who dresses like Tarzan, has hair like Jane, and smells like Cheetah."[114] Maryland governor Spiro Agnew, who became Richard Nixon's vice president, also made fun of hippie styles and student protestors. At a speech at Brigham Young University, Agnew remarked that the campus "offers a refreshing change of pace. . . . Here the scenery is magnificent, the buildings are handsome, and you can still tell the boys from the girls. Now don't misunderstand me, I don't have anything against long hair, but I didn't raise my son to be my daughter."[115] Agnew's (and Wallace's) specifically gendered attacks on the hair and dress styles of student protestors were matched by their gendered attacks on the New Left and liberal politics more broadly. In one speech in New Orleans in 1969, Agnew famously called anti–Vietnam War protestors an "effete corps of impudent snobs," implying that antiwar protest and leftist activism were unmanly and signs of effeminate weakness.[116] In other speeches, Agnew warned that student protestors were turning America into an "effete society."[117] Wallace made similar gendered attacks in his speeches, deriding liberal, antiwar intellectuals as "bungling and effete."[118] Gendered attacks on liberal policies exacerbated their derision of longhaired student protestors, implying that leftist activists and their antiwar stance were "unmanly" and a threat to conventional gender norms.

Some antiwar politicians distanced themselves from the styles of self-fashioning that provoked so much ire among some Americans. The dress and grooming codes for Democrat Eugene McCarthy's 1968 presidential campaign volunteers—for which males cut their hair and shaved their beards, and females eschewed pants and miniskirts—epitomized this approach.[119] One magazine article described the efforts of McCarthy's young volunteers as follows: "To escape the hippie image, miniskirted girls went midi, and bearded boys either shaved or stayed in the back rooms, licking envelopes.... One youth cold-shaved his chin in a Concord street to get 'Clean for Gene,' while another hirsute canvasser, barred entry because of his beard by an irate housewife, borrowed a razor and tried to convert her while depilating."[120] The grooming and dress codes thus attempted to display a more moderate image of the antiwar movement to the public. As one student volunteer put it, "Many of our friends are hairy in their private lives, but when they are campaigning they know what is appropriate for the situation.... We aren't bothered by long hair, but we know how our mothers and grandmothers think."[121] The dress and grooming code of the McCarthy campaign therefore appealed to public sensibilities that favored traditional modes of grooming and dress and perhaps attempted to quell the symbolism of styles that seemed to suggest rebellion or untraditional views.

Perhaps nowhere could the backlash against leftist activism be seen more clearly than in the increasingly violent reactions to New Left protests in the late 1960s. As dissent against the war and antiwar protest mounted, so too did the number of counter-protesters at rallies and marches.[122] Opponents of the antiwar movement often focused on students with unconventional looks, and sometimes became violent towards them.[123] Violent police interventions also became prevalent at marches and demonstrations. During "Stop the Draft Week" in 1967, police famously attacked protesters at an Oakland, California, induction center in a riot that became known as "Bloody Tuesday"; police violence and intimidation occurred at other antiwar protests as well.[124] The riots and police brutality at the 1968 Democratic National Convention in Chicago have also become famous in narratives of the 1960s for unraveling the New Left and altering the course of the 1968 election, paving the way for Nixon's victory as the Republican candidate.[125]

Certainly, violent reactions by police and others were seen as a response to the unruly tactics that were allegedly used by student activists themselves. But the self-presentation of antiwar protestors was also a factor; whether due to the reality of students' styles or to media exaggerations of those styles, student protestors were believed to be longhaired, strangely dressed "freaks" who transgressed norms of respectability and propriety.[126] As the *New York Times* explained of the protests in Chicago, "The police were confronted by a large group of young people who had rejected much of what the policeman, as a man, had grown up believing to be right. These youngsters were ... nonconformists who wore long hair and garish clothes, and espoused unpopular, anti-establishment and even outrageous viewpoints. Their very appearances inflamed the policemen with hostility."[127] The hair, clothes, and "very appearances" of these activists thus symbolized, for their opponents, the disorder they seemed to cause and helped to incite anger against the movement.

Some police officers reacted to the self-presentation of student protestors just as much as they reacted to any violence on the part of protestors themselves. Sociologist Rodney Stark studied police behavior in the late 1960s and found that some police officers, many of whom grew up in working-class Catholic families, were particularly irked by unconventional gender and sexual behavior: "They are easily shocked by sexual freedom, casual nudity, 'filthy' speech ... 'strange' clothing, [and] long hair," he explained.[128] Along with other countercultural behaviors like drugs and nudity, "sexual freedom" and "long hair" challenged a police officer's sense of "conventional morality and sexuality," and Stark found that anger toward sexual and gender deviance could incite the police to violently abuse their power. Accounts of police violence at antiwar rallies illustrated that allusions to gender and sexuality were prevalent in their verbal attacks on students. Abbie Hoffman recalled that police in New York City called protestors "fairies," and would yell, "You pull dese guys' pants off and they ain't got no pecker"—implying that male student protesters weren't masculine enough to be "real" men.[129] The Walker Commission Report, a study commissioned by the federal government to determine the causes of the violence at the Chicago convention, found that the police were to blame for provoking the crowd, often committing acts of "malicious" and "mindless" violence toward the protestors. The report discovered instances in which the police had targeted youths with long hair, called male protestors "queers," "fags," and "cocksuckers," ripped off the skirts of female protestors, and kicked activists in the groin.[130]

The personal appearance of student protestors informed the gendered and sexual overtones of these police attacks. While the Walker Report recognized that to "characterize the crowd . . . as entirely hippie-Yippie, entirely 'New Left,' entirely anarchist, or entirely youthful political dissenters is both wrong and dangerous," the commission conceded that "the stereotyping that did occur helps to explain the emotional reactions of both police and public during and after the violence that occurred." The predominant image of the protestors in the minds of both the police and the public was one of sexual and gender transgression: "the long hair and love beads, the calculated unwashedness, the flagrant banners, the open lovemaking and disdain for the constraints of conventional society," the Walker Report explained.[131] And the police were not alone in their negative reaction to the student protestors; public opinion polls found that the vast majority of Americans sided with the police's actions at the convention.[132] While the assumption that protestors were violent and unlawful certainly fueled public opinion against them, so too did perceptions of protestors' deviance in self-presentation. "I do not think that the hippies and the yippies realized how much they confused the police and madden them," contributed one writer to an editorial in the *Chicago Defender*. "The long hair, the clothes, the nature of their protest, all conspire to make a policeman feel he is dealing with people more menacing than Communists whom he has never seen anyway."[133] It was easy for the police and the public to conflate the self-presentation of leftist activists with the actual political content of their protests; according to the media, the FBI, and conservative politicians, the student-led antiwar movement fueled threats of communism and threatened notions of gender, sexual, and social order by challenging middle-class respectability and traditional American values.

The violence provoked by social protests of the era can thus be understood as part of a longer history of hostility toward changing norms of self-presentation among youths and student activists. For students and youth, conflicts over self-presentation were yet another example of the problems of conformist, capitalist, and middle-class America, in which masculine respectability was predicated on a culture of warfare and militarism and feminine respectability was determined by a culture of capitalist conformity and artifice. For their opponents, the self-presentation styles of activists challenged norms of gender, sexuality, and respectability, symbolizing the social disorder caused by these movements more broadly. The politics of self-presentation among social movement activists thus aided the backlash that fomented against these movements by the end of the 1960s—movements that, to their opponents, seemed to threaten the very fabric of America.

3

"NO WOMAN CAN BE FREE . . . UNTIL SHE LOSES HER FEMININITY"

The Politics of Self-Presentation in Feminist Activism

In 1971 a woman writing in the Iowa City feminist journal *Ain't I A Woman?* described her decision to cut her hair as the definitive experience of women's liberation. Previously, her hair "grew down to [her] waist," and thinking of cutting it made her stomach "contract in terror." After she cut it extremely short, however, she discovered a newfound self-confidence and independence. "In classes I didn't have to bother about how I was coming across," she explained. "When I walk through the commons, I feel much less on display." Refusing to look like, in her words, "an attractive female," she no longer had to worry about men's unwanted stares and advances. Most of all, by cutting her hair, she rejected the notion that her identity was tied to femininity. "So now when I look in the mirror I see a person who really doesn't look like a girl. She doesn't look like a boy. Really, what she looks like hasn't been labeled yet. She looks like ME."[1]

Cutting one's hair was just one example of how some feminists in the 1960s and 1970s rejected traditional standards of feminine beauty as oppressive and objectifying of women. Criticisms of makeup, high heels, and miniskirts by women's liberation activists of the 1960s have been well-documented by many scholars.[2] But this Iowa City feminist illustrated how the self-fashioning techniques of women's liberationists were also, in some cases, part of the feminist quest to reject gender binaries that strictly separated masculine and feminine roles. By failing to look like a traditional woman, this activist challenged the notion that men and women were as different as socially constructed roles of gender made them out to be.

While not all feminists cut their hair or rejected feminine beauty culture, the politicization of hairstyles, dress, and self-presentation became central to the cultural politics of the second-wave feminist movement, widely discussed in feminist and mainstream periodicals alike. Women's liberationists and lesbian feminists borrowed from popular cultural styles that challenged gender norms as well as from the politicization of dress and hairstyles by hippies, New Left activists, and Black Power advocates. Women's liberationists, however, were the first 1960s activists to connect self-presentation styles to an explicit politics of gender. Feminists did not reject makeup, dresses, and high heels simply as expensive or objectifying accoutrements of a female lifestyle; rather, they rejected normative self-presentations of womanhood as part and parcel of socially constructed sex roles that defined, marginalized, sexualized, and oppressed women. Dress and personal appearance thus became an explicit part of some feminists' political goals of challenging broader conceptions of gender and traditional femininity.

The study of self-presentation as a political tactic of women's liberation during the 1960s and early 1970s highlights some of the successes, challenges, and divisions within second-wave feminism. The politics of self-presentation became a contentious issue among feminists and their observers, highlighting broader conflicts between groups of feminists and the skepticism that some women and men felt toward the movement. Within feminist circles, activists disagreed over the meaning and efficacy of self-fashioning as a political statement. While no opinion was monolithic within any one group, trends emerged in feminist periodicals that illustrated specific divides that formed among activist women, often (though not always) along lines of age, sexuality, class, and race.

Debates on feminist gender presentation also revealed deeper conflicts among feminists and nonfeminists alike over the meaning of female identity and womanhood. Did nontraditional, androgynous or "masculine" self-presentations help to create a new feminist version of womanhood, free from socially constructed gender roles? Or did rejecting traditional feminine gender presentation signal that feminists sought to abandon their heterosexual female identities? Those who believed the former often embraced new forms of self-styling; those who believed the latter often rejected politicized self-presentation as further proof of the radical nature of feminist activism. Antifeminists, most notably Phyllis Schlafly and opponents of the Equal Rights Amendment, capitalized on these "unfeminine" self-presentation styles to prove that feminists sought to destroy gender distinctions that antifeminists believed were real and important. As mainstream media focused on the hair and dress styles of feminist activists and journalists derided women's liberationists as "ugly" and "unfeminine," some Americans were led to believe that by failing to "look like" traditional women, feminists hoped to destroy womanhood and gender difference altogether. Women's dress, hair, and fashion styles thus became the sites of cultural battles over the meanings of feminism and womanhood.

WOMEN'S LIBERATIONISTS, LESBIAN FEMINISTS, AND THE POLITICIZATION OF SELF-PRESENTATION

The women's liberation movement introduced itself to America in 1968, when a number of women's liberation groups staged a massive protest at the Miss America Pageant in Atlantic City. The protest garnered the reputation of feminists as "bra-burners," as the women threw bras, along with cosmetics, girdles, high-heeled shoes, and issues of *Playboy* and *Cosmopolitan* into a "Freedom Trash Can."[3] While the

FIG. 6. Protestors at the Miss America Pageant in Atlantic City, 1968. AP Images.

media misrepresented the method of protest at the pageant—nothing was burned—these activists sent a message that feminism rejected a culture that defined women by how they looked. In a leaflet handed out at the protest, the feminist group New York Radical Women compared the pageant to a county fair, "where the nervous animals are judged for teeth, fleece, etc., and where the best 'specimen' gets the blue ribbon. So are women in our society forced daily, to compete for male approval, enslaved by ludicrous 'beauty' standards we ourselves are conditioned to take seriously."[4]

The Miss America protest was not the beginning of feminist activism in the 1960s; earlier in the decade, new visibility for feminist concerns, and new organizations to fight for women's rights, had emerged.

The publication of Betty Friedan's book *The Feminine Mystique* in 1963 called for increased education and work opportunities for women, and the book drew new attention to the plight of middle- and upper-class housewives.[5] In 1966 Friedan and other activist women, many of whom had been active in women's issues in the 1940s and 1950s, formed the National Organization for Women (NOW), a civil rights organization for women modeled after African American organizations like the NAACP.[6] The primary goals of NOW were legal and legislative. Two years earlier, Title VII of the 1964 Civil Rights Act had been amended to ban employment discrimination based on sex as well as race.[7] When the Equal Employment Opportunity Commission (EEOC), the government organization created to enforce Title VII, refused to take seriously women's claims of employment discrimination, NOW lobbied for the commission to carry out investigations and file lawsuits based on women's complaints and also pressured the EEOC to restrict employers from specifying the preferred sex of employees in job advertisements.[8] Early "second wave" women's organizations such as NOW thus focused their efforts on legal channels to fight discrimination experienced by women in the workplace.[9]

At the same time that NOW and other women's organizations were focusing on legal and legislative change, a younger group of feminists was emerging that would challenge the priorities and politics of these older feminists. The women leaders of NOW were often older and more experienced in legislative channels of political activism than the younger women joining "women's liberation" groups like the ones that protested at the Miss America Pageant.[10] Most of these latter activists had developed their political consciousness from their experiences in civil rights and New Left activism earlier in the decade.[11] Many of these women also adopted hair and dress styles that were popular among the female counterculture; long hair, unshaved legs and underarms, and no makeup or brassieres were all considered symbols of a more "natural" state of womanhood.[12] Indeed, one New Left periodical's coverage of the protest of the Miss America Pageant identified the protestors not as feminists but as "hairy women" and "hippies," not recognizing their self-presentation as a sign of their feminism.[13]

Women's liberationists borrowed the notion, first developed by New Left activists, that "the personal is political."[14] Early women's liberationists discussed the ways that personal relationships shaped the roles of men and women in society; essays on housework, sexual relationships, marriage, and motherhood appeared regularly in women's liberation periodicals. Personal decisions such as changing one's last name upon marriage, they argued, held political ramifications and consequences that needed to be addressed in American culture just as much as codified forms of legal and economic discrimination needed to be addressed through legislative channels.[15] Indeed, some women's liberationists differentiated themselves from "mainstream" women's groups like NOW through their focus on personal politics. A feminist in Kansas City, Missouri, explained that while NOW fought for legislative change in "Congress and courtrooms," her women's liberation group fought for a "cultural revolution" to "end traditional notions of masculinity and femininity."[16]

Examining cultural ideas of feminine beauty became a significant aspect of the "personal politics" of women's liberationists. At first, these women focused on the sexism they experienced in New Left organizations, such as being relegated to menial tasks such as typing while men occupied decision-making roles. Moreover, they complained, men in New Left organizations treated them like sexual objects. They were "expected to look pretty," one woman explained, to "look [and] act feminine . . . and ugly women [were] scarce because they [were] actively discouraged."[17] New Left women were particularly enraged when a report on women's liberation in the newsletter of Students for a Democratic Society displayed a cartoon portraying a woman "with earrings, polka-dot minidress, and matching visible panties . . . holding a sign [that said] 'We Want Our Rights and We Want Them Now.'"[18] Similarly, the leftist *Ramparts* magazine referred to women's groups as "the Miniskirt Caucus" and emphasized women's clothes rather than their political demands. "It was obvious," one New Left woman complained, "that the playing up of fashions with regard to women perpetuates their status as sexual objects, and this is the basic form of oppression women must struggle against."[19] As a result of these experiences, many women began leaving New Left organizations to form separate women's liberation groups.[20]

These budding young feminists thus reacted to the era's "sexual revolution" in female dress differently than did many of the women who had at first embraced miniskirts and other sexualized styles earlier in the sixties. Rather than seeing miniskirts as a sign of "female emancipation," some women activists, although certainly not all, instead decried these fashions as objectifying women and focusing attention on their bodies rather than on their ideas. New Left men, however, were far from the only ones to focus on women as sexual objects. The American media was filled with sexualized images of women, particularly when it came to makeup, hair, and dress. One feminist explained that advertisements for cosmetics and feminine beauty products were really "aimed more at men than women. They encourage men to expect women to sport all the latest trappings of sexual slavery—expectations women must then fulfill if they are to survive. . . . One of a woman's jobs in this society is to be an attractive sexual object, and clothes and makeup are tools of the trade."[21] Women felt compelled to buy a myriad of beauty products to attain the standards of attractiveness and femininity that society required; in this way, capitalism and social expectations of beauty culture went hand in hand as mutually reinforcing the oppression of women.[22] "Makeup," one San Francisco feminist wrote, "is merely a toy that manufacturers have been pushing down our throats *for years* via TV commercials and ads which skillfully convince us that this miracle called makeup is the only way to ensure our success, love, and acceptance in this society."[23] Women's liberationists therefore based their rejection of beauty culture in part on arguments against consumer capitalism that the hippie counterculture had previously advanced.

Underlying these criticisms of consumer culture and sexualization were deeper feminist critiques of existing standards of femininity and womanhood. Women's liberationist Ellen Willis explained this concept in a 1969 issue of *Mademoiselle*: "In the typical American family," she explained, "a girl is trained from babyhood to be what the culture defines as feminine. . . . That means being preoccupied with clothes and makeup—with how she looks instead of what she does."[24] Womanhood as defined in American culture, Willis thus argued, was inextricably tied to clothes, makeup, and consumer culture. One women's liberationist compared high-heeled shoes to the tradition of foot-binding in traditional Chinese society; both fashions, she argued, not only deformed women's feet and restricted their movement but also reinforced the concept that "feminine" feet were small and dainty.[25] Makeup, similarly, not only concealed women's faces but also diverted women's time, energy, and money from useful pursuits like education and employment. "I was a slave to makeup," proclaimed one San Francisco feminist. "Always obsessed with my appearance.... I really believed that with makeup I was 'pretty,' while without makeup I wasn't."[26] Rejecting makeup, some women's liberationists contended, would help women to reclaim precious time and money as well as their self-esteem. Women's liberationists thus argued for the rejection of traditional feminine beauty standards in order to create their own definitions of female personhood through new forms of self-presentation.

In rejecting feminine beauty culture, women's liberationists also claimed to discard patriarchal standards of female beauty. It was men, women's liberationists argued, who created traditional feminine fashions and beauty culture as a means to keep women oppressed, stealing their time and money and harming their mobility by forcing them to wear expensive, constricting makeup and fashions. "Women have been forced to dress as objects since the invention of patriarchy," one woman explained. "Why are women forced to dress certain ways? Because our clothes help keep us oppressed. They are a constant reminder of our position."[27] "Who is the Man?" another group of feminists asked. "He values women according to our physical appearance. He imposes his idea of womanhood on us, rewarding us for being weak and defenseless."[28] By rejecting patriarchal definitions of femininity, women's liberationists claimed to advance an ideal of womanhood free from the judgments of male expectations of female beauty.

Lesbian feminists further articulated connections between patri-

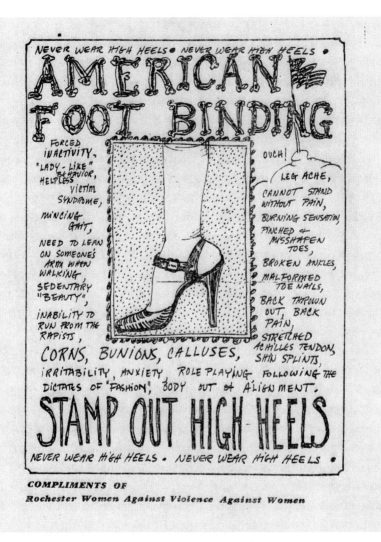

FIG. 7. A flyer from a women's liberation organization in Rochester, New York. Sophia Smith Collection, Smith College.

archy and traditional feminine gender presentation. These lesbians, who often formed separate organizations in the 1970s because they felt marginalized in so-called mainstream women's groups, argued that lesbianism was a political statement against traditional definitions of womanhood.[29] Lesbians, they claimed, should not be afraid to shed stereotypical feminine dress and gender presentation as part of this statement. In the 1970 manifesto "The Women-Identified Woman," members of the organization Radicalesbians explained that lesbianism provided women the ultimate escape from "male culture" by rejecting all social definitions of what women ought to be—not only that women were sexual objects at the service of men, but also that women needed to look "feminine" in order to be desirable to men.[30] Some lesbian feminists thus claimed to discard both social expectations of heterosexuality, which bound women to men, and cultural expectations of femininity, which bound women to *look* a certain way *for* men. "I am in deeper and more righteous revolt," explained lesbian feminist Sally Gearhart, "against the exploitative capitalistic economy which . . . tells me (as it does not tell a man) that [my] body is an object of male pleasure on which I am expected to expend thirty tubes of lipstick every year."[31] Lesbians could thus reject feminine beauty standards since they had already eschewed male-defined standards of heterosexual femininity.

Moreover, alternate styles of gender presentation visually challenged sex and gender roles. Earlier writings by anthropologist Margaret Mead and psychologist John Money had introduced terms like "sex roles" and "gender" to differentiate the biological manifestations of sex from the social enactment of masculine and feminine behavior.[32] Women's liberationists borrowed this terminology, using it to argue that differences between men and women were socially created, rather than natural components of biological difference, and that gender inequality resulted from these socialized differences. "The explanation [for women's oppression] does not lie in 'nature,' that scapegoat which has been used for eons to justify the subjugation of all minority groups," women's liberationist Jo Freeman explained. "Rather, the answer lies among the hazy myths about women and the traditional beliefs of the proper sex-roles. . . . To be 'feminine' is to be weak, gentle, submissive, emotional, and above all, sexual."[33] Traditional fashions, feminists argued, exacerbated these sex roles: high heels restricted women's movement, makeup obscured women's faces, and skirts left women cold, uncomfortable, and sexually accessible to men.[34] Separate fashions for men and women, more-over, perpetuated the false conception of women as naturally differ-ent from men. Lesbian feminist Coletta Reid perhaps put it best: "Female clothing, just like female hair styles ... are all aimed at mak-ing the differences between men and women readily apparent. If men and women dressed and acted alike ... how would men know who to treat as inferior, who to hire as secretaries, who to rape?"[35] Some feminists thus used dress and hairstyles to explicitly dispute gender differences and conceptions of womanhood they saw as oppressive, objectifying, and fallacious.

A number of feminists thus advocated a cultural politics of self-presentation that rejected what they considered to be patriarchal and socially constructed prescriptions of feminine dress. Feminist consciousness-raising workshops included discussions of how much time women spent on applying makeup and whether or not they wore nylons and bras, asking them to consider the role of fashion and beauty culture in their lives.[36] Women's liberationist and lesbian feminist writings encouraged women to discard their makeup, high heels, skirts, and dresses, opting for the mobility and comfort pro-vided by pants and blue jeans.[37] As one group of feminists explained, "Clothing is a political statement. We have thrown off our former mindless and painful conformity to fashion. We show what women's liberation is all about: The individuality of women showing through in every facet of life, including the clothes we wear."[38] Perhaps the most controversial decision that some feminists made was to cut their hair, ridding themselves of the long locks that defined both traditional femininity (at least for white women) and membership in the 1960s counterculture. "Hair is political," proclaimed one New York City lesbian feminist. "Short hair is a symbol of emancipation. Long hair requires effort, time-consuming and frequently expensive care. It is accepted, in fact, almost required by patriarchal culture."[39] Cutting one's hair was thus a symbolic escape from patriarchal stan-dards of feminine beauty. Some feminist women also refused to shave the hair on their legs and underarms, imbuing new political mean-ing on a self-presentation tactic previously employed by countercultural women. "A woman must shave her legs and armpits because hairiness is 'masculine,'" another woman explained. "But that hair is part of Me, the Me I've finally begun to get in touch with. . . . Why should I shave twice a week to satisfy *someone else's* standards of feminine beauty?"[40]

By adopting what would come to be known as an "androgynous uniform" (or for lesbians, a "dyke uniform")—often consisting of jeans, button-down work shirts, and work boots, often without makeup and bras, and sometimes with short hair—these women's liberationists and lesbian feminists visually displayed their political goal of creating a society free of gender distinctions, defying expectations that men and women ought to "look different" from each other.[41] Some feminists embraced the "masculine" connotations of their new appearance; one Boston woman not only cut her hair, but also started wearing men's clothes, playing football, and told family and friends, "Don't call me Ellen; I'm Ellis," thus connecting her new self-fashioning to a traditionally masculine identity.[42] A San Francisco lesbian feminist explained her embrace of the "dyke uniform" in similar terms: "True, many women fear having any labels attached to them which may accuse them of being masculine, truck-driving, combat-boot-stomping 'Dykes.' But many women are proud to be identified as masculine, truck-driving, combat-boot-stomping 'Dykes!'"[43]

Other feminists imbued unisex styles, which had become increasingly popular in American culture, with new political meaning.[44] Some feminist writers advocated androgyny as an ideal (non)gendered state of being. Carolyn Heilbrun most famously articulated the "androgynous ideal" in her 1973 book *Toward a Recognition of Androgyny*: "Our future salvation lies in a movement away from sexual polarization and the prison of gender toward a world in which individual roles and the modes of personal behavior can be freely chosen," she wrote.[45] The hair and dress styles of some women's liberationists visually accomplished this state of androgyny by eschewing traditional feminine dress, adopting some aspects of masculine self-presentation, and defying expectations that men and women ought to "look different" from each other. "Today's fashions reflect the increasing con-

This is a candid picture of JoAnn (L) and Ann (R) before they became feminists. Note how their clothing objectifies their bodies and submerges their true individuality.

This is a candid picture of JoAnn (L) and Ann (R) after they became feminists. Note how the individuality of each radiates from the clothes they have each chosen. Note that they are free from pressure to conform to sexist fashion.

FIG. 8. Before and after photographs of the dress of two women's liberationists, 1973. Jeanne Cordova for *Lesbian Tide*. Courtesy of the Gay, Lesbian, Bisexual, Transgender Historical Society.

vergence of men's and women's roles and recognize similarities long ignored for the sake of exaggerated differences," explained one feminist. "It may be hoped that unisex fashions represent a move toward equality in roles and responsibilities."[46] Unisex or androgynous fashions were thus explicitly tied to the feminist project of erasing socially enforced distinctions between the sexes that contributed to gender inequality. As one activist succinctly explained in 1968, "No woman can be free, as a person, until she loses her femininity."[47]

Alternative styles of self-presentation also allowed women to identify themselves as members of women's liberation and lesbian feminist communities. One member of the San Francisco lesbian feminist group Dykes and Gorgons initially cut her hair "after a man attacked me and spun me around by my long hair because I repelled his advances." She soon discovered, however, that her short hair made a "statement" of lesbian identity: "I cut my hair not just as a symbolic gesture of no longer being a sex object for men but as a way of aligning and identifying with other Lesbians."[48] Sharon Deevey of the Furies, a lesbian separatist group in Washington DC, concurred: "I cut my hair as a symbolic cut with my past, and because I wanted to look like a 'real' lesbian."[49] Conversely, some feminists expressed criticism of women who kept their long hair, makeup, and traditionally feminine dress. "I'm slightly suspicious of women who dress the way our culture has taught us to," Liza Cowan, a lesbian feminist in New York City, wrote. "I know how those clothes and makeup make me feel and it's hard to believe that they're not affected too."[50] Rejecting traditionally feminine styles thus allowed some women to claim solidarity with the feminist movement and with each other. "The time has come to stop blending in with the 'feminized' masses of women, to stop being that invisible minority," proclaimed the lesbian feminist group Dykes and Gorgons.[51]

Alternative styles of self-presentation thus allowed feminists to reject the alleged discomfort of standard women's clothes, freeing them from stereotypes of submissive femininity that were reinforced by traditional dress. "We wear what makes us feel strong on the streets, gives us freedom of movement, and frees us as much as possible from sexist attacks by men," explained one member of Dykes and Gorgons.[52] "I discovered the comfort and practicality of boots—men's boots with thicker soles and longer wear than women's," explained another lesbian feminist. "Levis with all their pockets (purses were an image of the sexual sell which I rejected) and shirts with long tails (so they'd stay tucked in . . . women's blouses are cut short and it's impossible, if you're an active person, to keep them in). It wasn't a masculine image I was creating. It was convenience and practicality."[53] As Cowan concluded, "The clothes I wear help me to know my own power."[54]

NOW, CLASS, RACE, AND "CHOICE": GENDER PRESENTATION AND FEMINIST POLARIZATION

But not all women's liberationists followed these tenets of personal style. At one feminist rally in San Francisco in 1970, some women wore dungarees and blue jeans, while others wore miniskirts and high heels; some women wore makeup while others purposely did not. One young woman told a reporter that she wore "heavy sandals, denim pants, and olive drab sweatshirt" because she feared that men would otherwise see her only as a sex object rather than as a "human being." She admitted, however, that she missed her former, feminine attire: "I'd like to dress up and look sexy," she confessed. Another "mini-skirted participant" explained that she could not get a job unless she arrived to interviews wearing makeup and a skirt, thus constraining her ability to participate in the feminist politics of self-presentation. Other women simply maintained that they *liked* dressing femininely. "It's fun to put a scarf around your waist and a cap on your head," explained one participant from Sacramento. "I like to wear makeup once in a while," said another. This was fine, she argued, as long as she was dressing to please herself, not men: "It's fun as long as it's not controlling you," she explained. "Clothes should be an extension of yourself."[55]

These discussions highlighted many of the conflicts that arose among feminists in the 1970s over the politics of self-presentation. Some began to debate precisely who, if anyone, was excluded from the movement by these styles, while others questioned whether women needed to dress in a certain way in order to be truly "liberated," or whether having the choice to dress as one wished was liberation enough. Within feminist groups, women became divided over the meaning, goals, and propriety of self-presentation politics, often questioning the relationship between new styles of feminist self-presentation and their personal understandings of womanhood and female identity.

How did NOW, the largest and most famous organization of the second wave, respond to these calls for new forms of personal presentation? Some NOW leaders and members, particularly in local chapter settings, participated in these critiques of fashion and beauty culture.[56] But many NOW members continued to wear makeup, high heels, and dresses.[57] The national leadership of NOW was significantly older than the members of many women's liberation groups, and some were wary of the self-fashioning tactics of women's liberationists. One organization leader worried that focusing on fashion and dress would distract the movement from crucial legal battles. "I know you, as I, have to steer interviewers away from critical topics like the maxiskirt, hot pants, makeup, bras, and the shaving of legs," she complained in a letter to a fellow board member. "I cannot spend time nor energy, *nor can any of us,*" on diversionary issues like fashion. In order to "liberate ... women where it counts," she argued, NOW needed to downplay issues of dress and fashion in order to remain focused on legal changes that they believed were more important to the quest for women's equality.[58]

Other organization leaders feared that the self-presentation of women's liberationists would exacerbate stereotypes of feminism, particularly that feminist women were "ugly" or "unfeminine." As older, middle- and upper-class professional women, early NOW organization leaders staked their reputations on respectable, conventional self-presentation "to avoid becoming stereotyped in the public eye."[59] In 1967 the New York NOW chapter described its members as "articulate" and "attractive" professionals, implicitly basing the legitimacy of the organization on both the class status and traditional femininity of its members.[60] Some NOW leaders therefore balked at the politicized self-presentation styles of younger activists. Betty Friedan, NOW's founder, criticized their tactics at the 1969 Congress to Unite Women in New York City, when a group of young women from Boston's Cell 16, a radical feminist group, went on stage and began to chop off each others' hair. "The message some were trying to push," she lamented, "was that to be a liberated woman you had to *make yourself ugly*, to stop shaving under your arms, to stop wearing makeup or pretty dresses—any skirts at all."[61] The implication of Friedan's horror over "ugly" feminists without long hair, makeup, or dresses was that being attractive was part of a feminine identity, and that "ugly" women's liberationists were therefore unfeminine. Friedan's fears of "unfeminine" women were undoubtedly related to her initial stance that lesbian members were a liability for NOW and the women's movement.[62] Long-held medical and cultural beliefs that lesbians were gender deviants—unnaturally "masculine" women, or perhaps men trapped in women's bodies—continued to shape the public image of lesbianism in the 1960s and 1970s.[63] Women's liberationists donning men's clothing and short hair would exacerbate the belief that all feminists were both lesbians and gender deviants.

Self-fashioning styles also became implicated in ongoing discussions of racial and class politics within feminist groups. Many working-class women and women of color felt alienated from NOW and women's liberation groups in the 1960s and 1970s, claiming that the predominantly white, upper-class leadership ignored concerns of race and class.[64] As a result, feminists often vied over which types of strategies and groups were most inclusive of working-class and minority women. Some feminists argued that rejecting feminine fashion styles allowed them to express solidarity with working-class women who needed to wear masculine clothes to blend into predominantly male workplaces like factories. If "cheap, simple work-shirts ... are good enough for the oppressed working class of this country, they're good enough for me," one lesbian feminist wrote.[65] But other feminists argued that androgynous dress excluded other groups of working-class women who, as Robin Morgan put it, were "forced to wear [women's dresses] for survival."[66] "Women who work must continue to dress traditionally," one women's liberationist acknowledged. "Secretaries cannot go to work in blue jeans or slacks without arousing hostility and often dismissal. Waitresses, restaurant hostesses, [and] airline stewardesses have to wear uniforms which are sometimes degrading and submit to personal appearance checks whereby gaining or losing a pound can sometimes mean their job."[67] Nontraditional dress, this feminist argued, was simply not an option for many working women. Other feminists, however, noted that the upkeep of a traditionally feminine appearance was expensive and thus prohibitive for those same women. "Androgyny isn't a luxury of the middle class; femininity is," one feminist wrote.[68]

Other women chafed at cultural assumptions that ascribed unfeminine identities to working-class or minority women. One woman of color complained that "Third World lesbians" were often ascribed a "butch" role by white lesbians due to racist assumptions about the "animalistic," "unusually strong," and "unfeminine" nature of nonwhite women.[69] Similarly, one black lesbian argued that wearing dresses and makeup were part of her quest for respectability in a society that consistently made her feel inferior due to her race. Wearing a dress simply made her feel good and empowered, she explained, in a society that often made her feel like "black trash."[70] Of course, many non-white, working-class lesbians found comfort in more masculine styles of dress, which facilitated working in blue-collar jobs traditionally reserved for men.[71] But other feminists of color felt excluded by the pressures they felt to eschew traditionally feminine dress. One Asian female immigrant explained how she felt rejected from the San Francisco lesbian community because she carried a purse. "I wasn't seen as a lesbian. I was seen as an Asian woman."[72] Similarly, when one Latina attended her first women's lib meeting dressed in her finest clothes, with makeup and jewelry, the other attendees told her that she looked like a whore.[73]

Especially for black women, the racial politics of self-presentation made gender presentation a particularly sensitive issue. Afro hairstyles were a hallmark of the Black Power movement in the latter half of the 1960s, but for some women, the Afro presented an uncomfortable challenge to normative definitions of feminine self-presentation. Some black activists used the Afro to redefine what natural beauty and femininity ought to mean for African American women. Black feminist Michelle Wallace, for example, recounted her struggles with "white" definitions of feminine beauty and shed her "makeup, high heels, stockings, garter belts, [and] girdles" along with her pressed hair, as she discovered for herself a black feminist politics of style.[74] But even at the height of the Afro's popularity in the late 1960s, many black women continued to straighten their hair in order to look more traditionally feminine.[75] In the context of these debates on the Afro, it made sense that some black women might be wary of the more explicit rejection of traditional feminine self-presentation by some women's activists.

A number of feminists of all classes and races, moreover, expressed discomfort with self-presentation styles that appeared to be too "unfeminine." They worried that androgynous dress merely replaced their feminine gender presentation with an equally oppressive masculine one.[76] "Perhaps I am in the minority," one lesbian wrote, "but those who advocate wearing men's clothes should remember the adage, 'imitation is the sincerest form of flattery.'"[77] Other lesbian feminists agreed that the androgynous "dyke" look was too dull, too conforming, but most of all, too *masculine* for women. "I refuse to look to the dull dead male and his dull dead clothes for my inspiration," one woman wrote. "I'm a gay *woman*, free and beautiful to myself—I put bright new colors on my face and nails and body. . . . I like long hair and makeup."[78] Beyond simply criticizing the alleged conformity of feminist self-fashioning, complaints of discomfort with androgynous dress also suggested that some women did not want to choose between "feminism" and a "feminine" identity, and that androgynous dress simply seemed too *masculine* for women. "The 'Dyke look' is representative of the male supremacy concept and most Lesbians are repulsed by worshipping maleness," one woman charged. "I believe that Dyke-ism is a pattern of behavior that only exemplifies the male is superior myth. . . . We do not need to dress like male images."[79] Another woman complained of her feminist androgynous dress, "When someone mistakes me on the street for a boy, it freaks me out."[80]

The butch-femme styles that had been popular in lesbian communities of the 1950s exacerbated concerns about masculine styles of self-presentation among lesbian feminists. In butch-femme relationships, which most often occurred among lesbians in working-class communities, the "butch" partner dressed in masculine clothes while the "femme" dressed in traditional feminine attire. While some have argued that butch-femme styles constituted a radical statement of lesbian visibility and female sexual pleasure, the butch lesbian also epitomized the supposed innate masculine nature of the lesbian, and butch-femme relationships seemed to mimic heterosexual roles.[81] Concerned that butch lesbian styles exacerbated stereotypes of lesbians as masculine, the Daughters of Bilitis (DOB), a lesbian organization that formed in San Francisco in the 1950s, instructed its female members to wear dresses and to avoid "butch" styles of dress.[82] Del Martin and Phyllis Lyon, founders of DOB, were among the first to speak out against butch styles: "The Lesbian is attracted to a woman— not a cheap imitation of a man," they wrote.[83] Implicit in their critiques of butch styles was the notion that lesbians, as *women*, ought to dress like women as well.

Butch styles became controversial among many women's activists of the late 1960s and 1970s. Some tried to downplay the prevalence of butch styles: "The obvious lesbians, the ones who look boyish ... are a minority within a minority," wrote two NOW leaders in 1971.[84] Criticism of butch styles also became prevalent in the writings of younger lesbians of the era. "Because we are conditioned for definite man or woman roles, many Lesbians begin to question where they are as women. After all, only *men* are supposed to turn on women," explained an essay by Berkeley Gay Women's Liberation in 1969. "Therefore, the logical solution to your identity crisis is to cut your hair short, wear T-shirts (with a pocket to keep your cigarettes in), flatten your chest, and wear tight Levis and leather boots. . . . Hopefully, we as Lesbians can become 'liberated' to the self and realize that we have been co-opted into role-playing. Outward dress *does not* make the woman, but it *may* conceal a woman from herself."[85] These authors claimed that by rejecting butch styles, lesbians would find their authentic female selves, unconditioned by the social conceptions of masculinity and femininity taught in heterosexual relationships. Younger lesbians thus appealed to older lesbians to abandon their butch-femme roles. "Feminism is breaking up roles in heterosexual society," explained one younger lesbian in 1971. "The new lesbianism is breaking up role-playing in old gay life. The styles no doubt came from heterosexual society. . . . New gays don't follow these roles, they're creating a new style."[86] Another lesbian feminist explicitly compared the dyke look to the butch styles of the previous era: "The new dykes are visually almost indistinguishable from the 'old dykes' who used to haunt the bars before feminism made it clear that a woman who wants a 'man' wants a 'man' and that roles are definitely not good."[87] The implication of these criticisms was that dyke fashions imitated masculine roles, which were simply too *masculine* for lesbian *women* to accept.

Perhaps to downplay this discomfort with self-presentation styles that seemed too masculine, a number of feminists appropriated the language of choice in describing their fashion decisions. The concept of "choice" emerged early in second-wave feminist rhetoric; NOW's statement of purpose, written in 1966, used the language of choice to defend their legislative goals for women, arguing that the laws and mores of contemporary society "prevent women from enjoying the equality of opportunity and freedom of choice which is their right, as individual Americans, and as human beings."[88] While NOW's statement of purpose focused on expanding career choices for women, the rhetoric of choice was most famously applied in the realm of reproductive rights, as women activists sought to nullify laws that restricted or outlawed abortion.[89] Shirley Chisholm, at the first press conference for the National Association for the Repeal of Abortion Laws (NARAL) in 1969, succinctly stated that each woman deserved "to choose whether or not she will bear children."[90] By the mid-1970s, the concept of "choice feminism" became a central tenet of liberal feminist leaders, who argued that "choice" was the basic goal of the women's movement. As Robert Self explains, "Their central claim was deceptively simple: women ought to be free to choose the content of their lives. Marriage and motherhood were choices. Women could choose to have careers or become homemakers."[91] Perhaps as a response to antifeminist forces of the 1970s, women's activists maintained that allowing women broader choices in their lives—and not necessarily mandating a certain lifestyle for women—was the ultimate goal of feminist activism.

Feminist arguments that liberated women deserved a wider array of choices in their careers and family lives also became applied to the realms of dress and fashion. "Liberation" came not from the actual clothes a woman decided to wear, but from the knowledge that the choice was hers to make. Prescribed fashion choices "would simply be substituting one restriction for another," one women's liberationist complained in 1968. "The problem is not current fashion per se; it's the rigidity with which it is prescribed by the fashion industry. We are not liberated unless we can choose [our fashions] freely," she concluded.[92] "Play up the drag queen in you with a lavender ruffle, or censor that sensuous body in a pair of overalls," wrote a fashion columnist in one feminist periodical in 1972. "It's still a woman's prerogative to change her mind, and fashions this fall are swinging . . . from the butch look to the femme and everything in between."[93] Women adopting the language of choice thus implied that they could embrace traditional conceptions of femininity in their dress and hairstyles and still be liberated women. One feminist described her slow transformation away from jeans, work shirts, and boots, toward a more feminine style of dress: "I don't have to be a sex symbol or a male replica to wear clothing that is an extension of myself. I'm discovering colors and pants that fit my body and don't hide it. . . . Someday I might even be comfortable in a dress," she concluded.[94] Another woman wrote of growing her hair long, and stated, "I feel beautiful. I learned from this to make the choice to take back control of my own body."[95] "I am not masculine *or* feminine, or masculine *and* feminine; I am a person with myriad characteristics," wrote another feminist on her decision to re-embrace traditional feminine clothing. "Now, at thirty-one, I wear jeans and yellow ruffled dresses, too."[96]

Some lesbian feminists also used this language of choice when dissenting from the dyke look. "Having long hair doesn't make one passive or 'femme,'" one lesbian feminist wrote, "it makes one a woman with long hair. . . . I do not have to take on or adopt a certain way of dress, length of hair, style or approach in order to be validly me."[97] "I am a woman. I like being a woman, wearing clothes fanciful or fantastic, according to my caprice," another lesbian explained. "I do not wish to pontificate on how any of you should dress or behave; you do your thing but let me do mine."[98] Even NOW leaders adopted the language of choice when discussing the relationship between feminism and fashion. In 1973, for example, the Task Force on the Image of Women celebrated women's newfound choice as a triumph of feminism: "We have freed large numbers of women from the constraints of 'fashion,'" proclaimed a task force memo, as "more and more women are making a free choice of what to wear and how to look based on what is uniquely suited to their personal style and individual lives."[99]

The language of choice in dress, hairstyles, and fashion allowed feminists to incorporate a more diverse array of women and styles into the feminist politics of self-presentation. Yet some feminists complained that the concept of choice allowed women to return to traditional styles without fully realizing the political consequences. Heather Booth and Naomi Weisstein lamented the return of feminine fashions among women's liberationists: "Now, the con goes, a *truly* liberated woman can *choose* to do these things," they wrote.[100] Choosing feminine fashions, they suggested, was a form of false consciousness among women. "When a [woman] says, 'I think enough of myself to dress how I please,' I wonder, 'Is she really sure that she is dressing only how she pleases?'" another feminist asked. "How can we be sure?"[101]

The politics of self-presentation thus created conflicts within the second-wave feminist movement, often dividing women along the lines of age, class, and race but also revealing differing concepts of femininity and womanhood among activists. Did women have to dress a certain way in order to be liberated? Was it possible to look "feminine" and still be a "feminist"? Did politicized self-presentation styles imitate masculinity and foster stereotypes of "masculine" feminists and lesbians, or enable a lifestyle free from societal expectations of gender? How did self-presentation politics affect the public image of the women's movement? Significantly, these questions were asked not only by members of women's groups but also by outside observers of the second-wave feminist movement. The different answers given to these questions shaped the ways in which the public perceived the meaning and goals of feminism.

THE MEDIA AND THE PUBLIC IMAGE
OF WOMEN'S LIBERATION

Friedan and other NOW leaders were not necessarily incorrect in their concerns that women's liberationists' self-presentation styles would exacerbate images of "ugly" and "unfeminine" feminists in the public eye and distract attention from their legislative goals. Media coverage of feminists in the late 1960s and early 1970s often focused on the hair and dress styles of younger feminist activists, often portraying them as both unattractive and lacking in femininity. One *Boston Globe* article described Roxanne Dunbar of Boston's Cell 16 as having "dull" chin-length hair, "sallow skin and beaten-dead brown eyes." "She was the very portrait of her Liberated Woman," the author wrote with irony.[102] The *San Francisco Chronicle* depicted another feminist as "a slim girl in jeans, shades and baggy sweater who used to dance in topless joints in North Beach," implying that the former dancer could have been attractive if she did not ascribe to the self-presentation norms promoted by feminists.[103] While the mainstream media also publicized "attractive" women's liberationists like Gloria Steinem and Germaine Greer, the typical feminist activist was portrayed as a dowdy, unattractive, unfeminine woman who was unconcerned with how she looked.[104]

By the early 1970s, a number of journalists began to openly criticize the feminist movement's alleged assault on female identity. Feminist styles of self-presentation played a central role in these popular critiques. One female author in the *San Francisco Examiner* decried that women's liberationists had "lost their femininity . . . by devoting so much time to defeminizing women, denouncing cosmetics, [and] pretty clothes."[105] An author in *Playboy* in 1970 similarly derided feminists for their "rejection of distinctly feminine clothing and of the pursuit of beauty." His main example of feminist extremism, pointedly, was the hair-cutting episode at the 1969 Congress to Unite Women.[106] A female author in *Esquire* was even more vicious. "Demands for equal political and legal rights, for child-care centers and equal pay for equal work are reasonable enough," the author wrote, "but these have been submerged in a hair-raising emotional orgy . . . directed at love, marriage, children, the home . . . the penis, the pill, false eyelashes, brassieres, [and] Barbie dolls." The author particularly derided feminist rejections of makeup and beauty culture: "Women enjoy using makeup, trying out new kinds, playing around with it," she claimed, "primarily to make themselves desirable to men (a goal which is anathema to Lib members) and, secondarily, for the sheer pleasure of self-adornment." Women who did not care about looking good, either for themselves or for men, were missing an essential component of womanhood, she concluded: "These are not normal women. I think they are freaks."[107]

These journalists were not alone in equating feminism with being "unfeminine." Some American women, influenced by these media images, expressed discomfort with the women's movement not because they disagreed with its legislative goals, but because they believed that women's liberation meant renouncing womanhood and femininity. An informal poll conducted by the *San Francisco Chronicle* in 1970 asked a group of women whether or not they planned to join the women's liberation movement; they all said no. "Independence is very important to me but I think you can be independent without losing your femininity," one woman explained. Another woman said, "No. I don't want to be the same as men." "No. I like being a girl," another woman echoed. "If all women wanted to be the same as men, women would become masculine and men would become feminine," a fourth woman concluded.[108] Opinion polls in the 1970s came to similar conclusions, finding that the majority of American women "favor efforts to improve women's status" but were still "unsympathetic to women's liberation groups," and found the actions of activists to be "unwomanly."[109]

These surveys suggest that a significant number of women perceived the feminist movement to be rejecting femininity altogether, an identity that for many women reflected their important and *real* differences from men. It was also an identity that, for some women, afforded significant privileges: the ability to be a homemaker, free from the pressures of the workforce, and to be provided for financially by a husband.[110] While many women might have agreed with the tenet that they had the right to choose what they wore—dresses or skirts, makeup or none, short hair or long—feminists that seemed to eschew traditional feminine dress entirely also seemed to reject the notion that they were different from men. But if men and women were innately different in some ways, as many women believed, ought they not look different in some ways as well? For these women, feminist criticisms of female beauty culture and adoption of androgynous dress symbolized a rejection of femininity in which they had no interest, and perhaps even seemed threatening to what they believed to be a woman's privileged position. While women might deserve equality under the law and choices in their work and personal lives, these critics contended, they were still different from men.

It was this fear of feminism erasing gender differences entirely that antifeminists used in their successful fight against the Equal Rights Amendment. Led by Phyllis Schlafly and other groups aligned with the growing conservative New Right, antifeminist women and men waged a campaign against the ERA, which had become the leading legislative goal of NOW and other women's rights organizations in the 1970s. Although the ERA—which stated simply that "equality of rights under the law shall not be denied or abridged by the United States or by any state on account of sex"—was originally introduced to Congress in the 1920s, it was not until 1972 that both houses of Congress, after intense lobbying by NOW, passed the amendment. Within a year, thirty states had approved the ERA, and the amendment seemed destined for ratification. But a number of grassroots organizations, most famously Phyllis Schlafly's Stop ERA, mounted campaigns against the amendment that halted its further ratification; even a three-year extension by Congress in 1979 failed to make any gains for the amendment at the state level. By 1982, the amendment was dead.[111]

Schlafly and other grassroots activists against the amendment staked their arguments on the notion that the ERA would "promote a 'gender-free,' unisex society"—significantly, borrowing the phrase used to describe the gender-bending fashion styles of the 1960s.[112] Activists argued that the ERA would eliminate sex-segregated bathrooms, legalize same-sex marriage, and—particularly poignant in the Vietnam War era—force the government to include women in the draft. Anti-ERA activists thus argued that the amendment would erase gender distinctions in the law that antifeminists believed were important and real differences between men and women, and afforded women certain legal privileges in recognition of those differences. Implicit in their concept of feminism, then, was the idea that feminists sought to erase gender distinctions in society. "I am absolutely certain that a major motive force behind the feminist movement is a search for an identity and role which permits them to live out a pseudo-male identity," wrote one ERA opponent, implying that feminists really wanted to be men.[113]

Traditionally feminine gender presentation was a significant, though rarely explicitly discussed, aspect of antifeminists' lobbying strategies. Recognizing that "looking feminine is important" to defeat the ERA, Schlafly instructed anti-ERA activists to wear dresses and makeup when they went to their state capitols.[114] Other groups of anti-ERA activists became known as the "Pink Ladies" for the pink dresses they wore when lobbying.[115] These strategies of dress and gender presentation, along with the home-baked cookies and pies that these women often brought with them to give to state legislators, provided symbolic reminders that anti-ERA women were *real* women— and implied that feminists, with their antimarriage, antichildren, and antifeminine dress stances, might not be.

The specific focus on dress and hairstyles among antifeminists and anti-ERA activists suggests that some of the backlash against feminism in the 1970s was fostered by the cultural politics of women's liberation just as much as by the political goals of feminist activism. While many women and men expressed agreement with the concepts of legal equality for the sexes and choice in women's lives, feminist activism that seemed to ignore differences between men and women—including androgynous dress styles that obscured gender distinctions—seemed to push feminist reasoning too far for some would-be supporters of the movement. "Millions of Americans . . . deplore the practice of paying women less just because they are women, or denying women equal rights to the ownership and disposition of property," wrote one ERA supporter in 1973. "But what has the urgent need to erase these discriminations got to do with whether women wear bras?"[116] Legal equality between men and women, in other words, seemed reasonable to many Americans; but cultural challenges to gender differences seemed to take the principles of feminism too far. Capitalizing on these doubts, antifeminist activists argued that the ERA would do more than merely guarantee women equal rights; rather, they argued, the amendment would erase gender distinctions entirely. The traditionally feminine dress styles of anti-ERA lobbyists, alongside public derision of feminist androgyny, provided subtle reminders of the concepts of womanhood that antifeminists believed were at stake. Self-presentation thus became a symbol of deeper cultural debates over the meaning of feminism and its challenges to traditional womanhood.

FEMINISM, WOMANHOOD, AND THE POLITICS OF SELF-PRESENTATION

These debates over the meaning of particular styles of feminist self-presentation—among women's liberationists and lesbian feminists, among middle-class and working-class feminists and women of color, and among the media and antifeminist lobbyists against the ERA— illustrate how the politics of self-presentation, for both its advocates and its dissenters, implicated deeper questions about femininity and womanhood in the context of feminist activism of the 1960s and 1970s. For some women, new styles of self-presentation eschewed patriarchal definitions of femininity and created a new model of liberated womanhood, in which women could claim freedom of choice in their dress. For others, shedding traditional feminine dress and hairstyles suggested a form of womanhood at odds with their cultural conception of gender. For these individuals, the politics of self-presentation symbolized their interpretation that feminists sought to erase gender differences between the sexes that were widely considered to be real and important. What was liberating for some women—to declare one's lesbianism, to avoid marriage, to choose to end a pregnancy, or to cut one's hair—was for other women an abhorrent rejection of their personal conception of womanhood. Debates over the politics of self-presentation thus reflected deep disagreements both inside and outside of feminism on the central question of what it meant to be a woman in the era of women's liberation.

These debates continue today, whether in media discussions of Hillary Clinton's pantsuits and Sarah Palin's "fashionable" styles and high heels during the 2008 presidential campaign, or critiques of the popular television show *Toddlers & Tiaras*. Despite the legal and cultural gains of the second-wave feminist movement—including the acceptance of women in the workforce, as athletes, and as political leaders—for some Americans, the assumption still remains that to be a feminist means giving up one's femininity. And dress remains a potent symbol of the challenges that feminists face. Even as two women seriously contended for the highest political offices in the United States, their choices of dress were scrutinized and politicized as signs of their femininity and allegiance to feminism.[117] The current incarnation of "third-wave" feminism, and the emphasis on feminine dress for some of its participants, highlights the ways that self-identifying feminists continue to debate the implications of self-presentation styles. Not unlike second-wave feminists who championed women's "choices" in self-fashioning, third-wavers argue that women can adopt traditional feminine accoutrements such as makeup and jewelry and appropriate these as signs of their personal independence and sexual freedom, arguing that women's liberation is strengthened when women can reclaim femininity as part of their individuality.[118] The fashion politics of third-wave feminists highlights how choices in self-fashioning remain a politicized and contentious issue among feminists and women into the twenty-first century. This chapter has demonstrated one of the origins of these modern debates—the self-presentation politics of the second-wave of feminism, and their implications for broader understandings of gender. These debates did not end in the 1960s or 1970s and continue to shape the world that second-wave feminism has made.

4

"WEARING A DRESS IS A REVOLUTIONARY ACT"

Political Drag and Self-Presentation in the Gay Liberation Movement

In 1971 Frank Hartin, a member of the Berkeley Gay Liberation Front (GLF), decided to attend his organization's meeting in unconventional attire. He put on pantyhose, a blouse, and a brown velveteen skirt. He felt strange walking down the street with the wind hitting his legs "more sharply than I'm accustomed to," and at the meeting he felt even more uncomfortable. While one member, Mike Silverstein, welcomed him "with open arms," other attendees averted their eyes. Another member, Tom Peel, became angry and yelled, "A dress is a prison cell." When Hartin left the meeting, his friend walking beside him seemed uncomfortable, "paying close attention to how other people are reacting to me," Hartin noted. But his friend insisted that it "really doesn't make any difference, just another set of clothes, maybe like a pair of crimson pants." Even though Hartin was "freaking out" on the inside, he tried to brush it off: "So what if I look like a Vassar girl with a beard," he decided.[1]

Hartin's account, printed in the Bay Area gay periodical *Gay Sunshine*, failed to explain why he decided to attend the Berkeley GLF meeting in women's clothes. At first glance, Hartin might have appeared to be "coming out" as a male-to-female transsexual; however, a transsexual would rarely cross-dress with a beard. Hartin was more likely engaging in a political tactic that some gay activists at the time called "gender fuck," in which "elements of both male and female dress were worn together in order to confuse the gender signals given by those pieces of clothing."[2] By dressing in drag, these activists were not attempting to pass for women; since Hartin had a beard, his appearance still signaled maleness. Rather, these activists hoped to challenge gender norms of masculinity through their dress and outward appearance. By wearing women's clothes and refusing to look like a "typical" man, Hartin perhaps hoped to challenge the societal expectations of masculinity to which he himself had become accustomed.

Just as women's liberationists and lesbian feminists defied societal conceptions of femininity through their dress, Frank Hartin's appearance in drag epitomizes how gender transgression in dress became a political tactic for some gay liberationist men of the late 1960s and early 1970s.[3] Many of these activists emerged from the political milieu of leftist social activism in the 1960s and had used popular hair and dress styles to protest concepts of American conformity and "respectability" just as hippie, antiwar, and New Left activists had done. But some radical gay liberationist men, similarly to some women's liberationists, recognized the implications of self-presentation styles for protesting gender norms and made gender-bending dress an explicit part of their political activism. A closer exploration of the uses of self-fashioning as a political tactic among gay liberationists reveals how critiques of gender norms played a significant ideological role in the politics of the early gay liberation movement.

However, gay liberationists also had to contend with popular stereotypes of homosexuals that made gender transgression a risky political endeavor. Historically, homosexuality and gender deviance have long been intertwined in both medical and cultural discourse. As the category of "homosexual" appeared in the late nineteenth and early twentieth centuries, early sexologists such as Richard von Krafft-Ebing defined homosexuality as a form of "gender inversion," denoting that a person of the opposite sex was trapped in the wrong body.[4] Homosexual organizations in the 1950s and early 1960s took measures to separate their sexual identities from concepts of gender deviance. But images of "effeminate" homosexual men, as well as "mannish" lesbians, still commonly characterized homosexuality.

Because of this longstanding cultural connection between sexual and gender deviance, gender transgression held particularly complex meanings for the gay rights activism that emerged in the late 1960s. While some gay liberationists wished to challenge gender norms as part of their multi-issue leftist politics, other gay activists believed that these gender-bending styles were a political liability that exacerbated stereotypes of homosexuality and, as feminist critics argued, of women. Debates on self-presentation, moreover, raised questions about who belonged among the constituents of gay liberation, as transvestites, drag queens, and transsexuals attempted to carve out a place for themselves within the movement. While drag remained a marker of gay community at pride parades and events throughout the 1970s, proper self-presentation in everyday dress remained hotly contested within the gay movement. Perhaps most significantly, drag and gender transgression in dress became political liabilities for the gay movement as antigay activists—most notably, Anita Bryant—used gender nonconformity as an argument against affording gays equal rights and protection from discrimination. With legal gains seeming to hang in the balance, voices in favor of gender transgression were drowned out by those who advocated gender normativity, alleging that gays, in their dress and everyday lifestyles, were "just like everyone else."

It remains a popular misconception that the gay rights movement began at the June 1969 rebellion at the Stonewall Inn in New York City.[5] While the Stonewall Rebellion certainly marked a turning point in the growth of the modern gay movement, historians have illustrated how homosexual activists first began forming "homophile" organizations to fight for their rights in the 1950s.[6] For these early homophile groups, combating stereotypes about gender-deviant homosexuality became one of their primary goals. Dress codes requiring suits for men and dresses for women at official functions of the Mattachine Society, a nationwide homophile group established in the 1950s, underscored how gender-normative presentation was a central tactic in their quests for rights and respectability.[7] New homophile organizations, such as the Society for Individual Rights (SIR) in San Francisco, grew and became increasingly militant in the 1960s, as did some chapters of the Mattachine Society; but these organizations remained committed to maintaining "respectability" in their dress, mirroring the personal presentation tactics of civil rights and SDS activists of the early 1960s. When the Mattachine Society chapters of Washington DC and Philadelphia held pickets in front of the White House and Independence Hall in the late 1960s, they still required a strict dress code of suits, ties, and neatly cut short hair for men and dresses for women.[8]

By the late 1960s, a new group of gay activists began to emerge out of the same political and cultural milieu as the New Left, Black Power, and anti–Vietnam War movements, forming new organizations such as Vanguard (1966) and the Committee for Homosexual Freedom (1969) in San Francisco, and the Gay Liberation Front (1969) in New York City. These activists were often younger than the members of the Mattachine Society or SIR, and many of them had been involved in New Left organizations and antiwar protests. In contrast to older homophile leaders, who fought for the rights of homosexuals to serve in the military, young gay men, like their younger straight counterparts, criticized the Vietnam War and the conventional markers of masculinity that went along with military service. They also borrowed "revolutionary" rhetoric from their New Left and Black Power counterparts, "display[ing] a distinctly countercultural style at odds with the staid decorum and liberal nationalism of the homophiles," according to Justin Suran.[9]

Hair and dress were significant aspects of the "distinctly countercultural style" of these new gay activists. Many young gay activists adopted the long hair, blue jeans, and unconventional attire of the hippie counterculture.[10] As (mostly male) leaders of these new gay organizations began to emerge in the public eye, the media often focused, as they did with the hippies, on their long hairstyles. In November 1969, when the *San Francisco Chronicle* covered the court hearing of gay activists who were arrested after a public demonstration, it could not help but comment on the "long blond hair" of twenty-four-year-old Patrick Brown, who made a point of "sweeping back his ... hair" when speaking to the judge.[11] Other newspapers commented on the "hippie" styles of young gay activists who often kissed in public, illustrating their nonconformity to both sexual and self-presentation norms.[12]

These new styles of self-presentation created conflicts with the older generation of homophile leaders, many of whom still wanted activists to follow "respectable" modes of dress during public protests. The clash became apparent at a 1969 demonstration organized by the Mattachine Society in Philadelphia. Occurring just days after the Stonewall Rebellion, a new crop of young gays from New York City came down to join in the march. Previous participants "noticed immediately the difference" between the 1969 protest and the pickets of previous years. What had normally been a crowd of ten or fifteen people had ballooned to 150, and younger participants did not follow the dress code; women and men both arrived in jeans, and many of the men wore their hair long and unkempt. At one point, one participant remembered, Washington DC activist Frank Kameny "almost [had] a cardiac" when two female participants held hands. But it was "the new attire" of the young gays that garnered the most whispering among older activists in the picket line.[13]

FIG. 9. Two gay activists at a rally in Albany, New York, 1971. Diana Davies.
Courtesy of the New York Public Library.

These new, younger gay liberationists had their own complaints about the staid attire and policies of older homophile activists. Being gay, according to these new activists, meant automatically rejecting social norms of sexual respectability; arguing that the old guard activists were too accommodating to the norms of the so-called Establishment, these newer activists rejected the politics of respectability espoused by the older generation, including their dress codes. Gay activists Karla Jay and Allen Young remembered being turned off by the dress requirements at the demonstration in Philadelphia and therefore turned away from the homophile movement, declaring that "it seemed irrelevant to our goals" as gay liberationists.[14] Another gay activist wrote in 1970 that he was "tired of being a department store faggot: well dressed, cut your hair, shine your shoes," alluding to the attire that defined the "respectable" personal presentation espoused by homophile organizations.[15] Instead, gay liberationists called for militant activism that allowed them to be "blatant" in their nonconformity and their rejection of conventional American values and lifestyles. As Bay Area gay liberationist Charles Thorp explained, "It will not be until what straights call 'blatant behavior' is accepted with respect that we will be in any way, any of us, free."[16]

Gay liberationists' embrace of nonconformist attire and long hairstyles allowed them to deride homophile groups for their conformity in personal presentation, which they believed perpetuated discriminatory class, gender, and racial norms. Photos in the *San Francisco Free Press* of liberationists burning their SIR membership cards were accompanied with a piercing indictment of SIR's aesthetic politics: "The Society for Individual Rights, also known as the Society for Idle Rap, is a goodgrey organization dedicated to total integration within the establishment and to the proposition that, with a little help from a haircut and a suit and tie, all men can look equal. Passing for straight is SIR's ideal, and 'Really? You don't look it' the highest compliment it can receive."[17] Younger gays thus derided SIR and other homophile organizations for maintaining a middle-class image that allowed their members to "pass" as straight. SIR, perhaps in response, attempted to change this perception of its members' looks by featuring longhaired white and black men on the cover of their monthly newsletter in 1970, projecting a younger and less traditional image of their membership.[18]

Nonconformist hair and dress styles also allowed gay liberationists to make explicit their political challenge to gender as well as sexual norms. Some gay activists connected traditional gender roles to stereotypes that fostered discrimination against homosexuals. The New York Gay Liberation Front, which formed immediately after the Stonewall Rebellion, argued in the very first issue of their newsletter *Come Out!* that homosexual oppression was "based on sex and the sex roles which oppress us from infancy," borrowing language from women's liberationists who analyzed the social construction of gender roles as the cause of women's oppression.[19] Another group of Chicago gay liberationists explained the links between socialized gender roles and the stigmatization of homosexuality in their 1971 manifesto "Gay Revolution and Sex Roles." In order "to maintain sex roles," the manifesto explained, "heterosexual standards had to manufacture artificial definitions of male and female. A 'real man' and 'real woman' are not so by their chromosomes and genitals, but by their respective degrees of 'masculinity' and 'femininity,' and by how closely they follow the sex-role script."[20] Heterosexuality, the manifesto thus argued, was reinforced by societal concepts of masculinity and femininity that were assumed to be biological and "real." Another gay liberationist concurred with this notion that gender and sexual roles were socially constructed rather than biologically determined: "Masculinity and femininity are artificial categories, as are heterosexuality and homosexuality, exaggerations of biological differences."[21]

These authors not only recognized that biological sex was not determinative of social and cultural norms of gender—a cornerstone of feminist theory—but also that gender roles were inextricably linked to the social construction of heterosexuality as the norm for proper sexual behavior. Heterosexuality was part and parcel of society's definition of what it meant to be a man or a woman, they claimed: "Heterosexual 'normality' demands all-or-nothing outlines of 'masculine' and 'feminine,'" explained the Chicago activists.[22] Another GLF member wrote in a subsequent issue of *Come Out!*, "The straight world has told us that if we are not masculine we are homosexual, that to be a homosexual means not to be masculine."[23] In order to combat society's disapproval of homosexuality, gay males needed to challenge social constructions of masculinity, which were just as harmful to men as were constructions of femininity for women.[24]

One strategy to challenge social conceptions of gender, liberationists argued, was through one's personal presentation. Echoing women's liberationists, gay activists argued that dress standards were inextricably linked to socialized sex roles. New York GLF member Martha Shelley identified the "unease" that heterosexuals felt when faced with a "person whose sex is not readily apparent"—the "flaming faggot or diesel dyke" who failed to look like a "proper" man or woman. Shelley argued that these non-gender-normative gays and lesbians were actually performing a political and educative function: "We want you to be uneasy, to be a little less comfortable in your straight roles," she wrote.[25] Some gay liberationists therefore argued that gays (and lesbians) could break down socially enforced masculine and feminine roles through alternate self-presentations in their dress and outward appearance. "I hope," Berkeley GLF member Bill Miller concluded in his editorial in *Gay Sunshine*, "my barriers against femininity and especially queens can be broken down. . . . Maybe one way to break down these barriers is to go in drag occasionally—something I've never done and which would freak me."[26]

This was the origin of the "gender fuck" tactics adopted by some gay liberation activists in the early 1970s. An issue of *Life* magazine publicized this tactic in 1971, prominently displaying "three bearded, outlandishly dressed homosexuals parading through the streets of Hollywood" (with a "perplexed housewife" looking on). These men, the caption explained, "are not transvestites. They are demonstrators who claim they are trying to cultivate a life-style which will free men and women from the dictates of sharply defined 'sex roles.' . . They argue that the liberation of homosexuals will also free heterosexuals to adopt aspects of the less restrictive homosexual life-style. This includes the freedom to dress as one pleases, either as a man or a woman or both."[27]

Previously, homosexual men dressing in drag had been considered a festive aspect of gay culture or "camp"; the drag balls sponsored by homophile organizations such as SIR, however, were considered to be private events for attendance solely by the gay community.[28] In contrast, gay liberationists appropriated the gay cultural tradition of drag for a public, political purpose, using gender-transgressive dress to explicitly question and protest norms of gender and sexuality. As opposed to traditional drag attire, activists wearing political drag were not attempting to pass as women; indeed, the presence of beards and facial hair on many men in political drag easily signaled their true biological gender. Rather, political drag was used to protest culturally constructed gender norms. As one New York GLF member wrote, wearing makeup or dressing in drag allowed gay activists to "surrender [their] male privilege": "Together we are shedding the levis and leather jackets that secured us in our closets, and with them, our fear of being recognized as 'faggots.'"[29] Political drag not only allowed some homosexuals to be "blatant" about their sexuality, but also provided a symbolic protest of conceptions of masculinity that excluded homosexuality from its definition of normative gender.

For some gay liberationists, political drag often became a prominent mode of personal presentation at meetings, public protests, and demonstrations. Some male activists dressed in drag when attending gay organization meetings, arriving sporting unshaven beards and women's dresses.[30] "Wearing a dress is a revolutionary act," proclaimed GLF cofounder Jim Fouratt, an item which he sometimes wore to organization meetings.[31] Gay liberationists also sometimes wore political drag to marches and pride parades.[32] During the American Psychiatric Association's meeting in San Francisco in 1970, gay activist Konstantin Berlandt wore a "bright red dress" when he and others interrupted the meeting to protest the inclusion of homosexuality among the organization's list of psychiatric disorders.[33]

The use of political drag by gay activists also provided another means for some gay liberationists to critique the older generation

FIG. 10. A poster advertising political drag at the University of California, Berkeley. Charles Thorpe Papers, Folder 26, Gay, Lesbian, Bisexual, Transgender Historical Society and the San Francisco Public Library.

of homophile activists. When gay liberation groups picketed the San Francisco Tavern Guild's annual Halloween Ball in October 1969, they argued that such events not only promoted the capitalist exploitation of the gay community but also perpetuated gender oppression in the everyday world; drag was allowed only at private events "on these one or two special occasions per year" but discouraged as an everyday practice. "*Gays who dig Drag* don't need drag balls to do their thing," wrote one group of gay liberationists in a flyer. "*Do it in the road*, in the *streets*, where the *life* is!" At the picket, liberationists held signs proclaiming, "Do it in the streets!" and "Wear your gown all year round," and demonstrated their support of political drag with their own gender theater. One activist mimicked "going down" on a woman wearing short hair wig and a dildo, another drag queen flashed the crowd with her "very real bosom," and a number of participants dressed in drag but refused to shave their beards or legs. By protesting the drag ball with political drag, these gay activists decried the alleged conformist tactics of the older gay movement, while defending their own version of gender-transgressive dress as part of their liberation: "The Gay Establishment is doing as much to delay our Freedom as a thousand repression laws on the statute books," the activists concluded.[34]

While some gay liberationists embraced political drag and gender transgression in dress, other gay activists questioned whether such methods were appropriate political tactics for the gay movement. Some worried that these tactics exacerbated societal stereotypes that homosexual men were effeminate. Allen Young, a member of the New York GLF, advanced this argument when criticizing drag in a 1970 issue of *Gay Sunshine*: "It is straight society which tells us that to be Gay is to be womanly (read: inferior). Our fight to reject sex roles, and to reject heterosexual male chauvinism, is to reject terminology and humor which reinforces . . . those same straight roles."[35] Bay Area activist David Bertelston concurred that drag allowed the gay community to be "ensnared by stereotypes": "What at first may appear to be defiant nonconformity is really only a more subtle form of enslavement," he wrote.[36] These authors implied that political drag catered to oppressive stereotypes about homosexual men that activists should work to reject.

By combating stereotypes of "effeminate" homosexuality, gay liberationists could perhaps form alliances with other radical groups. Scholars have recognized the masculinist undertones of New Left and

Black Power organizations and how the activism of these movements was often predicated on the rhetoric of masculine power and manhood rights.[37] Particularly, the use of the term "faggot" by Students for a Democratic Society (SDS) and the Black Panthers as an "all-purpose insult" against their enemies revealed not only their gendered bias against homosexuality but also the masculinist assumptions of their political militancy.[38] When gay liberationists joined SDS brigades to Cuba in the late 1960s and early 1970s, they encountered homophobic slurs from other activists, evidence of the homophobic tensions that simmered under the surface of New Left organizations.[39] It is no small wonder, then, that some gay liberationists adopted traditional masculine rhetoric and presentation to combat this image of "weak" and "unmanly" homosexuals.

The Committee for Homosexual Freedom in San Francisco was one gay liberation organization that embraced masculinist rhetoric in its 1969 pickets of businesses accused of firing openly gay workers. "Join our [picket] line and declare yourself openly," its newsletter commanded, and "proclaim yourself a *man*," by fighting for rights as a homosexual face-to-face with the world.[40] One protestor explained his decision to leave SIR and join the CHF pickets by asking himself, "Bravery, manhood—do I possess them? Are my bravery and manhood involved in the States Lines confrontation? I concluded that they were, and they are what I had never committed to my belief in homosexual freedom."[41] This language of masculine militancy not only aligned these activists with the political rhetoric of other radical groups like the Black Panthers but also implicitly challenged the stereotype of homosexuals as "weak" and effeminate by asserting their manhood as the basis of their rights claims. But combating stereotypes of "weak" homosexuals with the rhetoric of masculine militancy left little room to include gender transgression in the politics of gay liberation. Unlike the gay activists who embraced political drag tactics at the 1969 picket of the Tavern Guild's Halloween Ball, the *Advocate* reported that other liberationists "opposed the ball because it perpetuates the faggoty stereotype of homosexuals ... and harms the cause of gay freedom."[42] For these gay liberationists, drag

FIG. 11. Two activists in drag at a rally in Albany, New York, 1971. Diana Davies. Courtesy of the New York Public Library.

furthered stereotypes of effeminate homosexuality that some activists were desperately trying to combat.

Male gay activists thus disagreed over the meanings of gender transgression in dress. Did political drag challenge norms of gender that helped to free gays from the norms of heterosexual society, or did political drag exacerbate stereotypes of homosexuals as effeminate? The answers to these questions were not always clear, and new groups of constituents in the gay movement would further complicate the issue of drag as a politicized style of self-presentation.

STREET QUEENS, TRANSSEXUALS, AND FEMINISTS: DIVISIONS OVER GENDER TRANSGRESSION

The gay liberation movement included many various groups of constituents; within these groups, gender-transgressive modes of self-presentation took on varied meanings, often dividing activists over the propriety of politicized forms of personal style. A significant complication for some gay liberationists was the potential confusion between gays dressed in drag (whether for political or cultural purposes) and transvestites or "street queens." These individuals transgressed gender boundaries in their everyday dress as a statement of their individual identities, rather than solely for festive occasions or political protest. While street queens participated in the Stonewall Rebellion, some gay activists remained unsure as to whether transvestites ought to be included in their advocacy, citing studies that many transvestites were in fact heterosexual.[43] But even for transvestites who clearly claimed a homosexual identity, confusion abounded about the role of these individuals in the gay movement. Indeed, some street queens created their own organizations, such as the Queens Liberation Front (QLF) and Street Transvestite Action Revolutionaries (STAR), claiming they felt excluded from gay liberation organizations.[44]

Some gay liberationists, following in the footsteps of their homophile predecessors, worried that the inclusion of street queens exacerbated stereotypes about homosexuality. In 1967 members of SIR debated the propriety of biological men dressing as the opposite gender in public. While many members argued that drag should be tolerated, explaining that "anyone should be able to dress anyway he wishes," other SIR members pointed to the damage that public drag could do to the reputation of homosexuals. "Our public behavior is of supreme importance," wrote one member. "Drag as a comedy in stage productions . . . is acceptable to the majority of our community. However, the homosexual who dresses as a woman for the purpose of solicitation or to declare his femininity should be rejected by SIR." Another member decried the stereotypes of homosexuals that drag exacerbated: "While a small minority of SIR members enjoy dressing in women's clothes, the majority . . . prefer to walk like men, talk like men, and dress like men." Overall, a majority of the surveyed members agreed that drag ought not to be tolerated in public, and that drag was "detrimental to the homophile community."[45]

In the 1970s, some gay liberationists echoed these concerns. "Transvestism oppresses Gay men by perpetuating society's stereotypes of us," wrote members of a gay organization at Hunter College in New York City. "These are the portrayals we see in movies, on news reports, and in magazines. Our oppression must end with our own Gay community before we can expect it to end in the minds of others. . . . Transvestism is a remnant of the ghetto and the first symbol of Gay oppression," they concluded.[46] "Whenever I am forced to endure a couple of screaming queens doing their best to embarrass or offend people around them, I am positively ashamed to be gay," wrote another individual in the *Advocate*. "Such unpleasant stereotypes can only strengthen prejudice, not help to alleviate it."[47] Other gay liberationists, of course, disagreed with this opinion, arguing that the gay community needed to be inclusive of all types of homosexuals. "Prejudice against transvestites divides us against ourselves in a way that plays into the hands of those who want to oppress *all* Gays, whether transvestites or not," one gay activist countered.[48]

Class differences perhaps provided another reason for some gay activists' concerns about transvestites. In San Francisco, many (although certainly not all) street queens lived in the Tenderloin, a neighborhood inhabited by immigrants and racial minorities and stricken with poverty. Many of the individuals who lived in the Tenderloin engaged in prostitution or hustling in order to survive, further increasing the lifestyle divides between them and middle-class gay activists.[49] One president of Vanguard, an organization for street queens and adolescents in the Tenderloin that briefly existed in the late 1960s, wrote in a statement to homophile organizations that Vanguard was "composed of the other 1 percent of homosexuals in this country. We are the hustlers, who are bought and paid for by the same people who will not hire us to a legimate [*sic*] job."[50] In New York City, many gender-transgressive individuals also lived on the streets, often kicked out of their homes by their families who disapproved of their homosexuality. Middle-class gay activists did not always recognize the poverty of street queens as part of the gay liberation struggle; when Sylvia Rivera, a drag queen who participated in the Stonewall Rebellion, begged at a gay pride rally for activists to remember their gay brothers and sisters in jail, some members of the mostly middle-class crowd did not want to listen, shouting at Rivera to leave the stage.[51]

For other gay liberationists, the class oppression of street queens was precisely the reason to include them in the movement. Seeing all forms of oppression—class, racial, gender, and sexual—as interconnected within the complex matrix of power relations in the capitalist state, some gay activists made a point of including street queens in their protests and marches to illustrate their acceptance of gays regardless of their class or racial backgrounds.[52] When various gay organizations in San Francisco banded together to hold an "Anti-Thanksgiving" rally and march in 1969, they invited "Tenderloin 'undesirables'" to join with them. The *San Francisco Free Press* reported: "Along the way two beautiful Queens in full drag were cheered by the throng as they came into the street to join the march. During the rest of the journey they walked, liberated, at the head of the line."[53]

Beyond enacting their commitment to racial and class inclusion, street queens helped contribute to the commitment that some gay activists had made to challenge gender norms through dress and outward appearance. Mike Silverstein, a leader of the Berkeley GLF, argued that street queens played an important political and ideological role through their appearance, which destroyed the masculine-feminine binary that contributed to gay oppression: "When a Street Queen walks down the street, she's a one-person rebellion, her being an affront and attack on the straight world around her.... The Street Queen denies the reality of the whole structure of Masculine-Feminine roles. She refuses to be either a man or a woman, and that is the most profoundly revolutionary act a homosexual can engage in."[54] In this statement, Silverstein explicitly placed street queens at the heart of gay liberation. Drag queens were not only homosexuals, but actually epitomized the rebellion that gay liberation hoped to achieve in challenging gender roles and norms of masculinity.

Other gay activists argued that street queens challenged the misguided goal of "respectability" that the earlier homophile movement had sought, and to which some gay activists still subscribed. "I question whether respectability is a respectable goal for the Gay Movement," New York gay activist Arthur Evans wrote in the *Advocate*. "Gays have always been told that it's respectable to dress like straights, love like straights, and not be noisy (that is, be invisible). It's 'bad taste' to hold hands in public, wear clothes that express who we really are, and hold big noisy demonstrations.... Transvestites are saying that straight role-playing is not respectable. They say that straight role-playing makes people deny their full humanity.... When we stop and think about it, isn't that what the gay movement is all about anyway—the right to be ourselves?"[55] The inclusion of transvestites and street queens in the gay movement, for these gay activists, provided another challenge to the concept that gays and lesbians needed to conform to straight society in order to be respected.

Underlying these debates about the inclusion of street queens and transvestites, however, lurked an additional question: Were transvestites and street queens actually *gay?* Awareness of transsexuality increased in the 1960s and sex-change surgeries became more readily available at major research hospitals, signaling a new form of cross-gender identity that psychiatrists attempted to differentiate from homosexuality.[56] Some number of former street queens and transvestites began to identify themselves, not as gay, but as transsexual. One article in *Vector*, sir's monthly magazine, was written by a "Tenderloin Transsexual," who described her shifting identity from homosexual to transsexual. While she had for years "live[d] constantly in the clothes of a woman" despite being a "biological male," she only recently had embraced her transsexual identity and identified as what she truly was—"a woman." "Not long ago I didn't know who I was," she lamented. "Now I know."[57] Gender transgression, in this case, was no longer a sign of homosexuality; rather, it was a marker of inner gender identity. Other "street queens" read about transsexual surgery in newspapers and discovered doctors who prescribed hormones for transsexual patients, putting a new name to their identities.[58]

Although many gay activists were welcoming of transsexuals, some were not. "Transvestites and particularly transsexuals are still another breed apart, and I have little patience for them," wrote one individual in the *Advocate*. "If a man dresses as a woman for a gag, or because he just plain enjoys it, that is one thing . . . but if he is actually convinced that he *is* a woman, then I cannot help believing that he is in serious, serious trouble."[59] Some lesbian feminists also criticized transsexuals, whom they saw as biological men attempting to invade women's spaces and usurp their movement by claiming to be women. In 1973 controversies arose when Beth Elliott, a male-to-female transsexual, tried to join the San Francisco chapter of Daughters of Bilitis (DOB), a lesbian organization; many lesbians expressed anger when Elliott performed later that year at the West Coast Lesbian Conference in Los Angeles (although other lesbians vocally defended her).[60] Whether transsexuals ought to be included in the gay and lesbian movement, thus, was a hotly contested question. For some activists, gender-transgressive dress seemed to confuse homosexual and transsexual identities in ways that made some gay activists uncomfortable.

Feminist and lesbian critiques of drag, transvestism, and transsexualism also complicated conceptions of drag as a political statement. Drag queens, feminists argued, portrayed a "hyper-feminine" image at odds with the feminist goal of deconstructing stereotypes of womanhood. "I cannot continue to be amused by men who think that the essence of a woman can be caught in the costume of high heels, wigs, falsies, and make-up," wrote one lesbian feminist. "They present this ridiculous figure and say, 'this is a woman—that is all she is."[61] Another lesbian feminist argued that drag was "a mockery and put-down of women. They dress up in clothes that no woman would wear and then make women out to be all of the stupid things that society ever said we were."[62] Men who dressed in women's clothes, these feminists claimed, were demonstrating their ignorance of women's oppression. "When men do women's drag they are making a joke out of the roles women have been forced into," one feminist explained.[63] Feminists thus criticized female impersonation as a cultural affront to women that mocked and stereotyped womanhood and thus projected normative gender roles onto them. As women's liberationist Robin Morgan stated in 1973,

"We know what's at work when whites wear blackface; the same thing is at work when men wear drag."[64]

Some gay liberationist men also recognized this feminist critique of drag. Mike Silverstein, the Berkeley GLF proponent of drag, noted how its practice could easily perpetuate stereotypes about femininity that were harmful to women. "When a woman presents herself as essentially frivolous and trivial," he wrote, "concerned with nothing except clothes and hair-style, make-up and other aspects of her appearance, when she acts child-like and unserious . . . she's playing out an oppressed role . . . when a Drag Queen acts in the same way, she's acting out the same oppression."[65] Bob Kohler, a member of the New York GLF, agreed: "The Drag Queen," he wrote, could easily be interpreted as "a caricature of the exploited woman."[66] Other gay liberationists, who called themselves "effeminists" and aligned themselves with the feminist movement, argued that drag was offensive to women *and* to effeminate men. Nick Benton, an effeminist activist in Berkeley, explained that drag was "a straight man's trip, and therefore oppressive to women and Gay people," because it exploited "those bearing the feminine qualities naturally—women and effeminate (young) men," and made these groups subject to "the domination of the . . . straight male." Gays in drag, Benton thus argued, "perpetuat[ed] their own oppression."[67] New York effeminists Steve Dansky, Kenneth Pitchford, and John Knoebel also criticized gay male drag in their writings. Drag, they argued, was based on the "sexist molecule of reciprocal role stereotyping" that oppressed both women and effeminate men by "allow[ing] [them] no alternative beyond the rigid roles it promotes."[68] These gay activists thus argued that drag, rather than deconstructing gender norms, actually reinforced stereotypical feminine roles that were harmful to both women and gay men.

For all of these reasons—fears that cross-dressing men perpetuated stereotypes of "effeminate" homosexuality, suspicions of transvestites, street queens, and transsexuals, feminist criticisms of drag—gender transgression in dress became a point of contention among gay activists. Conflicts arose in various settings. In San Francisco, Leo Laurence, the founder of the Committee for Homosexual Freedom, threw a fit when drag queens performed at a joint gay and women's liberation meeting; at another gay liberation meeting in the Bay Area, a transvestite was verbally attacked and accused of "castrating gay men" through his dress and makeup.[69] Del Martin, the longtime San Francisco lesbian activist and founder of DOB, issued a public statement in 1970 on her reasons for leaving the male-dominated gay liberation movement, including her criticism of gay male drag: "Goodbye to the Hallowe'en Balls, the drag shows and parties. It was fun, while it lasted. But the humor has gone out of the game. The exaggeration of the switching (or swishing) of sex roles has become the norm in the public eye. . . . It is time to stop mimicking the heterosexual society we've been trying to escape."[70] In New York City, effeminists boycotted the 1972 Gay Pride Parade, arguing that the presence of drag queens illustrated the "anti-womanism" inherent in the "male-supremacist" march.[71] And in 1973 Sylvia Rivera was derided onstage at the Gay Pride Rally in New York City by both gay men and lesbian feminists who objected to drag queens in the movement, until Lee Brewster, the president of Queens Liberation Front, mounted the stage to defend her.[72] During the rally, a number of lesbian feminists walked out, citing the sexism of the male-dominated event in which female impersonation allegedly went unquestioned by most of the participants.[73]

These debates on drag, drag queens, and transvestites illuminate the complications of gender-transgressive self-presentation as a political tactic of gay activism. While drag continued to play a cultural role in the gay community, its place within the politics of gay rights activism remained ambiguous—at times a marker of the community's acceptance of diversity, at times a political symbol against the constraints of gender at the root of homophobia, at times a perpetuator of stereotypes against women and homosexuals, and at times a political liability for the "respectability" of the movement. But perhaps the most poignant cause of conflict over drag and gender transgression in dress arose due not to these internal divisions within the movement but from an outside source: the rise of opposition to gay rights.

GAY RIGHTS ORDINANCES AND THE POLITICAL
LIABILITY OF GENDER TRANSGRESSION

One of the main legislative goals of the growing gay movement was to gain legal protections from discrimination. Modeling legislation passed in the 1960s that protected African Americans from discrimination in employment, public accommodations, and housing, gay organizations in the 1970s began to advocate for laws on the local, state, and national levels that would outlaw discrimination against gays and lesbians in these same areas. In some cities, these initiatives were successful: city councils in Washington DC, Detroit, Minneapolis, Los Angeles, and San Francisco passed ordinances in the 1970s that protected gays and lesbians from discrimination in employment. But gay activists experienced significant defeats in New York City as well as in statewide campaigns for laws in Massachusetts, Oregon, and California. Moreover, the rise of a national movement in opposition to gay rights laws, led most famously by Anita Bryant, fostered voter initiatives that repealed laws in Dade County (Florida), Wichita (Kansas), Eugene (Oregon), and St. Paul (Minnesota) which had been passed earlier in the decade.[74]

Multiple factors explain the turn against these initial gay rights gains in the 1970s: the rise of antihomosexual religious evangelicalism, increased political power of the conservative New Right, antifeminist backlash against the ERA, and cultural fears that openly gay teachers would introduce children to homosexuality. But in debates about antidiscrimination legislation, another concern continually arose: Would employers be forced to hire, as legislators or citizens often put it, "a man in a dress"? While some critics of antidiscrimination legislation asked this question merely to foil its impending passage, they implicated broader societal concerns about homosexuality as a form of gender deviance and identified how dress and self-presentation were central to this image.

The issue first arose in New York City, when Intro 475, a bill to protect homosexuals from discrimination in employment, housing, and public accommodations, was proposed in the General Welfare

Committee of the city council in 1971.[75] The bill was highly sought after by the Gay Activists Alliance (GAA), a powerful gay organization in New York City in the early 1970s, and became the cornerstone of their legislative advocacy for the next few years. However, despite multiple hearings and incarnations of the bill from 1971 to 1974 and a large, politically active gay population in New York City, the law never passed. Opponents of the bill questioned the advisability of "forcing" the city to hire homosexual firefighters and police officers (who would be working in close quarters with heterosexual men, they argued) and teachers (who would exert significant moral influence on children, they claimed), illustrating how stereotypes of homosexual deviance remained a formidable barrier to the bill.[76]

But another issue that arose in debates about the bill was its alleged protection of transvestites. During the first hearing on the bill held by the committee that was in charge of approving the bill before the full council vote, Assemblyman Olivieri, a supporter of the bill, was heavily questioned as to whether there might be "any circumstances in which ... discrimination might be justified" against homosexuals. "After much hesitation," he finally "admitted" that there was one circumstance that might fit: the case of employers hiring transvestites.[77] At the second hearing, Congressman Michael De Marco of the Bronx, an ardent opponent of the bill, further pursued the issue of whether the law would include protections of transvestites, pointing out the presence of transvestites at the hearing by derisively questioning the "people coming out of the men's room, who I assume are men." The transvestites allegedly responded by engaging in a screaming match with De Marco and seating themselves in the front row.[78] At the third hearing—which was also attended by a number of drag queens (and also included Jim Fouratt, one of the founders of the GLF, "wearing a purple miniskirt over his blue jeans")—De Marco once again raised the question: Would employers be forced to hire transvestites under the law?[79] Ultimately, the committee failed to pass the bill. Councilman Saul Sharison stated publicly on the bill's defeat that they "could not vote for a bill that might allow cross-dressing in public office employment."[80]

The issue of transvestism and gay rights became a major conundrum for the GAA as its members debated the proper course of action to defend the bill. Previously, the GAA had attempted to be inclusive of transvestites as part of its overall mission to defend "fundamental human rights for all"; its mission statement claimed that "no member may be discriminated against because of personal appearance, style of behavior, or sexual taste," and the group included among its political goals the repeal of laws against cross-dressing and the end to police harassment of transvestites.[81] But as transvestism became an issue at the Intro 475 hearings, GAA members became divided as to whether or not they should defend the inclusion of transvestites in the bill's protections. Some members began to question whether transvestites were members of the gay community; after all, some members asked, weren't most transvestites heterosexual? Other members argued that "the issue of transvestism is a hot potato" that should be dropped before it destroyed the bill. GAA member Ted Rauch, however, wrote a scathing criticism of these attempts to exclude transvestites in the organization's newsletter. "Are we so grateful for a scrap of protective legislation that we are about to sell out our own sisters and brothers, the transvestite gays?" he asked. "*All* gay people including transvestites are entitled to the same rights of employment, housing, and public accommodation as straight people.... Gay liberation implies liberation for all people."[82]

Other New York City gay organizations, however, agreed that the presence of transvestites at the hearings exacerbated concerns that the law would protect "men in dresses" from discrimination in employment. The Mattachine Society of New York wrote in their newsletter that they had "nothing against drag queens," but that "there is a time and a place for everything—and we . . . believe that for transvestites, in drag, to enter the rest room at City Hall during the City Council hearings on Intro. 475 was neither the right time nor the right place."[83] And after the uproar caused by the transvestites at the second hearing, GAA member Ted Rauch seemingly changed his mind in an article draft that went unpublished by the organization. "The presence of 'drag queens' . . . at the hearings couldn't help but to prejudice the minds of the legislative body," he wrote. "Transvestites and other disruptive forces at the hearings merely confirm their worst fears about faggots." Rauch also advocated that the GAA should "accept any amendment to the bill which is proposed. If the Councilmen want to exclude transvestites from the bill, so be it. They only make up a small portion of the community anyway, and a number of them are straight to boot! Why should the majority of homosexuals suffer because of a small and dissident minority?" Finally, Rauch suggested that "everyone attending the next hearings should come in suits and ties (except women) . . . to counteract the bad impression made last time," explicitly rejecting alternative styles in favor of a return to traditional "respectability" in dress.[84]

Transvestites, of course, complained that any exclusion of them from the bill was blatant discrimination on the part of gay activists. Queens Liberation Front founder Lee Brewster, in a meeting after the second hearing, accused the GAA of "offer[ing] [transvestites] up as a political sacrificial lamb" and "pointed out that it had been transvestites and queens who had turned on New York police at the Stonewall [Rebellion] in June 1969." "To be denied our rights by some straights is to be expected, but intolerable by our own community," Brewster concluded.[85] Indeed, the GAA in its official policies decided to stand by the inclusion of transvestites in the bill, claiming that it would "withdraw its support if the bill is amended to exclude any portion of the community." But GAA members continued to debate whether this was the correct stance for the organization to take.[86] And the issue of protection for transvestites continued to haunt the bill every time it was brought to the General Welfare Committee in subsequent years. In 1973, during the third vote on the bill, opponents once again raised the issue of whether or not the law would "permit transvestites to seek employment in schools and the Police and Fire Departments." While a lawyer assured them "that the bill excluded transvestites," opponents claimed that they were still not "satisfied with the answers," and the bill was once again defeated.[87] It was not until an amendment was added to the bill that explicitly excluded "attire or dress codes" from protection—an amendment that was supported by the newly formed National Gay Task Force (NGTF) and opposed by the GAA—that the bill was passed by the General Welfare Committee.[88]

The debates in New York City over the protection of transvestites in antidiscrimination laws foreshadowed similar issues that arose in fights for gay rights laws across the country. In Minnesota, in 1975, radical activists demanded that transvestites and transsexuals be included in a state bill protecting gays and lesbians from employment discrimination. The Democrats who introduced the bill opposed the addition of transvestites and transsexuals, arguing that "the inclusion of language regarding gender identification would absolutely doom the chance of passing gay rights legislation." When Republicans introduced an amendment to include transsexuals and transvestites in the bill, the Democrats convinced the House to vote it down. But the issue of transvestism continued to be raised by representatives during debates on the bill; one "elderly statesman" continued to ask "whether his wife would have to share 'lavatories' with 'men dressed up like women.'" Twenty representatives who had previously supported the bill changed their minds, and the bill lost by an eighteen-vote margin.[89] In Oregon, gay rights groups built a coalition with drag queens and lesbian feminists to pass a law banning discrimination in housing and employment, but after intense debate, the bill lost by one vote.[90] In Massachusetts, one legislator "fretted that passage of a bill would have drag queens infesting the state house bathrooms." The bill was voted down in the Senate after intense debate in the Massachusetts House of Representatives over the transvestite issue.[91] Overall, of the nine state legislatures considering gay rights bills in 1975, not a single one passed.[92]

Anita Bryant also exploited public fears of transvestism in her famous campaigns against gay rights in the 1970s. Bryant, a former beauty queen turned evangelical Christian, became a leader of religious conservative backlash against the gay movement in the late 1970s. Bryant's successful campaign to rescind a gay rights ordinance in Dade County, Florida, also inspired the repeal of similar laws in St. Paul, Wichita, and Eugene.[93] Concerns about gender transgression played a significant role in her antihomosexual rhetoric. When discussing the hiring of homosexual schoolteachers, Bryant's assertion that "men in dresses" would be teaching in public schools became ubiquitous in her speeches.[94] Television commercials against the ordinance showed clips from the San Francisco Gay Pride Parade, focusing on men "wearing dresses and makeup" and other "bizarre elements of the parade," stressing both the alleged sexual and gender deviance of homosexuals.[95] In the end, Dade County voters repealed the ordinance by a two-to-one margin.[96] A survey of Dade County voters after the referendum found that the majority of antigay respondents feared homosexuals because they were "effeminate or lack masculinity."[97] Concepts of gender transgression were therefore crucial in aiding the antigay backlash that harmed the legislative goals of gay activists in the 1970s.

In the face of growing opposition to gay rights initiatives, gay organizations in the mid- to late 1970s increasingly promoted strategies that emphasized gender and sexual normativity. The National Gay Task Force, formed in New York City in 1973 as an "American Civil Liberties Union for gays," hoped in their advocacy to "convince mainstream Americans that most gays were not that different—they were not all mannish women or Nellie men."[98] In 1977, for example, the NGTF led a campaign against the ABC sitcom *Soap*, which portrayed a gay man cross-dressing in his mother's clothes and claiming to desire sex-change surgery.[99] The QLF accused NGTF officials of standing in front of drag queens at the New York City pride parade in order to prevent the media from photographing them.[100] Other gay and lesbian media-watch organizations that formed in the mid-1970s, such as the Los Angeles Gay Media Task Force, sought to "eliminate inaccurate portrayals" of gays and lesbians in television shows, including depictions of homosexual men as drag queens.[101]

Gay organizations began to publish educational materials that focused on the gender-normative appearance of homosexuals. "Are Gay Men Effeminate and Lesbians Masculine?" asked a pamphlet distributed by Eugene Citizens for Human Rights in Oregon. "No," the pamphlet answered. "Most homosexual persons dress and act like everyone else. . . . The important thing to remember is that a person's sexuality has nothing to do with whether he or she appears to be more typically masculine or feminine."[102] A pamphlet by the Dallas Gay Political Caucus made similar arguments, assuring readers that "Homosexuals Persons" did *not* "Want to Be Members of the Opposite Sex."[103] While these arguments sought to clarify the differences between transsexuality and homosexuality, they also implied that gays and lesbians, as men and women who were "comfortable" with their biological sex, would also choose to *look like* members of their sex, without transgressing gender boundaries in appearance.

In their efforts to prove the gender conformity of homosexuals, some gay organizations in the mid-1970s began to stress the importance of gender-normative dress in public appearances. David B. Goodstein, a wealthy gay activist, urged gays and lesbians to "wear Establishment clothes" and "not confirm stereotypes" when acting as community representatives and placed particular blame on the "radicals who affect bizarre costumes" for doing so—an implicit jab at the gender-bending dress tactics of gay liberationists and transvestites.[104] In 1974, when gay activists in San Jose, California, lobbied the city council for the inclusion of gays in antidiscrimination laws, the leader of a local organization wore a "conservative suit" to the press conference; similarly, John Campbell, a gay rights leader in Dade County, dressed "conservatively in double-knit suits" in public appearances.[105]

In the same vein, Campbell "discouraged public participation by transvestites" in the Dade County campaign, fearing that such individuals would further exacerbate the stereotypes that Bryant's rhetoric invoked.[106] "Those gay men who insist on dressing up as women and parading themselves in public do nothing but create a 'negative image' so far as the 'straight' community is concerned," wrote one gay man in the *San Francisco Chronicle*. "The drag queen—but a small minority within our community, by the way—merely gives fuel to the fire, recently rekindled by St. Anita, which enflames the myth that we are all a bunch of 'freaks of nature.'"[107] After the referendum in Dade County, some gay activists specifically requested that drag queens not attend the upcoming pride parades that June. "Anita Bryant's forces will have photographers at the Gay Pride Week parade," activist Harvey Milk wrote in an editorial in the *San Francisco Sentinel*. "Each of us has to decide just what kind of image we will present to the photographers during the Gay Day parade."[108] While Milk did not explicitly single out drag queens, his message was implicitly understood. At the pride parade in Atlanta in 1977, marchers yelled at a television reporter who attempted to interview a man in drag; similarly, at the 1978 San Francisco parade, a "middle-aged marcher dressed in conservative casual clothes" told a reporter, as a drag queen on roller skates passed by, "Damn, I hope you don't focus on people like him . . . most people here aren't like that, but you'll look at the TV and see nothing but the freaks."[109]

Not all gay activists agreed with this dissent against transvestites, drag queens, and gender transgression in dress. Indeed, drag queens as cultural performers continue to be included in annual gay pride parades in cities across the country.[110] But activists who wore political drag and publicly embraced street queens became increasingly politically marginalized. In 1976 one activist wondered, "What happened to the gender confusion that used to be so strong on Christopher Street, in Piedmont Park, on North Clark Street, Westheimer, Castro?" He concluded, "Is personal liberation dead? Because if it is dead, so is gay liberation."[111] In some ways, gay liberation *was* dead; many of the original gay liberation organizations that had formed in the late 1960s had disbanded.[112] By donning suits, ties, and gender-normative dress, gay activists might have hoped to signal their willingness to work within established political channels, rather than portraying themselves as countercultural outsiders with long hair and unconventional attire. But the new mood of conservatism among gay activists by the mid-1970s also reflected the real challenges that gay organizations had faced in effecting legal change. As gender transgression in dress—whether as a political statement, a cultural production, or a marker of one's inner identity—became a political liability for the gay movement, "mainstream" gay organizations responded by muting gender politics and promoting an image of gender conformity.

In place of political drag, a new aesthetic emerged among gay men in the mid-1970s: the "macho man." Also known as the "gay clone" look, the macho-man image was epitomized by "mustached men with bulging biceps and hairy chests" that became ubiquitous not only among gay men themselves, but in advertisements in gay newspapers.[113] Sociologist Martin Levine elaborated on the macho-man aesthetic in his study of gay male culture in the late 1970s: "The clone was, in many ways, the manliest of men. He had a gym-defined body; after hours of rigorous body-building, his physique rippled with bulging muscles, looking more like competitive body builders than hairdressers or florists. He wore blue-collar garb—flannel shirts over muscle T-shirts, Levi's 501s over work boots, bomber jackets over hooded sweatshirts. He kept his hair short and had a thick mustache or closely cropped beard. There was nothing New Age or hippie about this reformed gay liberationist."[114]

The clone look attracted its share of dissenters in the late 1970s, with some arguing that the style uncritically promoted stereotypical masculinity and a new form of conformity.[115] But the macho-man aesthetic was also a product of its time: an era in which countercultural fashion and politics were losing their appeal among many gay men, and in which the gay movement shifted its tactics away from gender-transgressive dress and moved toward promoting gender normativity in one's personal appearance. Indeed, the macho-man look was not dissimilar from the styles adopted by many straight men of the 1970s, when mustaches became widely popular and a new interest in personal fitness among all Americans encouraged a more athletic aesthetic.

The macho-man style, however, perhaps held particular political implications for the gay community in the second half of the 1970s. Levine argued that the "masculinization of gay culture" arose from a psychological need among gay men "to challenge their stigmatization as failed men, as 'sissies.'"[116] Jacques Morali, the creator of the Village People, a macho-styled disco group that gained a large following among gay men in the late 1970s, explicitly revealed the political implications of the macho-man style for gay men: "I made a group

FIG. 12. Cover of the magazine of the Society for Individual Rights (SIR), *The Insider*, in 1975. Courtesy of the Gay, Lesbian, Bisexual, Transgender Historical Society.

that shows the world what gay *is* now—not this bullshit Anita Bryant says."[117] Morali thus implied that the macho aesthetic provided a political statement against Anita Bryant and the antigay backlash of the era, as well as against the public perception of homosexuality as a form of gender deviance.

Both gay men at the time and scholars today have recognized how the macho-man style was itself a form of gender performance.[118] But the macho-man aesthetic could be read by observers of gay culture as a sign of the gender normativity of gay men, in stark contrast to the political drag and public transvestism of the earlier gay liberation era. Dress and personal appearance remained political, but the message of the gay movement had shifted from challenging gender norms to upholding gender conventions. While gender-bending styles and drag never disappeared from gay styles or gay culture, the overall direction of the mainstream gay movement moved toward an adoption of gender conformity. This overview of the gay liberation movement has thus demonstrated the contentious nature of self-presentation in the politics of gay activism, as gender transgression in dress was liberating for some gays who wished to dispute norms of gender and constricting for others who believed that gender nonconformity was a liability in their quest for equal rights.

5

"EVERYONE SHOULD BE ACCUSTOMED TO SEEING LONG HAIR ON MEN BY NOW"

Style and Popular Culture in the Late 1960s to 1970s

In the late 1960s, the Clift Hotel in San Francisco enacted a policy banning longhaired males from their Redwood Room cocktail lounge. At first, the rule only affected the growing numbers of hippie youths congregating in the neighborhood near the hotel; by 1971, however, the policy made the front page of the *Wall Street Journal* when a lawyer from a "prestigious New York law firm" with "hair [that] extended below his shirt collar" was barred from meeting his clients in the lounge. "[The hotel's] policy probably would be little noticed if only a few stray hippies were involved," the reporter explained, "but it has barred the doors of the Redwood Room to stockbrokers, lawyers, businessmen and the like from the U.S. and around the world." One "put-off" business executive, a vice president at a manufacturing company, complained that the rule was "insulting" and that many "very important people" were being driven away from the hotel. The American Civil Liberties Union, moreover, filed a lawsuit claiming that the policy was an "arbitrary denial of service in [a] business establishment" and therefore illegal. The hotel's management, however, argued that they had the right to regulate the grooming of their clients, and claimed that most people supported the policy.[1]

But in 1974, the hotel relented and eliminated its hair-length policy (as well as its ban on women in pantsuits). "The transformation was brought about by a simple economic fact of life," the *Los Angeles Times* explained. "The Clift needed the longhairs more than vice versa, especially after male members of the Establishment such as young stockbrokers, lawyers and physicians adopted the hair styles." Continued "adverse publicity" of the hotel's policy as more and more longhaired clients were turned away had "cost the hotel dearly in loss of business." Moreover, the previous owner of the hotel had passed away; the new president, who wore his hair below his shirt collar, did not seem interested in the old hair-length policy.[2]

The demise of dress and grooming regulations at the Clift Hotel in San Francisco epitomized how new trends in hairstyles, dress, and self-presentation had become ubiquitous by the 1970s. Long hairstyles on men, pants on women, and unisex fashions were no longer restricted to baby-boomer youths or social movement activists; rather, Americans of all ages, classes, and political persuasions began to adopt these styles. The media and popular culture played a central role in promoting the ubiquity, if not acceptance, of these styles. American corporations and fashion producers aided in co-opting styles once seen as countercultural and marketed them to the mainstream, cashing in on alternative styles and promoting them to enhance business profits.[3] Movies, television shows, Broadway musicals, and musicians also displayed these styles to a national audience. Popular culture helped to shift the meaning of these styles from symbols of political and cultural conflict to playful and fashionable choices for Americans of all backgrounds.

Other changes at the end of the 1960s facilitated this shift. As male consumers became increasingly important to maintaining the consumer spending that had fueled the American economy in the post-war era, advertisers promoted the consumption-oriented male as an acceptable form of masculinity. As Thomas Frank has shown, the counterculture became both fashionable and profitable for American corporations.[4] Another factor was the aging baby-boom generation. Young men and women who, just years earlier, had been hippies, anti-war activists, or Beatles fans were now young adults entering the workforce. Some individuals, once they had the power to do so, changed policies with which they disagreed, as the new longhaired president of the Clift Hotel had done. Other adults persuaded employers and colleagues to embrace what had previously been seen as youth styles, as new modes of self-presentation became popular among adults.

Finally, as the power of radical social protest movements of the 1960s began to fade, so did the political implications of these styles. As the Black Power movement eclipsed nonviolent civil rights tactics in the late 1960s, fears of violence cramped the strength of black activism amidst riots in urban areas across the country.[5] In the aftermath of the riots during the 1968 Democratic National Convention in Chicago, the power of SDS eroded, as members of the organization splintered into radical organizations, like the Weather Underground, which met with little success.[6] As the previous two chapters have shown, the radical activism of women's and gay liberation groups of the late 1960s was overshadowed by a more mainstream brand of leaders into the 1970s, as these movements met increasing opposition from the growing conservative movement. As leftist social movement activism faded in the 1970s, the media helped to reframe the meanings of styles of self-presentation formerly seen as "radical." While conflicts over various modes of self-presentation never dissipated entirely, the seeming ubiquity of these styles began to overshadow the politically charged conflicts surrounding them, at least in popular culture.

HAIR AND STYLE IN POPULAR CULTURE

In 1968 the musical *Hair* debuted on Broadway. A melodious portrayal of the freewheeling, drug-enhanced hippie counterculture that had captured the attention of Americans nationwide, the musical received rave reviews from the *New York Times* and a horrified reaction from Strom Thurmond, the Republican senator from South Carolina. What the *New York Times* called "so likeable, so new, so fresh, so unassuming," Thurmond called "deprav[ed]": "There is something utterly perverted with our society's standards of art and entertainment if these examples . . . in any way actually reflect the temper of our time," he concluded.[7] While Thurmond was primarily concerned about depictions of drugs and sexuality in the show—particularly the famous "nude scene" at the end of the first act—much of the controversy surrounding the musical was symbolized by the long hair of the show's hippie men. "My hair like Jesus wore it, Hallelujah, I adore it!" proclaimed Berger, one of the main characters of the show, in defiance of cultural norms of masculine gender and respectability. And in the opening scene, in which Berger and Sheila cut a lock from the hair of Claude, the main protagonist, hair length provided a symbol of the two lives between which Claude would choose: the carefree life of the hippies who promoted freedom from social conventions, or a traditional masculine life of military service in Vietnam.

While *Hair* predominantly focused on the political and cultural conflicts of the era—the war in Vietnam, the sexual revolution, race relations, and the hippie counterculture—the title of the musical signaled that hair itself had become a popular symbol of these conflicts. Nor was the subject matter of *Hair* an anomaly; by the end of the decade, numerous movies and television shows began to portray changing self-presentation styles to a broad audience. Also addressing popular and controversial issues like the hippie counterculture, racial politics, and the Vietnam War, these films and television shows both reflected and shaped national sentiments on these styles. Illustrating the concerns that unconventional styles raised and the ideas of those who defended them, popular culture perhaps played its most important role in promoting the ubiquity of these styles.

Easy Rider, one of the highest grossing movies of 1969, was the first film to portray the styles and lifestyle of countercultural youth to a broad audience.[8] Starring Peter Fonda and Dennis Hopper (and introducing Jack Nicholson in a supporting role for which he received his first Oscar nomination), the movie tells the story of two young men traveling by motorcycle through the western United States, ostensibly to sell drugs but also to experience the "freedom" of the open west. Billy (played by Hopper) and Wyatt (played by Fonda) reflected popular stereotypes of teenage male youths, who rejected traditional jobs to embark on a cross-country journey, which included using and selling drugs. Their personal presentation symbolized their rejection of traditional American culture. Wyatt wore long sideburns and hair that covered his ears, and Billy had shoulder-length hair and a long mustache.

The long hair of these characters became a point of contention in scenes throughout the film. At the beginning of the film, when Billy and Wyatt are looking for a place to spend the night, a motel owner takes one look at them and slams the door, quickly changing his sign to "No Vacancy." The film thus reflected a concern raised by some hippies that individuals with long hair were rejected by society solely on the basis of their outward appearance. Later in the film, in a small, unidentified town, Billy, Wyatt, and George (played by Jack Nicholson, who joins their journey after they all meet in jail) walk into a restaurant and are immediately greeted by stares, whispers, and taunts. The older men in the restaurant refer to "the one with the long hair" as "she" and joke that they would need to put him in the "women's cell" in prison, thus emphasizing the challenges that their appearance presented to norms of masculinity. Other comments addressed their sexuality: "I saw two of 'em one time," one of the men remarks. "They were just kissin' away. Two males! Just think of it." And as the three protagonists left the restaurant, the older men refer to them derisively as "Yankee queers." While this scene suggested that regional and class differences were at play in perceptions of long hair—pitting working-class Southerners against middle-class urban youths—the scene also illustrated how gender and sexual norms provoked criticisms of long hair on men. Violence toward individuals with nontraditional styles of self-presentation was darkly portrayed in the film. Indeed, two of the three main characters are murdered in acts of violence directed at their hippie styles and outlooks. The working-class men from the restaurant hunt down the three travelers in the middle of the night, killing George and badly injuring Wyatt. The film's ending also highlighted violent reactions to the symbolism of long hair: two men in a pickup truck pull up alongside Billy and Wyatt and shoot them, asking before they do, "Why don't you get a haircut?"

This shocking end underscored the film's deeper criticism of society's treatment of unconventional individuals. Throughout most of the film, Wyatt is called "Captain America," a reference to the American flag decals that decorate his motorcycle and his leather jacket. The film thus portrays Wyatt as a symbol of American ideals that the film suggests are under attack. Moreover, the concept of freedom was emphasized as a major theme throughout the film. In one scene, when Wyatt and Billy stop at a farm for gas and lunch, Wyatt admires the freedom of the farm owner: "It's not every man that can live off the land, you know," he explains. "Do your own thing in your own time. You should be proud." Later in the woods after their experience in the restaurant, George explains that the taunts weren't really about their hair, but about the freedom that their hair and lifestyles represent. "What the hell's wrong with freedom, man?" Billy asks. "That's what it's all about." George replies, "But talkin' about it and bein' it, that's two different things. . . . But don't tell anybody that they ain't free, because they'll get busy killing and maiming to prove to you that they are." George thus identified long hair as a symbol of the freedom that was prized in American culture but rarely fully realized. Drugs and sexual encounters were similarly portrayed as forms of freedom that the protagonists could seize for only brief amounts of time. At the end of the film, notions of freedom and Americanism were symbolically highlighted one final time, when Wyatt wraps Billy, who is bleeding and dying from the gunshot wound, with his American flag jacket.

Easy Rider illustrated a quiet but unsubtle editorializing by the media in promoting the value of unconventional styles to a broad audience. A few years later, these styles were promoted with a significantly different tone. *All in the Family*, a sitcom that premiered on CBS in 1971 and remained a television hit throughout the decade, focused its plotlines on generational, class, gender, and racial conflict. The main character, Archie Bunker (played by Carroll O'Conner), was a working-class, middle-aged white man who faced conflicts in each episode with his daughter, Gloria (played by Sally Struthers), and her husband, Mike (played by Rob Reiner), over liberal politics and changing social norms. Episodes in the first season addressed controversial issues such as race relations, feminism, the sexual revolution, and homosexuality. Throughout these episodes, Archie is portrayed as the disgruntled, working-class elder who is dismayed and worried about these social and cultural changes, while Gloria and Mike represent the younger generation's embrace of change and dismay at Archie's outdated modes and ideas.[9]

Hair and dress styles were frequently portrayed in the sitcom's first season as symbols of these cultural and generational conflicts. In the very first episode, Gloria is shown wearing a miniskirt and reading *Cosmopolitan* magazine. Archie complains that the skirt is too revealing, and muses, "What the hell is it nowadays ... girls with skirts up to here, guys with hair down to there? I stopped in [the men's bathroom] the other day, [and] there was a guy in there with a ponytail. My heart nearly turned over in me, I thought I was in the wrong terminal." Archie thus identified changing hair and dress styles as symbols of the cultural changes surrounding him and echoed the famous complaint of the era that one "couldn't tell the boys from the girls." In response, Michael asks, "Why do you fight it? The world's changing," reflecting how clothing styles symbolized the conflict between traditional and modern social standards. In a later episode during the first season, conflicts over self-presentation again arose when Mike's "hippie" friend Paul comes to visit, donning long hair and outlandish clothes. When Archie opens the door to the house to greet him, he immediately turns to Mike and asks, "Who and what is this, and why is it here?" By referring to the male as "it" rather than "he," Archie seemed to deny the humanity, or at least the clear gender identity, of the individual. When Archie learns that Paul had attended Gloria and Mike's wedding, he expresses shock: "This is that nice boy with the combed hair and a pressed suit?" Archie laments how Paul dropped his engineering major: "He used to dream about building bridges and banks. Now he looks like someone who wants to blow 'em up!" In response, Mike chides, "There you go again, labeling people. Why can't you forget what Paul looks like and accept him for what he is?"

Archie's character thus symbolized the traditionalists of the older generation whose views would be overshadowed by those of their children. In the opening credits of each episode, Archie and his wife Edith sit at a piano, playing and singing the song "Those Were the Days." The song memorialized the "good old days" gone by and implicitly lamented the changes that had occurred in society and culture, including a reference to the "welfare state" that had grown large in the 1960s due to President Lyndon B. Johnson's Great Society programs. Another lyric recalls how, in the past, "girls were girls and men were men," a reference not only to changing sexual mores and women's roles but also to hairstyles and fashions that defied traditional gendered styles. In later seasons, the lyrics of the opening song were changed to make these concerns about hair and dress styles even more explicit: "Hair was short and skirts were long ... I don't know just what went wrong!" they sing. *All in the Family* thus used various styles of personal presentation to symbolize the broader changes in American society—such as gender roles, sexual mores, race relations, and political values—that seemed concerning to Americans who lamented these societal shifts.

There is no doubt that *All in the Family* was meant to be controversial; the first episode was aired on CBS "with a special announcement about the potentially shocking contents of the show ... while a battery of temporary telephone operators were in place to field complaints about the controversial show they were about to see."[10] However, the genre of the situational comedy (sitcom) served to couch these changes in humor and jest, rather than serious political conflict. Jefferson Cowie notes that *All in the Family* "served as a sort of national therapy session" in the post-1960s era, using a unique combination of comedy and conflict to bring "the generations, the races, the genders, and the classes" together.[11] Audience laughter after many of Archie's statements implied that these conflicts were humorous, and de-emphasized any fundamental seriousness of his claims. While the show discussed controversial political and social issues, each scenario was couched in humor rather than in serious conflict. Unlike *Easy Rider*, rarely was real violence a part of the plot; indeed, many episodes end with Archie showing sympathy for opposing views or alternative lifestyles, even if he does so grudgingly. *All in the Family* thus seemed to call for an end to the harsh conflicts surrounding the politically charged issues of the 1960s, including conflicts over personal presentation. Archie and Mike could agree to disagree on these issues, and the social order would not explode.

The contrasts between *Easy Rider* and *All in the Family* suggest a shifting vision in popular culture over styles of personal presentation, one that de-emphasized the political nature of fashion choices and instead portrayed these styles as choices upon which reasonable people could disagree. While conflicts remained, fights over personal presentation and other political issues could end with a laugh rather than a riot. As self-presentation trends of the 1960s became more ubiquitous in the 1970s, popular culture reframed styles with messages that denied their political edge.

MEN'S STYLES AND THE POPULARIZATION OF THE PEACOCK

In 1971 a teenager wrote to advice columnist Ellen Peck in the *Chicago Tribune* asking for help with her brother. "My father insists that my brother Jim get a haircut," she explained. "My father makes Jim wear our big sister's clothes around the house. First it was just her dresses. Now it's her lipstick, too. . . . What can we do to convince Jim to stop being so stubborn and get a haircut?" Peck replied that the problem was not with her brother, but with her father. "In my opinion, your brother deserves no punishment at all," she wrote. "Your father should understand that men's (especially young men's) hairstyles change over the years, from long to short to crew cut to slicked-back long, and a parent should not feel threatened by a style change. Long hair on young men today certainly should not be regarded as girlish or feminine. After all, men's long hair represented virility—remember Samson?"[12]

Peck's response to Jim's long hairstyle became the norm in popular culture rather than the exception. Journalists, letters to the editor, and interviews with ordinary citizens expressed increasing acceptance of long hair on men and no longer automatically questioned the masculinity, propriety, or cleanliness of men who adopted longer hairstyles. Abigail Van Buren, the author of the syndicated advice column Dear Abby, best summarized the emerging attitude: "It seems to me that everyone should be accustomed to seeing long hair on men by now. If it's clean and well cared for, what is there to criticize?"[13] The media also portrayed longer hairstyles on men as a growing national trend: "From Portland, Maine, to Portland, Oregon, more and more men at home in the culture of the nation's heartland are succumbing to the siren call of the hair stylist and his panoply of grooming aids," wrote the *New York Times* in 1970. Across all ages, classes, and professions, the media claimed, longer hairstyles became increasingly common.[14]

Helping the acceptance of long hair on men was the gradual incorporation of peacock fashions into standard middle-class male wardrobes. The media and clothing designers marketed bright patterns and bold colors to business professionals.[15] "Men of all ages have broken out of the white shirt, white collar picture," an article in the *Los Angeles Times* explained in 1970. "And for fall you are going to find even peach and orchid offered for leisure wear."[16] One wife complained tongue-in-cheek about her husband's new clothing styles, "My red lace dress clashes terribly with his mauve shirt."[17] Even Herbert Klein, the White House director of communications and "guardian of President Nixon's sober image" was seen in 1971 wearing a "yellow shirt and bright blue-and-striped, tab pocketed suit."[18] Growing ubiquity of these clothing styles among men in the professional world signaled a redefinition of middle-class respectability in dress; for men, the business executive's image was no longer defined by the white shirt, dark suit, clean shave and crew cut of the past.

But the media took pains to differentiate these styles from those of hippies or radical activists. By the 1970s, as the social movements

"S.E.C.? I would have said H.E.W."

FIG. 13. A cartoon from the *New Yorker*, in 1972, illustrating the ubiquity of long hairstyles on men. Condé Nast.

of the previous decade dissipated, long hairstyles on men no longer signified a commitment to radical politics. Indeed, differentiating themselves from "hippies" became important for many of the wearers and designers of these new styles. One twenty-two-year-old construction worker explained that, despite his "cascading hair" and "flowered shirt, flared jeans and a string of love beads," he was still against drugs and in support of the war. "I'm just changing with the times," he claimed. "Girls like my long hair."[19] Other individuals noted that long hair should not necessarily define a person as a "hippie."[20] The media helped to combat this image of longhaired males as hippies or radicals by focusing on politically conservative young men who adopted these styles. In 1972 the *Washington Post* profiled a twenty-year-old, longhaired, male Nixon campaign volunteer. "One thing that really bothers me is the idea that McGovern people are the only cool ones, the only ones with long hair," he stated. "I can think of two Nixon volunteers, guys, with hair to their waist. McGovern has no corner on the counterculture."[21] The *Los Angeles Times* similarly profiled a "long of hair and mod of dress" thirty-year-old campus organizer who was hired to attract younger voters to the Republican Party.[22] The upscale nature of men's peacock styles, moreover, were differentiated from the "grubby" styles of hippies: it was still "far-fetched to imagine the head of a successful firm, directing activities in blue jeans, a grubby shirt, battered boots, long hair and a beard," one journalist wrote.[23]

The media also promoted styling and grooming techniques for men's longer styles, which helped to differentiate mainstream long-hair wearers from "hippie types." While the "real short cut of the 1950s" was out, "the new look is neater and slightly shorter" than the long hippie styles of the 1960s, explained one Chicago barber. "No longer than the shirt collar" became some barbers' catch phrase to describe the haircuts.[24] Other barbers described the most popular styles as "full" haircuts or "radial styles" in which "the hair is the same length all over: it's a short haircut that looks long." While layered, styled, and coiffed hairstyles reflected the demise of the crew cut as a popular men's style, these longer hairstyles were different from those of longhaired women; as one barber concluded, "Real long hair is going out."[25] These styles also helped to differentiate masculine long hair from feminine hairstyles. "Longer hair lengths are for women," explained a Los Angeles hairdresser.[26]

Moreover, male adopters of long hair and peacock fashions pro-moted the masculinity of their fashion choices. Some men explained their decision to grow their hair as an assertion of their rights to free-dom of choice and self-expression, adopting the arguments of defend-ers of long hair in the 1960s. "I feel like less of a man when I am told I have to wear my hair short," explained one individual. "It's an indi-vidual's decision." Another longhaired individual concurred: "It's a basic freedom that a man can wear his hair as he chooses."[27] While adopting the reasoning that long hair was symbolic of the right to self-expression at the core of the American creed, they also portrayed long hair as an assertion of masculine autonomy, implying that "real" men treasured their "freedom" above all. Others argued that long hair on men represented a more natural version of masculinity, borrowing the reasoning of some hippie advocates of long hair. One individual told the *Chicago Tribune* that long hair was "a more masculine look. A more natural look."[28] Another explained that long hair was "symbolic of a sophisticated cave man," the epitome of original masculinity.[29] Advertisements for peacock fashions and products stressed the sensuality, sexuality, and masculinity of their wearers.[30] Defenders of new styles for men thus asserted the masculinity of their choices, stressing the value of personal liberty in their fashion decisions. It was the act itself of exercising the choice to wear one's hair short or long that allowed an individual the freedom to be a man.

Shampoo, one of the highest-grossing films of 1975, reinforced this popular perspective of the "peacock" male as a fun-loving, apolitical individual, firm in both his masculinity and his heterosexuality. The central character is a thirty-something, philandering male hairdresser named George (played by the handsome and equally sexually adventurous Warren Beatty). With hair to his collar, sideburns, medallions around his neck, and ruffled shirts, George epitomized the Peacock Revolution in men's fashion from the late 1960s and early 1970s. His multiple sexual partners, moreover, signified his participation in the "sexual revolution," in which sexual relationships outside of marriage were not only acceptable, but also served to symbolize George's virile masculinity. Despite his longer hair and peacock fashions, George's rampant masculine heterosexuality was emphasized in the film. In one scene, George confesses his love of women—all women: "I go into that [hairstyling] shop, and they're so great-looking. . . . I'm doing their hair, and they feel great, and they smell great . . . and that's it! It makes my day. . . . It makes me feel like I'm going to live forever." With this explicit statement of his attraction to women—along with his multiple sexual encounters with women throughout the film— George's long locks and stylistic fashions belie any indication that either his masculinity or his heterosexuality might be questioned.

Shampoo defined long hair and peacock fashions not only as compatible with heterosexual masculinity, but also as divorced from political activism. The film takes place, significantly, on the day of Nixon's win over Humphrey and Wallace in the 1968 presidential election. But politics is not the focus of the movie; indeed, George is unable to pay any attention to politics amidst his own self-destructing personal life. While the film makes the impending election obvious, with climactic scenes taking place at two very different election-night parties—a black-tie affair for Republican supporters, and a gathering of "hippie"-style youths involving pot smoking and public nudity— George not only fails to fit into either crowd, but is seemingly oblivious to it all. Significantly, George does not seem to care that he is attending a Republican gala, implying that his longish hair would not preclude him from siding with the Republican candidate. But George also does not seem to fit in with, or even notice, the long-haired hippies and their escapades at the second party, signifying that his long hair did not automatically align him with this group of activists, either. Indeed, the film never reveals who George (or any of the other characters) voted for in the election—or if he voted at all. The implicit message of the film epitomized the prevailing message in popular culture on men's long hairstyles and peacock fashions in the 1970s: that these styles were predominantly cultural, not political, and bore no significance for the masculinity, heterosexuality, or political views of their wearers.

Men's long hair and peacock fashions, which had inspired so much anxiety and contention in the 1960s, thus became promoted in the 1970s as a valid style of masculine self-presentation. Long hair grew increasingly ubiquitous, as men adapted these styles to fit into a framework of masculinity that was no longer threatening to concepts of gender, cleanliness, or respectability. As the social activism of the 1960s faded, so too did connotations of long hair on men as a symbol of rebelliousness, radicalism, or effeminacy.

WOMEN'S STYLES AND "FASHION FEMINISTS"

In 1970 fashion designers introduced a new line of skirts for women ranging from mid-calf to ankle lengths. These "midi" and "maxi" skirts were meant to replace miniskirts in women's wardrobes; designers touted the longer styles as a return to femininity and sensuality, spurning the hypersexualized miniskirt. But while some women in the 1970s embraced the midi, many women rejected these longer skirt lengths; they argued that the midi was a ploy by manufacturers to increase their profits by arbitrarily declaring the miniskirt to be out of style and forcing women to buy the midi as a replacement. Moreover, women complained that the longer-length skirts were "dowdy," "ugly," and old-fashioned. Women across the country formed protest groups against the midi, arguing that fashion designers were dictating to women rather than listening to their fashion desires. Skirt sales plummeted, and clothing boutiques quickly promised to bring back shorter skirts. By 1971 miniskirts were back in stores to the delight of many female clients (and their male admirers).[31]

The mini-midi controversy highlighted the growing acceptance of shorter skirt styles for women. In the 1960s some commentators had derided the miniskirt as unfeminine for its attention to female sexuality rather than traditional modesty. But while designers in 1970 claimed that the midiskirt was a return to femininity, most commentators disagreed, arguing that it was the *midiskirt* that was unfeminine.[32] "Won't women look less feminine" in midiskirts, journalists wondered, "and won't men resent the absence of the flash of legs and thighs that seem to enlighten every subway ride?"[33] Thus, the ubiquity of miniskirts suggested that the public was becoming more accepting of sexualized imagery in women's fashions. Moreover, journalists in 1970 portrayed the mini-midi controversy as emblematic of changes in women's consciousness due to women's liberation. Women, journalists claimed, were now too independent—too emancipated—to blindly follow the whims of fashion designers. Just as women deserved to choose their own careers and sexual partners, they also deserved to be able to choose their mode of dress—some of the basic tenets of the growing women's liberation movement.[34]

Increasing acceptance of women's pantsuits signaled an even more significant change. By the fall of 1970, pants had come into their own as a popular mainstream fashion for women. A survey in the *Los Angeles Times* in September 1970 found that 84 percent of women

FIG. 14. In 1970 a protest group called Fight Against Dictating Designers (FADD) featured a woman cutting off the bottom of a long skirt to create the preferred midiskirt. Bettmann/Corbis /AP Images.

planned to wear pants that fall, including 97 percent of the teenage females surveyed. "To us, *this* is the fashion revolution," the *Times* concluded.[35] Both fashion marketers and the media were crucial in promoting pants as an acceptable fashion for women. "The pantsuit, for both daywear and social dressing, has achieved enormous popularity and ready acceptance," claimed a retailer quoted in the *Los Angeles Times*.[36] Pants on women began to show up "everywhere," according to *Business Week* in 1971, "from offices to formal parties." Photographs in the magazine revealed that pants were now worn by women of all ages, from young women on motorcycles wearing jeans to older women in elegant pantsuits.[37]

Institutions that had balked at women's pantsuits in the 1960s began to change, gradually accepting these styles. School districts that had previously forbidden female students from wearing pants or jeans began to modify their dress codes in the 1970s, allowing pants to be worn as everyday school attire.[38] Fancy restaurants began to allow female patrons in pantsuits, and Hollywood celebrities began appearing in pantsuits at industry events.[39] "The pantsuit is no longer controversial," one journalist concluded in 1971. "It is now accepted at any social gathering, has become almost a uniform for offices and certainly is the most comfortable, practical garment in any woman's wardrobe."[40] By 1975 the *New York Times* asserted that "nobody raises an eyebrow anymore" to pants on women.[41]

Newspapers and magazines often portrayed the growing popularity of pantsuits and miniskirts as indications of the spread of feminist values among mainstream American women. Syndicated columnist Art Seidenbaum argued that pants-wearing women were not the "karate choppers or even dues-paying members of the movement," but that their adoption of pants was evidence that they "hear[d] militant complaints loud and clear" and agreed with some of the tenets of feminist politics.[42] Some women concurred with this assessment, linking their choice to wear pants to their growing awareness of the need for women to assert their right to dress as they wished.[43] As one pantsuit wearer, Mrs. Olin Wellborn III, told the *Los Angeles Times*, "I stand for freedom of choice."[44] Another supporter of "freedom of choice" in dress, seventy-year-old Mrs. Harold M. Stern, sent money to one of the anti-midi protest groups "with a note that she wants to help them defend the right of American girls to dress as they please."[45] Even some fashion designers recognized the broader claims of these fashion battles: "It seems to me that your fight is more than just for length," one designer stated. "It's for a way of life. You want to be able to choose."[46] Growing societal acknowledgement of the right of women to wear pants or miniskirts thus illustrated how feminist concepts of choice—despite the controversial nature of the "choice" argument for women's abortion and reproductive rights—had in fact gained some mainstream acceptance by the 1970s. Alongside increasing acceptance of a new range of choices for women in their work and personal lives, the right of women to choose their own styles of dress became commonly acknowledged.

But many journalists and pants-wearing women carefully distinguished wearing pants from feminism. While some women saw their dress styles as reflecting their adherence to the values of women's liberation, many women and their media advocates claimed that there was nothing political about the decision to wear pants. "Pants do not have to march militantly in a feminist parade to prove that they can stand on their own two feet," explained an article in the Los Angeles Times in 1970.[47] One twenty-three-year-old engineer wore pants and cut her hair short to make herself comfortable as she biked to work, but explained that her style had nothing to do with women's liberation "because I already feel liberated."[48]

Moreover, some women and journalists maintained that the decision to wear pantsuits did not mean that they would forever eschew skirts or traditional feminine attire. Indeed, the mini-midi controversy and subsequent return of miniskirts to the racks of fashion retailers revealed that many American women were not planning to give up skirts anytime soon. "The Spring '71 woman," according to the Los Angeles Times, wore pants, skirts, and jeans as part of her "new picture of femininity."[49] Women adopted pantsuits alongside skirts and dresses in their wardrobes; "I want clothes that are understated and classic without being masculine," one woman explained.[50] These "fashion feminists," as some journalists labeled them, stood up for "choice" in women's clothing within the confines of a feminine identity that was not overtly political. "The 1971 Fashion Feminist suits herself in many individual ways," described the *Philadelphia Tribune*. "She is free to select pantsuits with any of the new and exciting pants looks" or "skirts that move with the rhythm of the body."[51] "All-in-all, the fashion feminist goes her own way," wrote an article in the *Los Angeles Times*. "She uses her own special style to give her clothes meaning. She's all woman."[52] "Fashion feminists" could choose to wear pants *or* skirts, but never gave up their feminine identities; in other words, they could be "liberated" but still be "women."

Fashion designers and women pants-wearers also described how their particular styles allowed them to maintain a feminine look while wearing pantsuits. Designers made pantsuits look feminine by showing them with ruffled blouses and long tunics, making the styles "pretty," "soft" and "tasteful" even for the most feminine of women.[53] Accessories were another way to feminize the pantsuit style. "For daytime wear, these suits look best with casual leather shoes, a scarf at the neckline, a turtleneck, or a gold chain," instructed a fashion columnist for the *Chicago Tribune*. "At night, change the look with higher, dressier shoes, pearls instead of casual chains, a pretty blouse instead of the more formal, tailored shirts and sweaters."[54] Paired with the correct blouse, colors, and accessories, there would be no reason for a female in a pantsuit to project a masculine image. While designers in the 1960s had also attempted to promote women's pantsuits as feminine, the growing ubiquity of women's pants provided new acceptance for these claims that pants and femininity were not mutually exclusive. One seventy-four-year-old woman explained of her recent decision to buy a pantsuit, "With a color that suits you best, plus a necklace and earrings, it really is feminine."[55]

The growing acceptance of miniskirts and pantsuits signaled changes in societal definitions of womanhood, allowing for sexual independence and a new range of choices for women in their fashion decisions. However, women's fashions remained tied to feminine identities that weren't overtly political. The popular film *Annie Hall* epitomized this message about the meanings of new fashion styles for women. The main character, Annie (played by Diane Keaton, who won an Oscar for the role; the film also won the Academy Award for Best Picture of 1977), was characterized by her nontraditional fashion choices. In the pivotal scene in the film in which she first meets her love interest, Alvy (Woody Allen), Annie wears a stereotypical men's outfit: vest, tie, khaki pants, and a black full-brimmed hat. "I love your outfit," Alvy remarks as a sign of approval. While her attire in this one important scene became her trademark, Annie's dress during the rest of the film is "quirky," but rarely explicitly gender bending; often, her outfits include feminine pants, long skirts, and dresses. Moreover, Alvy and Annie's relationship in the film rarely exhibits any hint of relaxed gender boundaries, nor is Annie portrayed as either a feminist or as a woman willing to step far outside the bounds of normative womanhood. Annie may be a free spirit, but she is resolutely heterosexual and feminine in her mannerisms; even at her first meeting with Alvy, despite her potentially masculine dress style, Annie's demeanor is shy and nervous, trying to make a good impression for her love interest.

Nor is Annie portrayed, at least at first, as an independent woman. Instead, through most of the film, Annie is dependent on and highly influenced by Alvy, who convinces her to take classes and to see an analyst to work through her insecurities. In one scene, Annie calls Alvy to come over to her apartment in the middle of the night because she is scared of a spider in her bathroom. By the end of their relationship, and through the help of her analyst, Annie does grow more independent, eventually breaking up with Alvy when he becomes jealous of her singing career, and moving to Los Angeles with a new lover. But even at the end of the film, when Annie refuses to accept Alvy's marriage proposal and move back to New York with him, she frames her decision in terms of the support he gave her in their relationship: "You're the reason that I got out of my room, and that I was able to sing. . . . And get more in touch with my feelings and all that crap." While Annie may have become more independent by the end of the film, it was through her relationship with a man that she gained her autonomy. Annie is not a feminist, nor does she ever reject heterosexuality, men, or an expressly feminine identity; the film remains focused on the lessons of heterosexual relationships rather than on feminism or women's independence.

It was ironic, perhaps, that changes in women's fashions implicated some of the key values of the women's liberation movement at the same time that the movement fell under criticism in the American media. The difference, however, was one of interpretation. The broader public often conceptualized popular styles such as pantsuits and miniskirts as "choices" for women; this rationale did not go beyond a growing consensus that women deserved equal legal rights to challenge deeper concepts of gender difference. Pants and miniskirts were *options* for women alongside dresses and makeup, and it was the choice itself that allowed women to be liberated. But styles of self-presentation that were explicitly political, intentionally challenging gender differences, seemed to take the principle of choice too far. Popular culture portrayals of women's fashions in the 1970s thus allowed women to be "liberated" in their fashion choices, as long as they remained "feminine" in doing so.

AFRICAN AMERICAN STYLES AND AFROS IN POPULAR CULTURE

One of the most popular films of 1971 was *Shaft*, today considered the epitome of blaxploitation films of the 1970s. The film begins with the main character, Shaft, walking around the streets (and in the streets) of New York City with a long leather jacket, natural hair, and a mustache. He is the quintessential black "cool cat," introduced by a narrator in the film's opening minutes as follows: "Who's the black private dick who's a sex machine with all the chicks?" Two years later, Pam Grier graced the silver screen in *Coffy*, another blaxploitation film, with a large Afro. Both films focused on the sex appeal and street smarts of their characters, with little hint of black politics in their overall message. The presence of natural hairstyles in these widely viewed films demonstrates how, by the 1970s, the Afro had moved into the mainstream.

By the end of the 1960s, the Afro became widely recognized as a style among African Americans. The *New York Amsterdam News* wrote in 1969, "Afro wearers are multiplying in areas where once there was criticism and scorn toward the natural hair wearer. . . . Middle-class women, doctor's wives, professional entertainers, white-collar workers, school teachers, social workers, and students alike are wearing the Afro."[56] A number of male African American celebrities, such as Bill Cosby, Sammy Davis Jr., and James Brown, adopted natural hairstyles, as did African American actresses, models, and some candidates and winners of the Miss Black America Pageant.[57] As Susannah Walker concludes, "By the late 1960s and early 1970s . . . the Afro was as fashionable as it was political."[58]

The "fashionability" of the Afro was promoted by the black beauty industry, which had traditionally focused on hair-straightening products and techniques in their marketing to African Americans. By the late 1960s, capitalizing on the idea of "Black Is Beautiful," the black beauty industry began to promote natural hairstyles and products that they claimed would enhance these styles. As Walker explains, "Advertisements for Afro products frequently invoked black pride, particularly when the company producing them was owned by African Americans."[59] "Afro-Sheen, Soul Brother, Mr. Natural, and Duke" were just some of the names of new lines of beauty products that "reflect[ed] the wave of black pride," according to the *Los Angeles Times*.[60] "The natural offers a new-found freedom to Black women," wrote an article in the first issue of *Essence*, a magazine targeted to African American women. "But please, since your natural does so much for you, why not do something for it," the article pleaded, as it advertised shampoos and sprays that women allegedly needed to maintain their Afro styles.[61] Thus, the beauty industry helped to commodify the Afro, which "transform[ed] the style from political statement to fashion commodity" in helping the fashion to move into the mainstream.[62]

In response to the growing popularity of the Afro and the beauty industry that developed to support it, some African Americans became critical of the style. Some black activists decried the Afro "fad" as "part of a cultural invasion from imperialist and capitalist America."[63] One black newspaper criticized, "Your black pride dollars go to white manufacturers. All of your Afro picks, cakecutters, sprays and other embellishments that allow your hair to be wooly, are manufactured by white companies."[64] The Black Panthers also began to denounce the commercialization of Afro styles, which they claimed fed capitalistic profit and ignored the true political and economic problems facing African Americans. "Not one stitch of false hair or manufacturer thread will contribute anything to Black freedom," wrote one party member in 1968.[65] Other Black Power intellectuals agreed that the media's attention to black self-presentation styles might obscure true political progress. "These are the *symbols* of the new awareness," wrote Black Power philosopher Charles V. Hamilton, "[but] they do not necessarily relate to the *substance* of what the struggle is all about."[66]

Indeed, as Afros began appearing as a common black style in movies and television shows, scriptwriters attempted to strip them of their political meanings. In the first episode of *All in the Family*, Lionel, Mike's African American friend, sports an Afro hairstyle and is portrayed as a quick-witted and insightful young man who gently prods Archie into implicitly recognizing some of his racist views. Lionel's attitude, however, is portrayed as one of ironic reconciliation, rather than one of political militancy or activism. "What's new on campus with you angry white social Democrats?" Lionel asks Mike, implying that Mike's radical activism is not shared with Lionel. Then, Lionel explains how Archie bugs him by making him explain his choice of career—"I want to be a 'lectrical engineer!" Lionel practices, in a derogatory imitation of a Southern black accent. Mike expresses outrage that Lionel would say this to Archie. "Give the people what they want, man," Lionel explains. "How else am I going to *become* an electrical engineer?" In this exchange, Lionel implies that accommodation and acceptance of politically incorrect attitudes, rather than militancy or angry provocation, is the correct tactic for achieving his goals. Despite Lionel's Afro hairstyle, he does not preach explicit Black Power politics or hint at militant goals.

Another popular show of the 1970s, *Good Times*, also portrayed these nonmilitant versions of the Afro. The show, one of the most popular of the 1970s, centered on a poor African American family and their economic and familial struggles. In an early episode that was originally intended as the show's pilot, one of the main characters, Thelma (played by Bern Nadette Stanis), opens the episode with a large Afro hairstyle, cooking breakfast for her siblings as her mother recovers from surgery. Two jokes about the Black Power movement are made in the first five minutes of the episode. When Thelma serves her little brother his food, he cries, "Black is Beautiful, Thelma, but not when it's oatmeal!" A few minutes later, their mother comes into the living room while the children are bickering, and the children freeze. Their mother quips, "It's comforting to know there is still some respect for Black Power around here." While other aspects of the episode suggest poking fun at militancy—jokes about Michael, the little brother, receiving mail from the NAACP and other political organizations and playing "cops and militants" with friends—the sitcom nature of the show defies any serious political discussion. Thelma's Afro is portrayed as a fashion statement, not as an emblem of political militancy.

Along with these attempts to depoliticize the Afro, new styles began to emerge among African Americans that were promoted by the black beauty industry. Braids and cornrows, borrowed from West African female hairstyles, started to gain popularity in the 1970s.[67] While both men and women adopted the styles, long braids and cornrows allowed African American women to express their racial pride while also wearing their hair "longer," and thus closer to traditional feminine styles.[68] New forms of "relaxed" hair also became publicized. "Relaxed and partially relaxed hair is coming back," the *Los Angeles Times* claimed in 1972. One black stylist explained, "Ninety percent of my black clients here are having their hair at least partially relaxed. They may wear it short and curly—but far from frizzy. Many never wore the Afro and always had their hair completely relaxed in order to follow any style they like."[69] "Partially relaxed" hair was thus portrayed as a compromise between the strictness (and perhaps militance) of the Afro and a relaxed style that was marketed as more versatile.

Others in the media were more explicit in describing how some African Americans abandoned their Afro styles in the 1970s. "Critics of the 'Afro' say that too much time is required to maintain it, that it is too impractical or just plain boring," wrote one black newspaper.[70] Voices in the media claimed that straight hair gave women more "variety" in choosing among hairstyles. The Afro "wasn't versatile enough," explained a Chicago stylist. "It limited the female as to what she could do with her hair." Processed hairstyles, in contrast, allowed African American women to adopt "soft and fluid" hairstyles that appeared to be more traditionally feminine.[71] For women who maintained natural hairstyles, stylists and African American fashion magazines advocated ways for women to "soften" their overall look. "Society says you're feminine if you have long pretty hair," explained one Afro-wearing woman in 1975. "But when you cut it all off, you have to give them femininity in other ways like wearing lipstick, eyelashes, or eye shadow."[72] Magazines targeted to African American women promoted makeup, scarves, and hair-care products for women to use and wear along with their natural hair, aimed at making them appear more traditionally feminine.[73] African American magazines also promoted "milder relaxers" to give short hairstyles "a more curly," and therefore more feminine, effect.[74]

The rhetoric used by the African American media also promoted choice in hairstyles as the true path to racial independence. "The cool breezes of this season and the next bring with them a special message for the black woman," wrote one African American journalist. "Freedom—it says, do your natural thing, chocolate woman. Wear your hair in the style that's natural for you. Wear it long, short, or somewhere in between; wear it straight, curled, bushed or waved."[75] Just as white "fashion feminists" could choose their own style, African Americans could now choose to wear their hair in different ways— straightened, braided, or natural—and it was the choice itself that offered them racial freedom and pride, rather than the particular style of the Afro. "Not every woman who has gone natural is a Black Power advocate and not every Negro who has ignored the trend is without racial loyalty," wrote one article in the *Los Angeles Times*. "To many it is just doing your own thing."[76] One African American woman stated that she had always "been proud of my heritage, and I don't think I have to change the way I wear my hair or my clothes now that it has become the chief thing to do." Another woman wrote, "Black women should be able to feel pride in themselves without having to wear African robes. . . . If you feel proud inside, it doesn't matter what you wear."[77] An advertisement for a hair-relaxing cream agreed with these sentiments that it was the choice in styles that mattered the most: "You can change your hair style as easily as you change your mind—with Ultra Sheen Permanent Crème Relaxer. After all, isn't that what doing your own thing is all about?"[78]

By the 1970s, then, natural hairstyles had become popularized as fashions at the same time that they began to lose their political meaning. The Black Power movement also faded in the 1970s, as groups like the Black Panthers disintegrated and black activism shifted from civil rights activism to municipal and state electoral politics.[79] As Ayana Byrd and Lori Tharps conclude, "The Afro had become a hairstyle, plain and simple. It was no longer a matter of what your 'fro stood for but of how high your 'fro stood."[80] While natural hairstyles never totally lost their political roots, Afros became just one choice in a range of black hairstyles that all signaled the "black pride" of their wearers—a pride that was increasingly divorced from the political activism of the previous decade.

UNISEX FASHIONS, GLITTER ROCK, AND "COMPLEMENTARITY" IN FASHION

As peacock fashions for men and pantsuits for women became more popular, unisex styles exploded in the early 1970s. Designers continued to show unisex fashion lines in their shows, and clothing stores nationwide increasingly marketed the styles. These fashions were not reserved solely for upscale fashion boutiques and designer clothes; stores that catered to middle-class Americans, like Montgomery Ward and Sears, also began to advertise unisex outfits.[81] Even in stores that did not officially sell unisex fashions, women and men shopped with an eye toward unisex style. At upscale Saks Fifth Avenue in New York, women raided the new "men's boutique" section to find belts, hats, and shoulder bags for their own closets. "Some of the most popular items" in the new boutique, the *New York Times* explained, "are unisex, and although a good many of them weren't intended to be that way, they are being worn by both men and women."[82] A similar phenomenon ensued at Yves Saint Laurent's specialty store for men. "It's not unisex, but that won't stop women from picking up shirts, sweaters, and even blazers for themselves. . . . The shirts are colorful, the sweaters patterned, and the blazers—well, everybody knows Saint Laurent put them on the fashion map for women."[83]

Some designers in the 1970s attempted to take unisex styles to new, more daring levels. One designer introduced "black and white–striped unisex bikinis" for both males and females.[84] Other designers advertised high heels, dresses, jewelry, and makeup for men.[85] In some crowds, particularly among teenagers and young adults, these daring styles caught on. The *Chicago Tribune* described one young fashion scene in 1971: "The young men are seen dancing . . . in old dresses, jewelry, and high-heeled boots, with their long hair and beards, all worn with blue jeans. Their girl friends are often in pants and shirts. . . . Other young men are wearing rhinestone-studded shirts, necklaces, and assorted bracelets. It's sometimes hard to tell who's the male in this new fashion mixup," the article concluded.[86]

Popular musicians who participated in the "glam rock" or "glitter rock" culture of the 1970s mirrored these fashions. Borrowing styles and techniques from the counterculture and from the shock tactics of many popular 1960s musicians, self-presentation became a means by which some musical acts in the 1970s attempted to gain publicity for themselves with "outrageous" dress styles and behavior. Rocker Alice Cooper and his band (of the same name) were some of the first popular musicians to adopt such tactics. "With chest-length hair, makeup, and dazzling lamé, silk and velvet, the Coopers' opening tactic is to confuse their audiences as to their sexual identity," wrote the *Los Angeles Times* in 1970. "Alice himself often appears in flashy miniskirts over his skin-tight trousers."[87] Even Cooper's name, the press often noted, paid homage to gender nonconformity—"Yes, Alice is a boy," the *Washington Post* snarked.[88] Iggy Pop was another musician who "flounced onstage in a weird winter wonderland flash, his face, torso and chest covered with specks of icicle glitter, his hair thickly dusted with silver."[89] British rocker David Bowie became the "central figure" of the glitter rock scene, whose "sequined, gleaming suits, spiky hair, and high-heeled boots" (and open bisexuality) made him the "showbiz standard-bearer for the gay and drag scene in London," although his music and shows attracted mainstream audiences as well.[90]

These singers and groups, along with many others—the Mothers of Invention, Parliament Funkadelic, Rod Stewart, the New York Dolls, and Queen, just to name a few—brought gender "theatricality" to a large audience.[91] And indeed, these rockers attracted significant mainstream attention, fame, and fans. But even with their broad attraction, the press portrayed these rock stars as outside of the mainstream. The *Chicago Tribune* in 1971 wrote that Alice Cooper and Iggy Pop were part of the "outer fringes" and "kinky spectacles" of current pop music, implying that they were outsiders in popular rock; the *New York Times* used the label "freak rock."[92] "Transvestite rock" was another term used to describe these stars, calling attention to their gender-bending tactics and their potential "deviance" within the mainstream rock scene.[93] Some radio stations even refused to play the music of the New York Dolls due to their extreme gender-bending styles.[94]

Female rock musicians, such as Joan Jett, Suzi Quatro, and Patti Smith, also transgressed boundaries of femininity by participating in the male-dominated rock scene of the 1970s. Joan Jett's leather jackets and Patti Smith's aggressive style, which one journalist described as similar to Mick Jagger's in that it "tend[ed] to erase gender," epitomized a "toughness" among some female rock stars that defied the stereotypical femininity and sensuality of female singers.[95] Few of these female musicians, however, attracted as much attention for challenging gender boundaries in their self-presentation as did male glitter rockers. One reason was that the dress of many female rockers—jeans, button-down shirts, and blazers—had become acceptable attire for women by the 1970s, as opposed to the miniskirts and makeup that some male rockers donned. For example, Patti Smith appeared on the cover of her 1975 hit album *Horses* "posed a la Frank Sinatra, standing with a suit jacket thrown over her shoulder"; but the *New York Times* interpreted this image as a sign of Smith's "parody" of stardom and her Sinatra-level potential, rather than as a sign of her potential masculinity or gender deviance.[96]

Female rockers themselves, however, were also wary of pushing gender boundaries in their self-presentation. Jett described the paradox of the female rocker in 1978: "It's kind of phony to act feminine on stage, because rock is like sports—it's aggressive and rough," she explained. "But just because rockers have traditionally been men doesn't mean women rockers have to act butch."[97] Female rockers in the 1970s might not have "dressed up sweetly," as Jett put it, but they were careful not to pose too much of a challenge to gender norms in their self-presentation. The *Los Angeles Times* described the Runaways, Jett's all-female rock band, as "young, female [and] fun"; a photograph of all five band members with long hair and makeup implicitly illustrated some of the ways that women maintained their femininity within the male-dominated rock scene.[98] Even Smith, despite her aggressive musical style, was featured in the *Washington Post* wearing a feminine scarf and mentioning her dream to be on the cover of *Vogue*, a testament to her interest in feminine fashion.[99]

The challenges posed by glitter rockers and their portrayals in popular culture suggested that the American media, and perhaps the broader public as well, were not quite ready to abandon gender distinctions in personal presentation. As unisex styles increased in popularity in the 1970s, the media began to describe the styles in ways that emphasized, not sameness, but difference in men's and women's fashions. As one designer put it, these clothes were "not Unisex," but rather were "complementing" styles for men and women: "They are His and Her garments and they are different."[100] One Italian designer explained his unisex line of evening wear as follows: "In the evening [a man] can wear a brilliantly coloured jacket, shirt, and ascot all in the same detailed paisley print with black trousers, while [a woman] wears a more fitted version of the jacket, matching paisley weskit and trousers and a black silk ascot hat. Often her outfit resembles his only in that it is made out of the same fabric."[101] Oscar de la Renta's line of unisex taffeta blazers also exhibited different styles for men and women. "The plain taffeta takes on a masculine look for the men and a soft feminine look when worn by women," one journalist explained. "The cut is changed slightly to accommodate the full-chested female figure."[102] When Ralph Lauren introduced a line of polo shirts for women in 1972, he used the same fabrics as his men's shirts, but provided a more "feminine" fit: "The neck is smaller, the sleeve slimmer, armhole cut high, the body trimmer." As a result, "There's no hint of unisex or a matched his-and-hers look" in the shirts, claimed the *Chicago Tribune*.[103] Lauren's "expanded" line featured "soft" and "trim" tailored shirts, jackets, and pants for women (but "no ties for women, no toughness"), with a result that was "decidedly feminine."[104] When gray flannel pantsuits became popular among both men and women in 1973, women could "soften any mannish look" of the outfits "with fluffy angora sweaters, flower-printed silk shirts, silver fox jackets . . . or argyle sweaters," differentiating their outfits from similar suits for men.[105]

This shift toward complementary rather than identical fashions made sense in the context of continued fears about unisex styles in the 1970s. Particularly, as anti-ERA activists claimed that the amendment would force the government to outlaw sex-segregated bathrooms, "unisex" became the buzzword for a society in which differences between men and women could no longer be acknowledged. "Combined men's and women's toilets to go along with unisex clothes and dormitories," was how one journalist described the fears that some Americans harbored toward the amendment.[106] It was perhaps not a coincidence that by the mid-1970s, as anti-ERA activism began to stymie the amendment's ratification, some media commentators began to reject unisex clothing styles as a lasting trend. In 1973 the *Los Angeles Times* reported that in the fashion world, "the bosom is back, the waistline has been recovered and the nation's clothes-makers have learned what the margarine commercial knew all along: You can't fool Mother Nature."[107] "Clothes are once again showing their gender," the *New York Times* concurred in 1974. "Unisex is happily fading away and all over the city men who like to look at women are pleased."[108] By 1974 newspapers claimed that "the unisex look" was "out" and that "unisex fabric[s] [are] all that's left of last year's idea of the happy couple dressing like identical twins."[109]

Unisex fashions, of course, never totally went out of style; throughout the 1970s and beyond, women continued to appropriate men's suits, pants, ties, and clothing for their own fashions, and men have never returned to the white shirt, dark suit hegemony of the 1950s. But the media portrayed unisex styles as maintaining gender distinctions between men and women. Unisex clothes for men and women were "complementary," but never identical; the biological sex of the clothing wearers remained obvious to the outside world, media commentators in the 1970s claimed. Maintaining gender distinctions in unisex fashions despite their growing popularity provided a means for fashion designers and the media to implicitly counter any remaining fears that they were perpetuating the rise of a "unisex society."

THE CONTRADICTIONS OF CHANGING SELF-PRESENTATION IN THE 1970S

By the 1970s, American styles of fashion had changed, perhaps permanently. Fueled by the growing commercialization of "hippie" styles and the aging baby-boom generation, long hairstyles and facial hair for men; miniskirts, jeans, and pantsuits for women; and natural hairstyles for African Americans became ubiquitous as options for self-fashioning. This chapter has shown how the media and popular culture helped to garner new acceptance for these styles. In doing so, the media helped to erase the political messages that had defined these styles in the 1960s. Styles came to be portrayed as fashionable, fun, and modern; popular culture largely rejected the messages of militancy, rebelliousness, feminism, or gender deviance that these styles signified in the previous decade. These styles were portrayed as "choices" among an array of fashion and grooming styles, rather than as political statements that fueled the conflicts of the previous decade. And, as the radical political activism of the previous decade subsided, more Americans were willing to believe these new messages about the styles.

But not all. Conflicts over self-presentation never completely disappeared in the 1970s; throughout the decade and even today, conflicts can be seen in various pockets of American society over men's long hair, natural hairstyles for African Americans, and short skirts and pants on women. As the last chapter will show, workplace conflicts over styles of self-presentation illustrate how the questions of the 1960s never totally dissipated, even as popular culture widely promoted broad acceptance of these styles. Styles were still controversial when they seemed to push the boundaries of gender, sexual, or cultural norms too far.

"OURS SHOULD NOT BE AN EFFORT TO ACHIEVE A UNISEX SOCIETY"

Legal Regulations of Personal Presentation in the Workplace

On March 5, 1975, the Ohio Supreme Court ruled that the city of Columbus's 127-year-old ordinance against cross-dressing in public was unconstitutional. The defendant in the case, John Terry Rogers, was a preoperative transsexual who had been arrested in 1973 while wearing a "curly wig, a flowered blouse, a pullover sweater, a bra, and bellbottoms" in public. Rogers's attorney argued that the ordinance had been used to subject gay men in drag, transvestites, and transsexuals to police harassment. The court, however, did not overturn the law based on the burgeoning movement for gay, lesbian, and transsexual rights. Instead, it based the decision on a different historical development: the ubiquitous wearing of "unisex clothing" by men and women across the country. Judge O'Neill, writing unanimously for the court, noted, "Modes of dress for both men and women are historically subject to changes in fashion. At the present time, clothing is sold for both sexes which is so similar in appearance that 'a person of ordinary intelligence' might not be able to identify it as male or female dress. In addition, it is not uncommon today for individuals to purposely, but innocently, wear apparel which is intended for wear by those of the opposite sex." As a result of these "contemporary dress habits," the law was deemed "void for vagueness," in that it was no longer specific enough to be enforced without violating the Fourteenth Amendment's guarantee of due process of law.[1]

While Rogers's conviction was overturned in part based on changing styles of fashion and dress, another pants-wearing individual was not so lucky. In 1974, the year after Rogers was arrested for "cross-dressing" while wearing women's pants, Data La Von Lanigan was fired from her job as a secretary when she wore a pantsuit to work, a violation of her company's dress code. Lanigan sued, claiming that she was the victim of employment discrimination due to her sex, a violation of Title VII of the 1964 Civil Rights Act. Men were allowed to wear pants in the office, so why not women? Despite the ubiquity of pantsuits as office attire for women by the 1970s, the U.S. District Court ruled against her. Title VII, the court explained, protected against discrimination based on "immutable" characteristics like sex or race; the ability to wear pants or skirts was not an "immutable" trait and thus did not bar her from employment. The policy, the court ruled, was not "sexist" nor "chauvinistic," as Lanigan claimed, but rather was part of a legitimate right of employers to set standards of attire for their employees, even if those standards were different for males and females. "Employment decisions . . . based on either dress codes or policies regarding hair length," the court explained, "are more closely related to the company's choice of how to run its business rather than to its obligation to provide equal employment opportunities."[2]

The judges in these two court cases reached seemingly contradictory conclusions: one recognized changing styles of dress for men and women as reason to strike down a law, while the other upheld gendered regulations of dress in the workplace. The disagreement in these cases mirrored the conflicts that remained in American society in the 1970s over changing styles of personal presentation. Court cases such as these provide an interesting window into these conflicts. Some judges acknowledged that new styles—long hair on men, pants on women, and unisex clothing—outmoded old regulations on gendered dress for individuals in public spaces and in the private workforce. Other judges were hesitant to rule against these regulations, recognizing the fears of both private employers and of some Americans more broadly if men and women crossed certain boundaries in their personal presentation. Legal decisions thus provide examples of how self-presentation was viewed by jurists when these styles became the subjects of scrutiny in courts of law.

This chapter will focus on court cases from the 1970s that challenged workplace regulations of the hair and dress styles of employees. These cases have inspired numerous articles by legal theorists trying to understand why the courts have continued to uphold gendered dress codes in workplaces even into the twenty-first century.[3] Many of these legal scholars have noted the historical circumstances surrounding the precedent-setting cases in these areas, particularly the battles of men with long hair in many employment discrimination cases. But no scholarship thus far has considered the broader historical context of changing mores of gendered self-presentation at the time that these cases were being filed in American courts. These cases thus provide a culmination of the previous chapters of this book, illustrating what happened in courts of law when social movement activists and individuals wanting freedom of choice in their self-presentation confronted American cultural anxieties over changing styles of dress.

While the decisions in these court cases often revolved around questions of law and legal precedent—what qualified as discrimination based on sex or race, or as an unconstitutional restriction of freedom of expression—judges and lawyers were not immune to the changes in society and culture around them. On the one hand, many judges recognized that modes of self-presentation had changed; on the other hand, some judicial decisions reflected societal anxieties over gender, sexual, and racial norms that remained strong in the 1970s—particularly, fears about the Equal Rights Amendment and antidiscrimination laws that included gays and lesbians, as discussed in chapters 3 and 4. Some jurists believed that striking down workplace regulations would exacerbate homosexuality, gender deviance, and the "unisex society" that anti-ERA activists decried. These fears, for some jurists, trumped arguments about the right to freedom of expression or the need to combat outdated stereotypes based on old modes of gendered dress. These court decisions, therefore, reflected continued ambivalence about changing dress and hairstyles into the 1970s despite their ubiquitous spread in popular culture.

CHANGING STYLES OF PERSONAL
PRESENTATION IN THE WORKPLACE

"The old order—in personal appearance—changeth," wrote an article in the *Christian Science Monitor* in 1969. But in the workplace, these changes were not so easily accepted: "In these 'mod' times, overabundance of hirsuteness is apparently a deterrent to getting hired." According to a survey of 150 companies, "nearly 80 percent ... regarded a male applicant's beard as a reason not to hire him.... And about three-fifths of the firms thought a miniskirt to be a negative factor with a woman applicant.... Ninety percent of the firms still objected to long hair and 'mod' attire on males. But sideburns can be long, and 'Afro' hair styles are okay for black applicants."[4] This article demonstrated the challenges and contradictions of new modes of self-presentation in the workplace at the start of the 1970s. In the 1960s, employers expressed vehement objections to many new or politicized styles: numerous workplaces placed restrictions on hair and beard lengths that cost some men their jobs.[5] Although many of these styles became increasingly ubiquitous in the 1970s, employers did not necessarily let up their criticism. Opinion polls in the early 1970s found that a significant majority of employers still disapproved of long hair on men, and many individuals continued to be fired from their jobs (or were refused employment) because of their long hair, mustaches, and beards.[6] Similar controversies ensued over Afro hairstyles or women who attempted to wear pantsuits or miniskirts to work against their employer's regulations.[7] One California judge made headlines when he chastised a female attorney for wearing a pantsuit in his courtroom in 1971, threatening to find her in contempt of court and send her to jail for five days if she did not "change into more appropriate clothing."[8]

However, many of these workplaces began to change their policies as new styles of self-presentation became more difficult to restrict. Some businesses worried that grooming codes would make them lose desirable employees; with increased societal attention to racial and sex discrimination in the workplace, moreover, some employers were fearful of claims that restrictions on long hair, Afros, or other politicized styles would constitute a violation of their workers' civil rights.[9] One employer decided to allow an African American employee to wear a dashiki to work because "it might project to minority applicants that we're an open-minded, tolerant organization," he explained.[10] In Hartford, Connecticut, controversy ensued when an African American police officer was fired for not cutting his Afro hairstyle. Black and white police officers banded together to protest the hair-length regulations, which they argued were a violation of their civil liberties.[11] Eventually, the department relented, reinstating the officer and revising their grooming regulations to "reflect current community standards."[12] In similar fashion, other workplaces across the country changed or eliminated their grooming regulations to appease increasing numbers of male employees with long hair.[13] By 1975, the New York Times claimed, "long hair and beards are in [at the workplace] as long as they're clean and neatly trimmed."[14]

Similar changes helped women's styles to find new acceptance in the workplace. Some employers began to accept short skirts as acceptable office attire, with some even vocally approving miniskirts over the "dowdy" fashion of longer skirts.[15] Pantsuits had gained "limited" acceptance in some workplaces in the late 1960s, but by the 1970s the number of women wearing pants to work and challenging workplace dress codes that forbade pants became too numerous for employers to ignore.[16] Nurses at a Los Angeles hospital "petitioned for and were granted permission to wear pantsuits to work," successfully convincing the hospital to allow them to order a pantsuit uniform that matched the previous one with a skirt.[17] Business firms, insurance companies, law firms, restaurants, and banks across the country also gave the nod to women's pantsuits as acceptable office attire.[18] Even some airlines began to allow female stewardesses, who had traditionally been promoted as the epitome of feminine sensuality, to wear pantsuits as part of their uniforms.[19] By late 1970, a survey of Atlanta businesses found that 83 percent of local businesses allowed women to wear pants to work.[20]

But not all workplaces or social institutions accepted pantsuits as attire for women. Some employers continued to implement dress codes that prohibited women from wearing pants, arguing that such styles were not "business-like" or "suitable" for women.[21] In 1972 the *New York Times* reported on the controversy at the offices of Revlon, which forbade its female employees from wearing pantsuits. While no woman had officially protested or quit over the policy, many female employees objected to the rule as "'awful,' 'dumb,' 'ridiculous,' 'archaic' and 'old hat,'" and the article noted that no other major cosmetics company had such restrictions on their female employees' attire. Regardless, the company stood by its dress code, with one corporate vice president explaining, "We felt pants are just simply not good business attire."[22]

Employers such as Revlon might have belonged to a minority of employers who "held the line" against changing fashion styles in the workplace. And as the *New York Times* article suggests, those employers who did not relent were sometimes threatened with quitting employees, public ridicule, or lawsuits. When United Airlines fired a black flight attendant due to her natural hairstyle, black organizations threatened to boycott the company and filed a complaint with the Illinois Fair Employment Commission. The airline relented, rehired her and paid her back wages.[23] Similarly, in 1975, women participated in a national boycott of sexist workplace practices, organized by the National Organization for Women (NOW); a number of the women protested workplace regulations that forbade pantsuits.[24] Over time, long hair, beards, and pantsuits became increasingly accepted in many workplaces, rendering such protest tactics unnecessary.

But those individuals whose employers maintained restrictions on modes of self-presentation found themselves with a choice to make. Some men decided to cut their hair and shave their mustaches and beards rather than face an employment drought; particularly in the downturned economy of the 1970s, some prospective employees felt they could not ignore the adage that "long hair means no job offer."[25] Other men and women filed lawsuits against employers who restricted their styles.[26] It is impossible to know precisely how many lawsuits arose in the 1970s; some cases were settled, some were dismissed, and many cases heard in smaller state or municipal courts never garnered opinions that made it to the national public record. But a number of cases from the 1970s can be found among the opinions issued in state and federal courts of appeals as well as in U.S. district courts. And when lawsuits over workplace dress codes did make it to court, jurists grappled with the extent to which employers could regulate the personal appearance of their employees while on the job.

EMPLOYMENT REGULATION OF HAIR
AND CONSTITUTIONAL FREEDOM
OF PERSONAL APPEARANCE

Of the court cases that are readily available in the public record, nearly all were brought to court by white male plaintiffs who had been denied employment over their long hair or facial hair. In deciding these cases, courts often looked to precedents set by high school hair-grooming cases, even though these cases usually dealt with minors rather than adults.[27] In turn, the courts applied the precedents set by these cases to other groups, such as women and African Americans. The courts, thus, needed to consider the fundamental question: Did employers have a legal right to restrict the grooming and attire of their employees, or were these restrictions discriminatory and unconstitutional?

One early case grappled with the multiple potential answers to this question. In *Ramsey v. Hopkins* (1970), a federal district court in Alabama reprimanded a school district for firing an African American male teacher for refusing to shave his mustache. The court rejected any evidence of racial discrimination, however, noting that "the person who took Ramsey's position and [a] teacher who has been permitted to continue wearing a mustache are both of the same race as Ramsey's." Instead, the opinion argued that the rule against mustaches was "an arbitrary, unreasonable and capricious regulation," which was unevenly enforced at the school. There was no clear reason, the court stated, that wearing a mustache needed to be restricted: "There must be some showing of justification for the rule related to the legitimate purposes of the institution," the court concluded. The implication, however, was that a "justifiable" rule with a "legitimate purpose" could be considered legal. But what reasons for restricting mustaches might be considered legitimate? The court in the *Ramsey* case gave a few suggestions: evidence that mustaches caused "disruption or disturbance," "health or sanitation problems" associated with facial hair, or "difficulties of any sort with mustaches."[28] Whether this last, broad category included cultural norms against alternative grooming styles, the court did not say. The *Ramsey* case thus left open the possibility of upholding grooming restrictions if the reasons were considered to be "legitimate" by the court.

To defend the right of employees to choose their grooming styles, some jurists gravitated to the right to freedom of expression implied in the Constitution. These arguments were only applicable to public employers, such as state agencies or public schools, which were required to follow constitutional limitations on employee regulation. In *Tinker v. Des Moines* (1969) and *Cohen v. California* (1971), the Supreme Court had accepted some forms of outward personal appearance as protected freedom of speech, upholding the right of high school students to wear black armbands in protest of the Vietnam War and allowing a man to wear a shirt with slurs against the draft printed on the front.[29] But not every hair or dress style represented a particular philosophy or idea, and the courts were divided as to whether or not hair and dress styles in themselves deserved constitutional protection as part of one's "fundamental right" to freedom of expression. Even if personal appearance was deemed to be a fundamental right, however, the question remained whether hair and dress styles were constitutionally protected in the workplace. If an employee voluntarily chose to work for a state employer, could that employer set regulations that violated the employee's constitutional rights, or did the concept of freedom of expression limit the rules a state employer could set?

Some courts ruled that the hair and dress styles of employees did deserve constitutional protection as a fundamental freedom and could not be subject to a state employer's rules. In 1971 the Supreme Court of New York ruled that the fire department could not restrict a volunteer firefighter from wearing long hair. Finding that personal appearance was a constitutionally protected fundamental liberty, absent any evidence that the hair-length regulations were necessary to protect the safety of volunteer firefighters, the fire department could not restrict the plaintiff's hairstyle. "Neither [the plaintiff's] oath of office nor the nature of his work subjects him to indiscriminate regulation of his hair style," the court explained.[30] In 1973 the U.S. Court of Appeals of the Second Circuit ruled similarly that a police department's regulations on hair length were unconstitutional, finding that only a "legitimate state interest" could justify a restriction on individual liberty. "A policeman does not . . . waive his right to be free from arbitrary and unjustifiable infringement of his personal liberty when he elects to join the force," the court wrote.[31] In 1975 the U.S. Court of Appeals for the Fifth Circuit ruled that a teacher at a public community college could not be fired for his hair length, quoting an earlier decision in concluding that "the adult's constitutional right to wear his hair as he chooses supersedes the State's right to intrude."[32] Significantly, many of these decisions still noted the possibility that "legitimate" rationales for restricting hairstyles might exist; in these cases, however, the courts found that the constitutional freedoms inherent in the right to choose one's style outweighed the arguments presented by employers.

Some courts recognized the political implications of particular grooming styles as additional reason to uphold their constitutionality as an aspect of freedom of expression. In 1969 a federal district court in Florida ruled that the firing of an African American schoolteacher with a goatee was unconstitutional since "the wearing of a beard by a teacher has been held to be a constitutionally protected liberty." Moreover, in this particular case the court deemed that the beard "is worn as 'an appropriate expression of his heritage, culture, and racial pride as a black man'" and was thus a form of protected expression under the First Amendment. The school showed "an intolerance of ethnic diversity and racial pride" in their regulation of the teacher's goatee, which the court found to be unreasonable: "No evidence has been presented . . . which would indicate that the wearing of a goatee by [the teacher] might reasonably be expected to cause a disruption . . . or to encourage inappropriate dress by its students." This ruling thus implied that political or cultural messages reflected in one's hair or grooming were constitutionally protected forms of speech. It acknowledged, however, that "reasonable regulations" of grooming styles would be accepted if evidence was presented that there was a legitimate reason for their restriction.[33]

Other courts, however, took the opposite view, ruling that there was no fundamental right to choose one's personal appearance, particularly when it came to voluntary employment. In *Schneider v. Ohio Youth Commission* (1972), an Ohio Court of Appeals ruled that it was not unconstitutional for an employee to be fired from his job in the juvenile justice system for refusing to abide by hair-length regulations. "Unless there is specifically shown to be such an expression of philosophy, idealism, or point of view through a style of one's hair," the court explained, hair length was not protected as freedom of speech under the First Amendment. Moreover, the court wrote, "the Constitution does not establish an absolute right to a free expression of ideas. Such constitutional right may be infringed by the state through law or administrative rule or regulation if there are compelling reasons to do so." In the case of an individual acting as a "role model" to delinquent youths, the court argued, the agency's request that male employees keep their hair short as an "example" to their clients was "reasonable." Finally, any potential constitutional right to wear one's hair as one wished was superseded by the right of state employers to regulate employee conduct: "One may have a constitutional right to wear his hair as he wishes free of state control, but there is no corresponding right to work anyplace that he might desire while adorned in a hirsute style of his choice."[34] Similar reasoning was invoked in other court decisions.[35]

Some of these rulings were hotly contested, producing strong dissenting opinions from judges who disagreed with the majority. In *Akridge v. Barres* (1974), the Supreme Court of New Jersey narrowly upheld a police department's hair regulations in a four-to-two decision. In two separate dissenting opinions, the disagreeing judges decried the majority's conclusion. Justice Pashman, a well-known advocate of free speech and the "rights of the underdog," wrote in his dissent, "It is a gross injustice to determine the merit and character of a person by his appearance alone."[36] Hair-length regulation, in his opinion, was an abuse of power on the part of employers who simply did not like long hair and had nothing to do with a long-haired individual's performance on the job: "Our differences in life-style are as distinct as our differences in religion and politics, and ... we should be able to hold and express such without undue interference." The other dissenting opinion, by Justice Clifford, was even more forceful in his critique of the majority decision as he quotes the "uncompromising libertarian" Supreme Court Justice William O. Douglas in linking an individual's choice of hairstyle to the fundamental freedoms upon which the nation was based: "I suppose that a nation bent on turning out robots might insist that every male have a crew cut and every female wear pigtails. But the ideas of 'life, liberty, and the pursuit of happiness,' expressed in the Declaration of Independence, later found specific definition in the Constitution itself, including of course freedom of expression and a wide zone of privacy. I had supposed those guarantees permitted idiosyncrasies to flourish, especially when they concern the image of one's personality and his philosophy towards government and his fellow men."[37] Echoing the arguments of high school students and hippies that restrictions on long hair were antithetical to the concept of American freedom, this judge argued that the regulation of long hair was a denial of the very liberties that the Constitution was meant to protect.

The virulence of these dissenting opinions illustrates how judges, attempting to make sense of workplace restrictions on hair, hotly contested whether the right to freedom of expression included one's personal appearance, and what limits, if any, could be placed on this right. On the one hand, debates among judges might have reflected a broader jurisprudential debate on the wisdom of granting constitutional protection to rights that were not expressly stated in the Constitution; backlash against recent Supreme Court decisions upholding an implied right to privacy in *Griswold v. Connecticut* (1965) and *Roe v. Wade* (1973) perhaps provided some incentive for some judges to limit the reach of their interpretations of constitutional rights.[38] On the other hand, the dissents in *Akridge v. Barres* suggested that broader public debates on men's long hair also informed these judicial disagreements. Was the right to wear one's hair as one wished part of a valid interest in combating conformity and asserting freedom of choice in one's personal appearance, or did cultural norms of respectability allow state employers to limit the styles of their employees?

Ultimately, the Supreme Court's decision in *Kelley v. Johnson* (1976) ended the debate on whether the right to choose one's personal appearance was subject to state employer regulation, although the opinion failed to decide whether or not the Constitution protected such a right. In upholding a police department's regulation of the hair lengths of its officers, the majority opinion sidestepped the issue of whether or not personal appearance was a "liberty interest" to be protected by the Constitution. Instead, the court ruled that the "desire to make police officers readily recognizable to the members of the public, or a desire for the esprit de corps which such similarity is felt to inculcate within the police force itself," were "rational" reasons to allow the police department to regulate the appearance of its officers, regardless of whether or not personal appearance was a constitutionally protected right. The Supreme Court thus tacitly adopted the earlier reasoning of the *Ramsey* decision in ruling that public employers could regulate grooming styles of employees for "legitimate" reasons.

But Justice Powell's concurring opinion and Justice Marshall's dissent (which was joined by Justice Brennan) argued that the choice of one's personal appearance was a constitutionally protected liberty. While Justice Powell agreed that the need to regulate the appearance of police officers outweighed the personal right in this case, such a regulation "would be an impermissible intrusion upon liberty in a different context." Justice Marshall took this reasoning further, arguing that restrictions on personal appearance were "fundamentally inconsistent with the values of privacy, self-identity, autonomy, and personal integrity that I have always assumed the Constitution was designed to protect." Indeed, Marshall pointed to restrictions on hair lengths enforced by the governments of Czechoslovakia, Libya, and South Korea as evidence of the risks involved in allowing the government the latitude to regulate their citizens' personal appearance. Simply belonging to the police force was not reason enough to allow the state to regulate an individual's hair length, Marshall concluded: "A policeman does not surrender his right in his own personal appearance simply by joining the police force."[39]

Thus, even as the Supreme Court upheld regulations on the hair length of police officers, at least three of the Justices—Marshall and Brennan in dissent, and Powell in a concurring opinion—argued that an individual's personal appearance *was* protected as a fundamental right under the Constitution. The majority opinion, however, set a precedent that state employers could regulate the personal appearance of employees for legitimate reasons. In some ways, the court's decision was politically predictable—Justices Rehnquist, Burger, Stewart, Blackmun, and Powell often joined in conservative decisions in the 1970s, while Marshall and Brennan more often joined the liberal wing.[40] But judicial ideologies alone cannot fully explain the split; Justices Blackmun, Burger, and Stewart, for example, had previously recognized an expanded constitutional right to privacy by upholding abortion rights in *Roe v. Wade* (1973). The decision in *Kelley v. Johnson* thus hinged on more than differing ideologies of constitutional interpretation. The case also posed the question of whether or not personal appearance in itself was a freedom that deserved respect in

American society, or whether cultural norms and employer preferences could trump the liberty of employees.

Lower courts used *Kelley v. Johnson* to rule against employee claims that the grooming codes of their state employers violated their constitutional freedoms. In *Jacobs v. Kunes* (1976), the U.S. Court of Appeals for the Ninth Circuit followed the precedent set by the Supreme Court. The court ruled that the hair length regulations of a county assessor's office were not "arbitrary," but rather were based in the rationale that customers were repelled by long hairstyles on men. Even if "the hair length requirements ... impinged upon ... constitutional rights," state employers could regulate personal styles so long as their reasons for doing so were not "irrational."[41] Significantly, the decision in *Jacobs v. Kunes* ruled that cultural norms of men's long hair could be deemed "rational" reasons to restrict personal styles, in acknowledging that public opinions against the styles trumped any potential violation of the personal liberty of employees. Since customers had expressed their dislike of long hair, the county assessor's office could "rationally" regulate it, the court concluded. Even if choosing one's personal appearance was a fundamental liberty protected by the Constitution, then, cultural views on the desirability of certain styles could legitimately limit the reach of constitutional protection for state employees.

Cultural views on men's long hair were changing, however, and many employers, both public and private, changed their regulations in the 1970s to allow men with long hair (and women in pants, and others sporting new hair and dress styles) to work without restriction. But these cases, and the conflicting opinions of judges, reflected continued debates in American society about the limits that could be placed on personal presentation. Did individuals have the right to choose their own styles of personal appearance, or did the discretion of individual employers, and their wish for adherence to prior cultural norms, trump any growing acceptance of these styles in popular culture? While legal precedent might have ultimately concluded that employer regulation was allowed, the broader issue of freedom of expression that underpinned these cases remained open for discussion.

Constitutional arguments for freedom of expression, however, could only be used in cases against state employers; private employers were not subject to the same constitutional limits on employee regulation. But fortunately for terminated employees, a law that prohibited discrimination by private employers was at their disposal. In the 1970s, male plaintiffs began to bring lawsuits under Title VII of the 1964 Civil Rights Act, claiming that terminating them from employment due to their long hair was discrimination based on their sex. Title VII was a relatively new law, and its passage held a strange history; originally meant to prevent discrimination in the hiring and employment of African Americans, the final wording of the law outlawed employment discrimination based on "race, color, religion, sex, or national origin." *Sex* was not originally part of the bill, but women's rights activists pushed for this addition to the bill's language, and some Southern congressmen decided to add their backing as well, perhaps hoping that this amendment would erode support for the bill. When the amended law passed, "sex" suddenly became a category of unlawful discrimination in employment.[42] While NOW made the enforcement of Title VII a priority for its women's rights agenda, in cases of workplace dress and grooming codes, many more men used Title VII to claim sex discrimination than did women. The law, however, was written broadly enough to apply to both males and females, and male plaintiffs claimed that employers could not restrict their hair lengths if they allowed their female employees to wear long hair.

The Equal Employment Opportunity Commission (EEOC), the governmental agency in charge of enforcing Title VII, initially took a clear stance on the issue of workplace grooming codes. In a number of EEOC decisions in the early 1970s, the agency found that employers who forbade women to wear pants, refused to hire male applicants with shoulder-length hair, enforced a "no bushy hair" policy targeted at Afro hairstyles, and forbade the long skirts required for individuals of the Muslim faith, all violated Title VII by discriminating in employment based on sex, race, or religion.[43] The EEOC thus agreed with the claims of longhaired male employees, as well as with African Americans who were fired from jobs for their Afro hairstyles, that such regulations constituted discrimination in the workplace. In the case of longhaired men, the EEOC argued that policies that restricted the hair length of men but not women were unlawfully discriminatory: "To maintain one employment standard for females and another for males discriminates because of sex within the meaning of . . . Title VII," the EEOC concluded.[44] Even when grooming policies were equally enforced, such as the rule against "bushy hair," the commission ruled that the regulation failed to take into account "racially different physiological and cultural characteristics," and thus "adversely affect[ed] Negroes because they have a texture of hair different from Caucasians."[45] Policies that disproportionately affected one race or one sex were thus also deemed by the EEOC to be discriminatory under Title VII.

With the backing of these EEOC rulings that the Supreme Court had said were "entitled to great deference" by courts when hearing Title VII cases, male plaintiffs began to bring lawsuits against employer regulations of men's long hair.[46] Initially, courts hearing their cases tended to agree with the EEOC. In *Roberts v. General Mills* (1971), a federal judge in Ohio ruled that the discharge of a male employee with long hair was discriminatory. General Mills' policy required that men's hair fit underneath the hats issued as part of their uniform; women, however, had the option of wearing hairnets to cover their long hair. Denying Roberts the opportunity to wear a hairnet, when such an opportunity was provided to women, constituted sex discrimination because it "deprived [him] of his employment opportunities" based on the "stereotype" that women, and not men, had long hair.[47] If women could not be discriminated against based on gender stereotypes, the opinion concluded, neither could men. Significantly, the judge assigned to the case, Don John Young, had been appointed by Lyndon B. Johnson and was an advocate of the rights of minorities in the workplace.[48]

The next year, in *Donohue v. Shoe Corporation of America* (1972), a federal judge in California similarly ruled that the firing of a long-haired male employee constituted sex discrimination. Judge Harry Pregerson cited the EEOC decisions in concluding that "the application of a hiring or retention standard to one sex but not to the other violates the Act." But Pregerson, a well-known liberal judge who had also been appointed by Lyndon B. Johnson, also decried the stereotypes that informed these grooming regulations, which he argued violated the very essence of the 1964 Civil Rights Act: "In our society we too often form opinions of people on the basis of skin color, religion, national origin, style of dress, hair length, and other superficial features. That tendency to stereotype people is at the root of some of the social ills that afflict the country, and in adopting the Civil Rights Act of 1964, Congress intended to attack these stereotyped characterizations so that people would be judged by their intrinsic worth."[49] Echoing the arguments of some hippie activists that individuals should be judged by their character rather than by their appearance, Pregerson argued that discrimination based on hair length was similar to discrimination based on stereotypes of different races, nationalities, or religions that Title VII meant to prohibit. Individual employees should be judged on their merit, he suggested, not upon whether they had long hair.

Other courts followed these or similar lines of reasoning to rule in favor of male plaintiffs with long hair. The Supreme Court of New York in 1972 ruled that a restaurant's refusal to hire men with long hair was discriminatory after being presented with evidentiary photographs of "female employees engaged in work at the [restaurant], all of whom [had] hair styles extending well below the shoulder line." The opinion concluded that an employer who "hires women with long hair but refuses to hire men with long hair" was clearly engaged in a form of sex discrimination. The opinion also noted that the ubiquitous nature of "uni-sex" hair and dress trends "belie[d]" the restaurant's assertion that long hairstyles on men would be "detrimental" to the image of their business.[50]

In a similar case, a federal judge in California ruled in *Aros v. McDonnell Douglas Corporation* (1972) that differential hair policies for male and female employees constituted sex discrimination because they "reflect[ed] a stereotyped attitude toward one of the sexes"— namely, the stereotype that men with long hair were "hippies" or "troublemakers." The entire point of the 1964 Civil Rights Act, the decision argued, was to prevent employers from hiring or retaining employees based on these stereotypes, forcing them instead to evaluate employees on their individual merits. "The message of the Act is clear," wrote Judge Ferguson, another Johnson appointee known for his liberal views on individual rights.[51] "Every person is to be treated as an individual, with respect and dignity.... Any stereotyped image of males with longer hair as 'troublemakers' unjustifiably punishes a large class of prospective, otherwise qualified and competent employees." Finally, Ferguson noted that "under the fashion norms of today it is quite permissible for men to wear their hair in longer styles than a few years ago. Longer male hair styles are now widely accepted and little burden is placed upon the average employer by prohibiting him from discriminating between the sexes on the basis of hair length."[52] Employers claiming that long hairstyles on male employees were "bad for business" were simply ignoring the vast popularity and growing societal acceptance of these styles, making the discriminatory nature of such regulations even more apparent.

Despite these first court and EEOC decisions arguing that differential hair-length regulations for men and women qualified as sex discrimination, subsequent decisions began to rule against these complaints. One factor in this shift was the appointment of new federal judges by Richard Nixon in the 1970s, many of whom were apt to take more conservative views in their interpretations of the law and less willing to extend the reach of the 1964 Civil Rights Act. Rulings in these cases, however, did not always split neatly along liberal/conservative lines. Perhaps more pressingly, growing societal concerns about feminism and homosexuality—particularly by 1973, as anti-ERA activists warned that same-sex marriages, gender-neutral bathrooms, and a "unisex society" would be legally enforced under the amendment—were reflected in this new wave of decisions on hair length and Title VII. In many cases, these rulings reflected a concern that *all* differential treatment of employees based on sex could be deemed discrimination under Title VII, even distinctions that were widely held to be common sense.

A federal judge in Washington DC was the first to rule against a longhaired male plaintiff in December 1972. In *Boyce v. Safeway Stores*, Judge Gesell, a "staunch liberal" who had been appointed by Johnson, ruled that having "separate written grooming standards" for male and female food clerks was not discriminatory so long as both sexes had a set of rules to follow.[53] Safeway hired both men and women for food clerk positions, the judge noted; in his opinion, "mild grooming rules [were] not shown to discriminate on the basis of sex any more than a condition of employment that requires males and females to use separate toilet facilities." An employer, he argued, had a right "to have its personnel meet grooming standards which in its judgment will appeal to the largest number of its customers." Customer preferences, therefore, made restrictions on men's long hair a "bona fide occupational qualification" that was exempt from prosecution under Title VII, according to the opinion. Finally, Judge Gesell argued that Title VII must be interpreted reasonably by the courts: "The laws outlawing sex discrimination are important.... They must be realistically interpreted, or they will be ignored or displaced. Ours should not be an effort to achieve a unisex society or an effort to eliminate all standards for modes of dress and grooming set out for employees who want to serve the public."[54] Focusing on the implications of a "unisex society" in which *no* differentiations between the sexes could be acknowledged by employers—perhaps even eliminating separate bathrooms for men and women—Gesell concluded that some "rational" differentiations in grooming standards for men and women had to be allowed. Gesell never criticized long hair itself; rather, he concluded that a grooming policy could differentiate between men and women to avoid the "unisex" implications of outlawing such a policy.

While other courts would affirm Gesell's opinion, his legal reasoning was shaky; in ruling that differential grooming standards for men and women were a bona fide occupational qualification, Judge

Gesell "ignored the rationale of earlier cases in which customer appeal was not accepted as a ground upon which to justify an employment requirement."[55] White customers, for example, might have "preferred" white employees over African Americans, but allowing this customer preference to stand as a "bona fide occupational qualification" would contradict the entire purpose of Title VII to restrict individual biases in employment decisions. Subsequent decisions therefore sought different rationales for upholding differential grooming requirements. The appellate court decision in *Fagan v. National Cash Register Company* (1973) demonstrates the "judicial gymnastics" that some courts used to justify employer hair-length regulations under Title VII.[56] In ruling against a longhaired plaintiff who had been fired from his job at the National Cash Register Company, the court (in a two-to-one decision pitting two conservative judges against a liberal) argued that the "Congressional purpose" of the 1964 Civil Rights Act was "to establish that persons of like qualifications are to be given employment opportunities irrespective of their sex. Certainly on our record there is no evidence of discrimination against women" by the company, the majority decision noted, since the company had hired both women and men as employees in the past.[57]

But what about the plaintiff's claim that it was discriminatory to regulate the hair lengths of men but not of women? While the majority opinion did not explicitly use the bona fide occupational qualification exception to justify the policy, it did note that "reasonable regulations prescribing good grooming standards are not at all uncommon in the business world," and that "taking account of basic differences in male and female physiques and common differences in customary dress of male and female employees" was standard practice in business dress codes. Fagan's claim, therefore, was "not . . . a challenge to the right of the employer to require Fagan to wear his hair in a shorter style but [an] urging that in order for the company legally to do so, it must require women to conform to the grooming style applicable to males." A non-gender-differentiated grooming policy, however, would fail to take into account legitimate differences between males and females. In a footnote, the opinion noted previous court cases that upheld employer regulations of male beards and female pregnancies because, the opinion exclaimed, "some men grow beards and some women become pregnant!" Men and women, this footnote implied, were different in some ways, and employers still needed to be able to take into account legitimate differences between the sexes in their regulations of employees: the "basic differences in male and female physiques" and the "customary dress of male and female employees," the opinion explained. Gender differentiation, the opinion implied, was part and parcel of "good grooming standards . . . in the business world," and thus needed to be "reasonably" allowed to employers.[58]

While other courts would use this concept of "employer rights" to uphold gender-differentiated grooming codes, other decisions latched on to a rationale that the *Fagan* decision only briefly explained: the idea that Title VII protected "immutable characteristics" rather than aspects of racial or sex identity that were deemed voluntary. According to this reasoning, an individual could not change his or her biological race or sex, but hair length was subject to individual choice; hair, therefore, was not an "immutable . . . classification" and therefore was not subject to protection under Title VII. In *Dodge v. Giant Food Company* (1973), the U.S. Court of Appeals in Washington DC, in a unanimous three-judge decision that included two Nixon appointees, expanded on the brief mention of immutable characteristics in *Fagan* to provide a rationale for their ruling.[59] "Since hair length is not an immutable characteristic but one which is easily altered," the court explained, "the sexual distinction embodied in the hair-length regulations does not significantly affect employment opportunities and thus does not violate the statute." A longhaired man, therefore, was not denied employment because of his sex, but rather because of his refusal to cut his hair. In *Dodge*, the court also differentiated between hair length and marital status (since earlier decisions had ruled that a sex-differentiated policy based on marital status was a violation of Title VII) by arguing that "marriage has a much more fundamental importance to and effect upon an individual's life." Marital status was thus implied to be a more fundamental right than hair length, and therefore was deserving of protection under Title VII, even though one's hairstyle was not.[60]

Subsequent court decisions borrowed this immutable characteristics reasoning to rule against longhaired plaintiffs. In *Bujel v. Borman Food Stores* (1974), a Nixon-appointed federal judge in Michigan ruled that the "regulations of employers based on personal, *mutable* characteristics of men, used by the employer to choose one or more men over other men in the various aspects of employment, do not discriminate against men on the basis of sex." In other words, men could still be hired, so long as they did not have long hair.[61] In *Baker v. California Land Title Company* (1974), an appellate court three-judge panel consisting of two Nixon appointees and one Johnson nominee ruled similarly: "Since race, national origin, and color represent immutable characteristics, logic dictates that sex is used in the same sense rather than to indicate personal modes of dress or cosmetic effects." Title VII was therefore not meant to protect "hair styles or modes of dress over which the job applicant has complete control," but rather to protect against discrimination due to "characteristics which the applicant, otherwise qualified, [has] no power to alter."[62]

While these opinions placed their emphasis on the legal reasoning that "immutable characteristics" were the sole protected categories under Title VII, lurking in the language of these decisions were continued fears about the implications of outlawing employers' gender-differentiated dress codes. In *Dodge*, the court compared "hair-length regulations to the requirement that men and women use separate toilet facilities or that men not wear dresses. Admittedly these are extreme examples, but they are important here because they are logically indistinguishable from hair-length regulations." Sex discrimination based on a woman's marital status might have legitimately violated Title VII, but discrimination based on a man's hair length seemed to take Title VII too far, the *Dodge* court argued. "The issue in these cases is one of degree. Few would disagree that an employer's blanket exclusion of women from certain positions constitutes 'discrimination' within the meaning of Title VII. At the same time, few would argue that separate toilet facilities for men and women constitute Title VII 'discrimination.' The line must be drawn some-where between these two extremes."[63] Hair-length regulation, even if the rules were different for men and women, seemed to this court to be a "reasonable" requirement of employment, just as separate toilets for men and women were also reasonable. In *Baker*, the court was blunt: "A private employer may require male employees to adhere to different modes of dress and grooming than those required of female employees," the ruling concluded.[64]

These judicial disagreements over whether or not male hair-length regulations constituted sex discrimination came to a head in the Fifth Circuit case *Willingham v. Macon Telegraph Company*. First heard by a three-judge panel in 1973, the decision was handed down just one day before the *Fagan* decision and was the first U.S. Court of Appeals decision to consider whether hair-length regulations for male employ-ees violated Title VII. In a two-to-one split, the majority overturned the district court and followed the reasoning in *Roberts*, *Donohue*, and *Aros* in ruling for the plaintiff: "We find that a grooming code requir-ing different hair lengths for male and female job applicants ... treats applicants differently because of a sex stereotype: only males are pro-hibited from wearing their hair long." Since Title VII outlawed the use of sex stereotypes in employment, hair-length regulations for men but not for women were found to be unacceptable. In a forceful dissent-ing opinion, however, Judge John Milton Bryan Simpson (a Johnson appointee) argued that the majority opinion defied "common sense":

> If this interpretation of the Act is expanded to its logical extent, employers would be powerless to prevent extremes in dress and behavior totally unacceptable according to prevailing standards and customs recognized by society. For example, if it be man-dated that men must be allowed to wear shoulder length hair ... because the employer allows women to wear hair that length, then it must logically follow that men ... could not be prevented by the employer from wearing dresses to work if the employer per-mitted women to wear dresses. ... Continuing the logical devel-opment of plaintiff's proposition, it would not be at all illogical

to include lipstick, eye shadow, earrings, and other items of typical female attire among the items which an employer would be
powerless to restrict to female attire and bedeckment.

The logical conclusion of these hair-grooming cases, in other words,
would be men in dresses and lipstick, and women with "shave[d]
head[s] as clean as a billiard ball," Judge Simpson argued. Employer
dress and grooming codes, therefore, had to be able to take into
consideration "biological and cultural differences" between male
and female self-presentation. The problem, once again, was not long
hair per se, but the implications of forcing employers to write their
grooming codes without regard to gender.[65]
    With a split decision and a powerful dissent, the *Willingham* rul-
ing was not a ringing endorsement of the discriminatory nature of
male hair-length regulations. Indeed, briefs of amicus curiae filed
after the initial decision was published, urging the entire Fifth Circuit
to rehear the case en banc, echoed the concerns of Judge Simpson
that this ruling would set a precedent that "virtually every difference between the sexes is unlawful discrimination." Grooming standards that were "sexually uniform," requiring both male and female
employees to wear crew cuts, dresses, or lipstick, would need to be
upheld by the courts, one brief argued.[66] Another brief warned, "The
effect of this holding will be far reaching. All employer grooming
and dress codes which do not enforce identical standards for males
and females will have to fall before it. . . . Although 'unisex' has not
appeared to be part of Title VII in the past, this opinion will certainly
become known as the opinion which required 'unisex.'"[67]
    Perhaps as a result of these briefs, and perhaps also due to the
contradicting decisions issued in *Boyce*, *Fagan*, and *Dodge*, the Fifth
Circuit agreed to rehear the case en banc, with all fifteen judges participating. This time, the court ruled eleven to four in favor of the
company's hair-length regulations, borrowing the "immutable characteristics" reasoning used in previous cases as well as the concept
of the employer's right to regulate its employees to guard its public
image. The full court was particularly persuaded by the company's

insistence that a music festival held nearby the city where the company was located had "soured" the public against "counter-culture types," and that male employees with long hair would create a particularly bad business image in their community.[68] While the court acknowledged that refusing to hire longhaired males was a form of discrimination, the discrimination was "based not upon sex, but rather upon grooming standards." Since hair length was neither an immutable characteristic nor a "fundamental right" like marriage or parenthood, the regulation did not count as sex discrimination under Title VII. The opinion admitted that male hair-length rules were based on a stereotype that men ought to have short hair; however, the court argued that "the elimination of sex stereotypes" was not necessarily the purpose of Title VII. The court opined, "Congress in all probability did not intend for its proscription of sexual discrimination to have significant and sweeping implications." In the end, the opinion concluded, "private employers are prohibited from using different hiring policies for men and women only when the distinctions used relate to immutable characteristics or legally protected rights."[69]

The decisions in the *Willingham* hearings cannot be easily explained by looking at the political ideologies of the judges involved. While the two judges ruling for the plaintiff on the original three-judge panel, John Minor Wisdom and Elbert Parr Tuttle, were known for their decisions upholding civil rights for African Americans in the South, the dissenting judge, Simpson (who also wrote the majority opinion in the en banc decision), was a Johnson appointee also known for his pro–civil rights decisions as a district court judge in Florida.[70] Moreover, eight of the judges on the fifteen-judge panel in the en banc hearing had been appointed by Johnson, and three of the judges in the majority opinion—Brown, Gewin, and Thornberry—ruled later that year in *Hander v. San Jancinto Junior College* that regulating the hair length of a public employee was a violation of his constitutional freedoms.[71] While the Fifth Circuit might have been more conservative than other U.S. Courts of Appeals based on its location in the Deep South, the judges involved were not necessarily hostile to civil rights nor to the 1964 Civil Rights Act, nor were they necessarily dismissive of the notion that hair length could be considered fundamental to an individual's freedom of expression.

Broader concerns about the implications of deregulating self-presentation, however, were implicit in the en banc decision. While the majority opinion did not focus on the gendered connotations of differential grooming codes, the decision noted that it was "persuaded by the arguments of Macon Telegraph and its amici supporters," and its mention of the "significant and sweeping implications" of striking down a differential grooming policy suggests that the court had their arguments about the impending "unisex society" in mind. By limiting employers' uses of differential policies for men and women to instances of protecting "immutable characteristics or legally protected rights," the court implicitly argued that employers *could* treat male and female employees differently when there was reason to do so. Implying that men and women did have "real" differences that needed to be respected, the court rejected interpretations that Title VII required identical treatment of men and women and instead argued that it *was* possible for employers to base their policies on sex stereotypes if there was a legitimate business reason to do so, assuming that those stereotypes did not violate a fundamental right or discriminate based on immutable characteristics. While employers could not discriminate based on parental or marital status, in other words, they *could* discriminate on the basis that men ought to look like men and women ought to look like women.

The second *Willingham* decision overturned the earlier three-judge-panel ruling and concurred with all of the other U.S. Court of Appeals rulings that male hair-length regulations were not a violation of Title VII. As a result, the en banc decision set a precedent that subsequent courts would follow in cases claiming sex discrimination based on differential grooming regulations and dress codes. One month after the decision was released, a federal court in Missouri ruled against a longhaired plaintiff in a very brief opinion, citing *Willingham* and the other appellate decisions.[72] Another federal judge in Missouri, Judge Regan (a John F. Kennedy nominee), followed the same reasoning of the *Willingham* decision in an opinion released the next month: "So far as we are aware, every appellate court which has considered this question has reached a similar conclusion."[73] The U.S. Court of Appeals for the Eighth Circuit cited *Willingham*, *Baker*, *Dodge*, and *Fagan* as "the more realistic and reasonable interpretation of [Title VII]" when ruling against a longhaired male plaintiff.[74] By 1976 the U.S. Court of Appeals for the Second Circuit did not even feel the need to explain its reasoning in ruling against the Title VII claim of a male longhaired employee. "All four courts of appeals that have ruled on the question have held that requiring short hair on men and not on women does not violate Title VII," the court wrote. "Without necessarily adopting all of the reasoning of those opinions, we are content to abide by this unanimous result."[75]

The *Willingham* decision set a precedent that gender-differentiated dress codes for men and women were legal and was used by subsequent courts in considering other cases in which plaintiffs claimed sex discrimination based on dress and grooming codes. In 1977, for example, a federal court upheld the firing of a male grocery-store worker who refused to wear a tie, which was a requirement of the workplace dress code for men. The court concluded that a workplace "may promulgate different personal appearance regulations for males and females," citing *Willingham* among other cases.[76] In Data La Von Lanigan's case, similarly, the court cited "haircut" cases like *Willingham* in arguing against her claim of sex discrimination for not being allowed to wear a pantsuit to work. Although Lanigan argued that "not allowing women to wear pants perpetuates the stereotype that men are more capable than women of making business decisions," and "perpetuates 'a sexist, chauvinistic attitude in employment,'" the court dismissed these arguments, stating that the "contention that the policies perpetuate a stereotype is simply a matter of opinion." Instead, the court cited the "immutable characteristics" reasoning in differentiating between sex discrimination and dress codes. "[The] Plaintiff does not contend that she is unable to wear clothes other than pantsuits or that she is in any way physically unable to comply with the dress code," the opinion wrote. "In other words, plaintiff's affection for pantsuits is not an 'immutable characteristic.'" The court thus reasoned that the regulation against pantsuits was not a matter of sex discrimination, but rather was simply part of a "company's choice of how to run its business."[77]

Willingham also set a precedent in racial discrimination cases that employers could restrict certain black hairstyles so long as grooming standards were applied equally to employees of all races. African American plaintiffs had some supportive rulings earlier in the decade, with some courts recognizing that the prohibition of Afros or "other natural hairstyles" could be considered a form of racial discrimination in employment.[78] These decisions agreed with EEOC rulings that restrictions on Afro hairstyles constituted racial discrimination because they disproportionately affected minority races. However, after the *Willingham* decision, courts began to interpret these rulings more narrowly. When a black male was fired from his position after growing a mustache, the court argued that his claim was not one of racial discrimination since the "grooming policy was obviously applied across the board and no man, white or Black, escaped its scrutiny. The Court fails to detect the slightest hint of a racially discriminatory application."[79] An earlier EEOC decision had noted that "goatees and various types of mustaches are more prevalent among minority group males than Caucasian males," and that restrictions against facial hair had a "foreseeable disproportionate impact upon Negro males because of their race."[80] However, in this case the court ruled against the African American plaintiff, stating that "neither facial hair nor hair length is an immutable or protected characteristic of either males or Black males."[81] Later, a federal judge in Georgia ruled that it was not racial discrimination to prohibit cornrows as a hairstyle so as long as the regulations were enforced equally for all races and sexes. Again citing *Willingham* as precedent, the court reasoned that a braided hairstyle was not an "immutable characteristic" that was protected by Title VII and argued that "an even-handed application of reasonable grooming standards does not constitute racial discrimination." The court also claimed that there was "no proof" that "black people are more likely to wear beads in their hair than white people," thus denying that the regulation had a "disproportionate impact on black people."[82] Thus, the decision in *Willingham* allowed legal backing for some restrictions on black hairstyles.

The decision in *Willingham* has continued to be applied in cases having nothing to do with men's long hair. In 2006, for example, the U.S Court of Appeals for the Ninth Circuit ruled in *Jespersen v. Harrah's Operating Company* that it was not a violation of Title VII to require female bartenders to wear makeup, garnering ire from many feminist legal scholars who disparaged the court for upholding a seemingly sexist grooming policy.[83] The *Jespersen* decision made the *Willingham* case, which it cited as precedent, seem illogical and outdated; why in the world should it be legal, many wondered, to force women to wear makeup as a condition of employment? In the historical context of the era, however, the decision in *Willingham* made sense. It is no coincidence that courts began to rule against long-haired male plaintiffs at the same time that anti-ERA activists were warning about unisex bathrooms and antigay rights activists were arguing that antidiscrimination laws would require employers to hire men in dresses. By upholding gender-differentiated grooming codes for men and women, these jurists implicitly acknowledged the concerns of political conservatives that the law—whether Title VII or the ERA—ought not be used to enforce a "unisex" society, in which "real" differences between men and women could not be taken into account by employers or by the public. The fear was not necessarily long hair itself, but the continued implications of the fights for gender and sexual equality under the law.

Indeed, one judge made these concerns explicit upon dissenting in a rare case that found a differential grooming policy to be an undue burden on women. In *Carroll v. Talman Federal Savings and Loan Association* (1979), the Seventh Circuit found that an employer policy requiring a company uniform for female, but not male, bank tellers was a violation of Title VII. In a scathing dissent, Judge Pell, a Nixon appointee and conservative judge, criticized the ruling as extremist and out of line with the meaning of the 1964 Civil Rights Act.[84] "With this decision of this court, Big Brother or perhaps in this case, Big Sister has encroached ... farther than the Congress intended or authorized into the domain of private enterprise," he wrote. Differential grooming policies for men and women were clearly allowed under Title VII, Judge Pell argued, and in no way prevented women from being hired or holding a job. Whether or not women *liked* the policies was beside the point. Implying that "Big Sister" women's liberationists were behind the majority's decision, the judge issued a warning that this ruling would lead the law down a path of feminist extremism. "Opponents of the Equal Rights amendment have argued that its adoption would be followed by extreme applications bordering on the ridiculous where no meaningful discrimination exists. The result reached by the majority opinion in the application of the statute I can only regard as adding strength to that argument."[85] In his dissent, Judge Pell made explicit what previous rulings on dress and grooming codes had only implied: if employers could not implement sex-differentiated grooming codes, the "unisex society" that anti-ERA activists feared would soon follow.

CULTURAL NORMS OF GENDER AND THE LEGAL REGULATION OF SELF-PRESENTATION

Legal cases dealing with hairstyles, dress, and grooming codes reflected many of the conflicts in America regarding changing self-presentation styles in the 1970s. Disparities among the conclusions of different courts reflected broader disagreements about the meaning of cultural changes in self-presentation. Nearly all of the courts acknowledged the ongoing changes in cultural mores of hairstyles and dress. But the courts were not always willing to legally sanction these changes. Certain styles might have been considered acceptable to some, such as men with long hair; other styles, such as men in dresses, were not. The legal solution, for the most part, was to leave the decisions to employers as to whether or not to regulate the personal presentation of employees, allowing public opinion to sanction the acceptability of cultural trends rather than the courts.

Judges and lawyers did not make their legal arguments in a vacuum; these cases demonstrate how jurists are affected by their historical context just as much as court decisions sometimes shape history. As long hair on men, pants on women, and unisex styles became increasingly ubiquitous, some judges acknowledged the growing cultural acceptance of these styles by striking down workplace dress codes and acknowledging that hair and dress styles were fundamental to individual freedom of expression. Other judges, however, reflected conservative fears about feminism, gay liberation, and the fate of gender difference in American society in the face of changing cultural norms of gender. While some changes, like long hair on men or pants on women, might have gained some cultural acceptance by the 1970s, other changes, like dresses on men, signified a much more troubling challenge to gender norms.

The courts, therefore, became a new front for "holding the line" against changing modes of self-presentation into the 1970s. While many employers decided on their own to allow their employees to don the new styles of the era while at work, the courts, for the most part, refused to force any employer to recognize these styles as valid. While self-presentation styles had changed by the 1970s, both popular culture and the law recognized that differences between men and women still existed, and the courts allowed employers to differentiate employee dress codes based on these cultural conceptions of gender. The precedents set in workplace grooming codes cases in the 1970s, however, did not arise without conflict, and the differences in opinions between judges reflected continued debates over the meanings of new modes of self-presentation in a rapidly changing American culture.

EPILOGUE

The Politics of Style in Retrospect

It is impossible to consider the tumultuous decade of the 1960s without images of long hair, miniskirts, hippie styles, and Afros appearing in one's mind. This book has shown how these styles of self-fashioning were not merely amusing cultural accoutrements of the 1960s, but rather became central symbols of the political conflicts of the era. As the 1960s ended, many of these styles lost their charged political meaning. But debates over various styles of self-presentation never fully ended, and in some cases arise as conflicts today. It is still not illegal for employers to restrict the hair and dress styles of their employees in many cases. Some employers still balk at longhaired or bearded male employees, women in pantsuits, and Afro hairstyles; in response, some individuals are willing to let their employers dictate their dress and hairstyles. Even as the gay rights movement has made large gains in the area of same-sex marriage, men in dresses are socially acceptable only in drag performances or as transgender individuals; certain boundaries of gendered dress still cannot be crossed without dramatic social conflict. And in 2010, a four-year-old boy was suspended from his preschool for having long hair.[1] Debates over styles of self-presentation did not end in the 1960s or 1970s, and continue to shape the world that these decades made.

An important question to consider is whether the social movements of the 1960s would have been strengthened or weakened if clothing and hairstyles had not been introduced into their politics. Certainly, this book has illustrated the ways that these styles sometimes provoked backlash against these movements. Conservatives such as George Wallace, Phyllis Schlafly, and Anita Bryant focused explicitly and implicitly on the perceived styles of activists and turned these styles against them. One might argue that the rise of the New Right political coalition was aided by the symbolism of these styles, which conservatives used to persuade their followers of the threats of these movements to the traditional social norms that they valued. Self-presentation styles were thus tools of opponents of liberal and radical social activists just as much as these styles provided tools for the social movements themselves. On the other hand, styles of self-fashioning provided an important cultural tool for the social movements of the era, fostering solidarity among activists and encouraging followers to their cause. Fashion styles might have even popularized these movements among American youths by exposing them to the politics of self-presentation. Restrictions on popular styles forced young Americans to stand up for themselves and consider the nature of the American creed of freedom and perhaps fostered political activism among individuals who may not have done so by themselves.

The 1960s era created vast changes in American society: legal protections for African Americans and women from discrimination in the workplace; unprecedented growth of the numbers of women in predominantly male professions; new recognitions of individual sexual autonomy outside of marital or heterosexual relationships; and new modes of hairstyles and dress that allowed women and men to express their individuality, free from constraints of norms of gender, class, race, or "respectability." The era also inspired the "culture wars" over race, social order, abortion, gay rights, and "family values" that American society continues to debate today. This book has illustrated how various self-presentation styles were often symbols of these culture wars, as visual markers of different interpretations of a changing American culture. What some Americans saw as stylistic freedom or political protest, others saw as signs of the demise of traditional American society. Self-presentation was, and still remains, a powerful visual symbol of the changes, continuities, and disagreements over what it means to be an American.

NOTES

ABBREVIATIONS

SFPL   San Francisco Public Library
GLBTHS   GLBT Historical Society of Northern California
LHA   Lesbian Herstory Archives Subject Files

INTRODUCTION

1. See Rising, *Clean for Gene*, 67; "Be Clean For Gene," *Newsweek*, March 18, 1968, 51–52; "Students Trim for McCarthy," *Hartford Courant*, March 20, 1968; "Mr. Clean Makes It in New Hampshire," *New Republic*, March 23, 1968, 13; Stavis, *We Were the Campaign*, 16; Stout, *People*, 164.
2. On the events of 1968, see Kaiser, *1968 in America*; on unisex fashion, see "Some Fashions Are for Boys and Girls, While Others Are Strictly for the Ladies," *New York Times*, August 15, 1968; on George Wallace, see "Wallace Hits Professors Who Support Viet Cong," *Hartford Courant*, September 15, 1968, and "The Wallace Boom: Third-Party Candidate Shakes Major Parties as He Wins Followers," *Wall Street Journal*, September 17 1968; on protests at the Miss America Pageant, see Echols, *Daring to Be Bad*, 92–101, and Rosen, *World Split Open*, 160.
3. Wilson, *Adorned in Dreams*, 3.

4. See Wilson, *Adorned in Dreams*; Parkins, *Fashioning the Body Politic*; Storm, *Functions of Dress*; Kidwell and Steele, *Men and Women*; Davis, *Fashion, Culture, and Identity*; Craik, *Face of Fashion*; Hollander, *Sex and Suits*; Rubinstein, *Dress Codes*; Barnard, *Fashion as Communication*; Entwistle, *Fashioned Body*; Crane, *Fashion and Its Social Agendas*.

5. See L. Cohen, *Consumer's Republic*; and Frank, *Conquest of Cool*.

6. See Spigel, *Make Room for TV*.

7. See Young, *Dissent in America*.

8. McGirr, *Suburban Warriors*; Sugrue, *Origins of the Urban Crisis*; Nicolaides, *My Blue Heaven*; Kruse, *White Flight*; Dan Carter, *Politics of Rage*; Lassiter, *Silent Majority*; Phillips-Fein, *Invisible Hands*; W. C. Martin, *With God on Our Side*; Perlstein, *Before the Storm* and *Nixonland*; Dochuk, *From Bible Belt to Sunbelt*.

9. See Frank, *What's the Matter with Kansas?*

1. "YOU CAN'T TELL THE GIRLS FROM THE BOYS"

1. "Norwalk School Suspends 53 in Hairline Dispute," *New York Times*, January 30, 1968; "'Hung by a Hair,' Students in Norwalk See ACLU," *Hartford Courant*, January 31, 1968; "Long Hair Battle Ends at Barber and Court," *New York Times*, February 6, 1968; "Norwalk Youths Lose Hair Fight," *New York Times*, February 8 1968.

2. See Lipsitz, "Who'll Stop the Rain?"; Frank, *Conquest of Cool*.

3. Bailey, *Sex in the Heartland*.

4. Ehrenreich, *Hearts of Men*, chapter 5; Breines, "The 'Other' Fifties," 399–400.

5. Allan Kozinn, "Critic's Notebook; They Came, They Sang, They Conquered," *New York Times*, February 6, 2004.

6. "Beatles Arrive on TV—and Girls Flip Wigs," *Chicago Tribune*, February 10, 1964.

7. "Now the Beatles Hold the Stage," *Hartford Courant*, February 17, 1964.

8. "The Boy-Girl Hero in Our Adolescent Folkways," *Hartford Courant*, September 22, 1964.

9. "Beatle Debate," *Chicago Tribune*, February 23, 1964.

10. Dialogue with Youth, *Christian Science Monitor*, November 24, 1964.

11. Dialogue with Youth, *Christian Science Monitor*, August 26, 1964.

12. Dialogue with Youth, *Christian Science Monitor*, November 5, 1964.

13. "Beatle Hair-Do Draws Cutting Remarks," *Washington Post*, January 26, 1964; "Thru the Looking Glass: Whew! Beatle Hair Style Could Sweep the Nation," *Chicago Tribune*, February 14, 1964.

14. "Hi Notes," *Washington Post*, January 26, 1964; "Here's How to Get Away from It All," *Hartford Courant*, January 31, 1964.

15. "The British Boys: High-Brows and No-Brows," *New York Times*, February 9, 1964.

16. "New British Invaders Outdo Beatles," *Washington Post*, May 26, 1964.

17. "Din Overpowers Dave Clark Five," *New York Times*, May 30, 1964.

18. See the DVD *Monterey Pop*.

19. "The New Far-Out Beatles," *Life*, June 16, 1967, 100; "The Messengers," *Time*, September 22, 1967.

20. "British 'His' and 'Her' Hairdos Blur 'Him-Her' Line," *New York Times*, July 23, 1964; "Shaggy Englishman Story," *New York Times*, September 6, 1964. See also E. Myers, "Burning Bras," 143.

21. "Youth Comments," *Hartford Courant*, February 25, 1968.

22. "British 'His' and 'Her' Hairdos Blur 'Him-Her' Line," *New York Times*, July 23, 1964.

23. "This Is the Year of the Great Rebellion—in Boys' Haircuts," *Chicago Tribune*, August 31, 1965.

24. "Big Sprout-Out of Male Mop-tops," *Life*, July 30, 1965, 58.

25. "Beatle Haircuts Opposed by Two Out of Three," *Hartford Courant*, October 6, 1965; "Support on Vietnam Down," *New York Times*, May 17, 1965.

26. Art Seidenbaum, "Teen Hair Problem: Long and Short of It," *Los Angeles Times*, April 24, 1966.

27. See, for example, Cory, *Homosexual in America*, chapter 8.

28. Art Seidenbaum, "Teen Hair Problem: Long and Short of It," *Los Angeles Times*, April 24, 1966.

29. Gilbert, *Cycle of Outrage*.

30. Art Seidenbaum, "Teen Hair Problem: Long and Short of It," *Los Angeles Times*, April 24, 1966.

31. "Rebellion, Boredom Affect Teen Dress," *Chicago Tribune*, December 8, 1966.

32. "The Kids Don't Get Their Hair Cut," *New York Times*, October 22, 1966.

33. "Voice of Youth—Students Tell Views: HAIR FARE," *Chicago Tribune*, October 22, 1967.

34. "Beatle Debate," *Chicago Tribune*, February 23, 1964.

35. "This Is the Year of the Great Rebellion—in Boys' Haircuts," *Chicago Tribune*, August 31, 1965.

36. "The Younger Generation Speaks—Two Viewpoints," *Los Angeles Times*, February 12, 1967.

37. Dialogue with Youth, *Christian Science Monitor*, November 5, 1964.

38. "The Younger Generation Speaks—Two Viewpoints," *Los Angeles Times*, February 12, 1967.

39. "Beatle Fans Let Their Hair Down!" *Chicago Tribune*, March 28, 1964.

40. "Observer: Hirsute, and So What?" *New York Times*, September 17, 1965.
41. "A Male Privilege," *Chicago Tribune*, July 18, 1967.
42. David Kuch, "'A Sad Tendency Revealed,'" *Los Angeles Times*, May 21, 1966.
43. Ralph J. Gleason, "Perspectives: The Final Paroxysm of Fear," *Rolling Stone*, April 6, 1968, 10.
44. "School Orders Boy: Brush Bangs Back and Go to Classes," *New York Times*, December 17, 1964; "Beatles' Mop Hair Style Banned at Hinsdale High," *Chicago Tribune*, September 3, 1965; "Long-Hair Boys in for Trimming," *Los Angeles Times*, September 12, 1965.
45. Graham, "Flaunting the Freak Flag," 523.
46. Graham, "Flaunting the Freak Flag," 528.
47. "School Battles over the Beatle Haircut," *Hartford Courant*, September 27, 1965.
48. "Norwalk School Suspends 53 Boys in Hair Squabble," *Hartford Courant*, January 30, 1968; "Schools in the Area Give Notice that Long Hair Is for Girls Only," *New York Times*, September 13, 1965.
49. Graham, "Flaunting the Freak Flag," 531.
50. "Norwalk School Suspends 53 in Hairline Dispute," *New York Times*, January 30, 1968.
51. "Forum," *The Illustrated Paper* (SF), no. 5 (October 1966): 9, reel 1, Underground Press Collection.
52. Harry E. Smith, "Schools, Skirts, Haircuts," *Los Angeles Times*, September 15, 1967.
53. "Observer: Hirsute, and So What?" *New York Times*, September 17, 1965.
54. "Forum," *The Illustrated Paper* (SF), no. 5 (October 1966): 9, reel 1, Underground Press Collection.
55. "'Hung by a Hair,' Students in Norwalk See ACLU," *Hartford Courant*, January 31, 1968.
56. Graham, "Flaunting the Freak Flag," 540.
57. "Billboard Hippie Is Shy Type," *Hartford Courant*, April 17, 1968; "Environment: Mysterious Billboard," *Time*, March 1, 1968.
58. "Post Office Bans Hippie Garb," *Washington Post*, February 1, 1968; "Hippie Hair Fashions Facing Ban in Cafes," *San Francisco Examiner*, August 4, 1967; "Long-Haired Waiters Ordered to Net It," *Washington Post*, August 5, 1967; "Brooklyn Precinct Tells Men to Shun the Hippie Look," *New York Times*, July 15, 1968.
59. Quoted in Morrison and Morrison, *From Camelot to Kent State*, 203.
60. "The New Student President," *Esquire*, no. 68 (September 1967): 93.
61. "Boy, 15, Partly Scalped as Hair Cut by 'Patriots,'" *Los Angeles Times*, May 8, 1970.

62. "Miniskirts Are Raising Some Retailing Eyebrows," *New York Times*, December 4, 1966.

63. "Miniskirts for the Bride? Girls Aren't Mod About It," *Los Angeles Times*, November 27, 1966; "Miniskirts Are Selling Out," *Oregonian*, October 30, 1965; "Miniskirts Are Raising Some Retailing Eyebrows," *New York Times*, December 4, 1966.

64. "Miniskirts Draw Looks and Plenty of Frowns," *Hartford Courant*, June 21, 1967.

65. "Miniskirts Are Raising Some Retailing Eyebrows," *New York Times*, December 4, 1966.

66. Melinkoff, *What We Wore*, 145–48.

67. Letters to the editor, *Washington Post*, July 13, 1967.

68. "Miniskirts Are Raising Some Retailing Eyebrows," *New York Times*, December 4, 1966; "Miniskirts Draw Looks and Plenty of Frowns," *Hartford Courant*, June 21, 1967.

69. Gerhard, *Desiring Revolution*, 21, 48.

70. May, *Homeward Bound*, 98.

71. "Women Got the Vote, Now What?" *Hartford Courant*, May 5, 1968.

72. "The Swinging English," *Augusta Chronicle*, May 9, 1967.

73. "Women Got the Vote, Now What?" *Hartford Courant*, May 5,1968.

74. "Long Hair Soothing to Male Ego," *Hartford Courant*, May 4, 1967.

75. "Miniskirts Are Raising Some Retailing Eyebrows," *New York Times*, December 4, 1966.

76. "'. . . A Knee Can Be Sexy!'" *Los Angeles Times*, April 17, 1967.

77. "Garment Makers Modifying Mod," *New York Times*, April 16, 1967.

78. "Short-Short Skirts," *Chicago Tribune*, March 7, 1966.

79. Letters to the editor, *Washington Post*, April 22, 1967.

80. "Grandmother Gives Short Shrift to Miniskirt Idea," *Los Angeles Times*, April 20, 1967.

81. "Standards for School-Clothes High So Skirts Better Be Low," *Los Angeles Times*, September 8, 1966.

82. "Pants Glamorized by Designers," *New York Times*, February 15, 1964; "Parisienne Stylists on Pants Kick," *Chicago Tribune*, July 30, 1964; "Courreges Puts Accent on Women-in-Pants Vogue," *Los Angeles Times*, August 4, 1964.

83. "Chanel Makes Pants Official," *Hartford Courant*, August 9, 1964; "Women in Pants? Don't Cuff That Idea, Critics," *Los Angeles Times*, April 6, 1967; "Bell Bottom Sailor Trousers Hit Paris," *Washington Post*, August 1, 1964.

84. "Uniform of the Day: Stylish Women Flock to Army Navy Stores," *Wall Street Journal*, July 7, 1966.

85. "Swingin' Bride Wears White—Bell Bottoms," *Los Angeles Times*, June 10, 1966.

86. "The Pants Suit People State Their Case Ubiquitously," *New York Times*, October 8, 1966; "Women Wear the Pants and with Approval, too," *Chicago Tribune*, October 29, 1966; "Pants: Success Story Is Big," *New York Amsterdam News*, October 8, 1966; "Summer's Miniskirt Brigade Leads the Rush to Pants for Fall," *New York Times*, September 6, 1968.

87. "Pattern Aids in Adjusting Fit of Pants," *New York Times*, October 15, 1964; "Pants Suits For the City Stir Debate," *New York Times*, August 20, 1964; "A Dilemma for Restauranteurs: Where Do Slacks End and Pants Start?" *New York Times*, August 3, 1966.

88. "Should Women in Pants Be Admitted?" *Chicago Tribune*, September 7, 1966; "Restauranteurs Cave in Before the Pants Suit Onslaught," *New York Times*, April 25, 1969; Women in Pants? No, Yes and Maybe," *Hartford Courant*, January 27, 1969; "Double-Duty Outfit Solves 'Pants' Dilemma," *Hartford Courant*, March 9, 1969; "Women in Pants? Where and When?" *Washington Post*, March 30, 1969.

89. "It Helps If Your Husband Isn't Running For Office," *New York Times*, November 7, 1966.

90. "Chicago Women Divided on Paris Pants Fashion," *Chicago Tribune*, September 4, 1964.

91. "Sophisticated Controversy: Pants for City Life," *New York Amsterdam News*, October 31, 1964.

92. "Pants Suits for the City Stir Debate," *New York Times*, August 20, 1964.

93. "Fashion Authority Gives Paris Fad 'Kick in Pants,'" *Chicago Daily Defender*, October 13, 1964.

94. "Pants Suits for the City Stir Debate," *New York Times*, August 20, 1964.

95. "Pants Suits for the City Stir Debate," *New York Times*, August 20, 1964.

96. "Miniskirts to Tux," *Hartford Courant*, December 19, 1966.

97. Grace Glueck, "Now His Is Hers," *New York Times Sunday Magazine*, September 20, 1964, 45.

98. "Wanted: Identity for Today's Woman," *Washington Post*, April 21, 1968.

99. "Fashion Authority Gives Paris Fad 'Kick in Pants,'" *Chicago Daily Defender*, October 13, 1964.

100. "The New Femininity," *Vogue*, January 15, 1967, 88.

101. "Kick Up Your Heels!" *Cosmopolitan*, January 1965, 38.

102. Amy Vanderbilt, "Let's Be Counted in the 'Battle of the Sexes,'" *Hartford Courant*, July 3, 1966.

103. Letters, *New York Times Sunday Magazine*, October 4, 1964, 118.

104. "Couture Collections," *Baltimore Sun*, January 3, 1967.

105. "Summer's Miniskirt Brigade Leads the Rush to Pants for Fall," *New York Times*, September 6, 1968.

106. "Restauranteurs Cave in Before the Pants Suit Onslaught," *New York Times*, April 25, 1969.

107. "'Hung by a Hair,' Students in Norwalk See ACLU," *Hartford Courant*, January 31, 1968; see also "Seniors Strike for Miniskirts," *Hartford Courant*, October 22, 1966.

108. "Uniform of the Day: Stylish Women Flock to Army Navy Stores," *Wall Street Journal*, July 7, 1966; "The Army-Navy Surplus Store: High Fashion on 42d Street," *New York Times*, September 2, 1965.

109. Anthony Carthew, "Dear Sir—or Madam?" *New York Times*, November 7, 1965.

110. "Sassoon and His Scissors," *Life*, July 9, 1965, 67–68; "Mia Farrow Sports Crew-Cut Now," *Washington Post*, December 18, 1965; "Cindy Makes Her Decision: Pigtail Goes," *Chicago Tribune*, November 14, 1966; "Short and Easy Hair-do Keeps the Stylists Busy," *Los Angeles Times*, June 10, 1967.

111. Bill Cunningham, "Men are starting to walk . . . ," *Chicago Tribune*, November 1, 1965.

112. "Uni-Sex," *Newsweek*, February 14, 1966.

113. "The Male Head: Now Even Squares Are Going Long-Haired," *New York Times*, September 22, 1967; "Longer Hair Is Not Necessarily Hippie," *Time*, October 27, 1967; "The Ladder of Success," *Newsweek*, July 15, 1968, 61.

114. "Off Again, On Again, It's the Latest Thing in Men's Whiskers," *New York Times*, June 8, 1968; "Gone Today, Hair Tomorrow: Artificial Moustaches, Beards, etc. Are Big Business," *Washington Post*, September 4, 1968.

115. "Men Shun Grey for Peacock Hues," *Hartford Courant*, April 7, 1968.

116. "Men's Fashions in the 1960s: The Peacock's Glory Was Regained," *New York Times*, December 15, 1969; "Male Plumage '68, *Newsweek*, November 25, 1968, 70; Frank, *Conquest of Cool*, 187.

117. "The Nehru," *Washington Post*, May 26, 1968.

118. "Penchant for Pendants," *Newsweek*, April 1, 1968, 99.

119. "Penchant for Pendants," *Newsweek*, April 1, 1968, 99.

120. "Male Plumage '68," *Newsweek*, November 25, 1968, 78.

121. "Men Shun Grey for Peacock Hues," *Hartford Courant*, April 7, 1968.

122. "The Age of Unisex," *Chicago Tribune*, July 8, 1968.

123. "Male Plumage '68," *Newsweek*, November 25, 1968, 78.

124. David Wilkerson, *Hope for Homosexuals: Teen Challenge* (Teen Challenge, 1964), 40–41, reel 303, box 1127, folder 18 (Lesbian and Gay Rights: Misc., 1965), ACLU subject files.

125. Tom Wolfe, "After WWII, Young Men in California Began to Create Their Own Statusspheres," *Los Angeles Times*, September 8, 1968.

126. "If a Fashion's Good Enough for Her, It's Good Enough for Him," *New York Times*, January 6, 1968.

127. "Uniworld of His and Hers," *Life*, June 21, 1968, 86–90.

128. "Retailers of 'Unisex' Apparel Wear Uncertain," *New York Times*, March 2, 1969.

129. Art Buchwald, "Skirts vs. Trousers," *Los Angeles Times*, August 4, 1966; "Wait 'Till Men's Skirts Catch On," *Hartford Courant*, March 12, 1967; "Who Wears the Pants?" *Hartford Courant*, December 31, 1967; "Men May Skirt New Fashions," *Los Angeles Times*, May 5, 1968.

130. Odenwald, *Disappearing Sexes*, 3, 4, 24, 140.

131. Winick, *New People*. See also E. Myers, "Burning Bras," 222.

132. See reviews by Isadore Rubin in *Annals of the American Academy of Political and Social Science*, 225; Beigel in *Journal of Sex Research*, 70–71; Blood in *Social Forces*, 359; and Robert W. Stock, *New York Times*, June 30, 1968.

133. "Books of the Times: It's Here to Stay—Are We?" *New York Times*, August 16, 1968.

134. "Vive La Difference," *Hartford Courant*, April 14, 1967.

135. "His, Hers, and Theirs," *Los Angeles Times*, May 25, 1969.

136. "The Age of Unisex," *Chicago Tribune*, July 8, 1968.

137. "Retailers of 'Unisex' Apparel Wear Uncertain," *New York Times*, March 2, 1969.

138. "Who's She? Why, Dear, That's He," *Washington Post*, March 13, 1968.

139. "Retailers of 'Unisex' Apparel Wear Uncertain," *New York Times*, March 2, 1969.

140. "The Real Change Has Just Begun," *Life*, January 9, 1970, 104–5.

141. Graham, "Flaunting the Freak Flag," 533.

2. "WHAT TO WEAR TO THE REVOLUTION"

1. "War Foes Here Attacked by Construction Workers," *New York Times*, May 9, 1970.

2. See Farber, "Silent Majority"; and Appy, *Working-Class War*.

3. See "Joe Kelly Has Reached His Boiling Point," *New York Times Magazine*, June 28, 1970.

4. J. B. Freeman, "Hardhats."

5. See Van Deburg, *New Day in Babylon*, 197–201.

6. Kelley, "Nap Time."

7. Kelley, "Nap Time"; Feldstein, "'I Don't Trust You Anymore'"

8. Chappell, Hutchinson, and Ward, "'Dress modestly, neatly . . . as if you were going to church!'"; E. Myers, "Burning Bras," 230–40.

9. See Carson, *In Struggle*, chapter 1.

10. E. Myers, "Burning Bras," 242–43.

11. Craig, *Ain't I a Beauty Queen?*, chapter 5.

12. Cleaver, "As Crinkly As Yours."

13. Ogbar, *Black Power*, 12.

14. "The Woman of Islam," *Muhammad Speaks* 1 (October–November 1961): 8–9; "Blackwoman Beauty Is A Standard," *Muhammad Speaks* 1.2 (December 1961): 16; "Be Satisfied with Self!" *Muhammad Speaks* 1.3 (January 1962): 21; "Why No Makeup?," *Muhammad Speaks* 1.4 (February 1962): 24; Cleaver, "As Crinkly As Yours, Brother," *Muhammad Speaks* 1.8 (June 1962): 4 (reprint of Eldridge Cleaver's article from the *Negro History Bulletin*); "The Natural Look Is Reborn in Brilliant New Show," *Muhammad Speaks* 2.10 (February 4, 1963): 12–13; "Many Negro Women Favor New African-Type Hairdos," *Muhammad Speaks* 2.15 (April 15, 1963): 17.

15. Craig, *Ain't I a Beauty Queen?*, 149–54; "Writer Rips Alleged 'Bad' and 'Good' Hair Standards," *Muhammad Speaks* 2.1 (September 30, 1962): 15.

16. "Should Women Wear Pants or Dresses?," *Muhammad Speaks* 1.4 (February 1962): 26.

17. Malcolm X, *Autobiography of Malcolm X*, 55.

18. Malcolm X, "Not Just an American Problem but a World Problem."

19. "Mainspring of Black Power: Stokely Carmichael," *London Observer*, July 23, 1967. See also "'Black Power' Rally Calm," *Los Angeles Sentinel*, December 1, 1966; Carmichael, *Stokely Speaks*, 72–73, 84.

20. Carmichael, *Stokely Speaks*, 73.

21. "The Natural Look," *Ebony*, June 1966, 142–43. See also Craig, *Ain't I a Beauty Queen?*, 93–94.

22. "Natural Hair: New Symbol of Race Pride," *Ebony*, December 1967, 139; "More Men Taking to the 'Natural' Hair Style," *Norfolk New Journal and Guide*, December 16, 1967; "'Nappy State' Marks New Trend, Says Mag," *Baltimore Afro-American*, December 23, 1967.

23. See Brown, *Fighting for us*, chapter 3.

24. "Black Nationalists Gain More Attention in Harlem," *New York Times*, July 3, 1966; "Students Observe Afro-American Week," *Los Angeles Sentinel*, March 7, 1968; "Fourth of July Is Marked in Afro Style," *New York Times*, July 7, 1969; Van Deburg, *New Day in Babylon*, 197–98.

25. E. Myers, "Burning Bras," 228.

26. "Report from Black America," *Newsweek*, June 30, 1969, 17.

27. "1968—The Year of Impact in Black Pride," *Baltimore Afro-American*, January 4, 1969.

28. "New Beauty Aids Created As Natural Hair Style Wearers Multiply," *New York Amsterdam News*, June 15, 1968. See also S. Walker, "Black Is Profitable."

29. "African Spreads Her Wings in Fashion," *Los Angeles Sentinel*, December 7, 1967; "About Dashikis and the New Breed Cat," *New York Times Sunday Magazine*, April 20, 1969, 93.

30. "1968—The Year of Impact in Black Pride," *Baltimore Afro-American*, January 4, 1969.

31. On the association of Afro hair with militance and violence, see "Angela Davis Third on FBI Wanted List," *Chicago Daily Defender*, August 19, 1970; "Cosmetics for Blacks Reflect Growing Pride," *Los Angeles Times*, December 27, 1970; "Natural Afro Losing Its Frizz as Relaxed Hair Comes Back," *Los Angeles Times*, October 27, 1972.

32. "Citizens Give Views on Survival of Afro as Hairstyle," *New York Amsterdam News*, March 3, 1973.

33. Letter to the editor, *Los Angeles Sentinel*, November 13, 1969.

34. "By the Way," *Chicago Daily Defender*, June 29, 1970. This advertisement also appeared in *Atlanta Daily World*, June 30, 1970; *Los Angeles Sentinel*, July 2, 1970; *New Pittsburgh Courier*, July 4, 1970; *New York Amsterdam News*, July 4, 1970.

35. Letter to the editor, *Los Angeles Sentinel*, November 13, 1969.

36. "More Men Taking to the 'Natural' Hair Style," *Norfolk New Journal and Guide*, December 16, 1967.

37. Letter to the editor, *Los Angeles Sentinel*, November 13, 1969.

38. "The Natural Look," *Ebony*, June 1966, 146; S. Walker, "Black Is Profitable," 270.

39. "The Afro: Black and Beautiful," *Washington Post*, August 18, 1968.

40. Letters to the editor, *Ebony*, August 1966, 12.

41. See "Black and Beautiful," *Black Panther* 1.5 (July 20, 1967): 15, 17, 18; *Black Power!* [periodical of the Northern California Chapter of the Black Panther Party, December 1967] 8, Special Collections, Bancroft Library, University of California–Berkeley; "Black Woman," *Black Panther* 2.6 (September 14, 1968): 6.

42. "Black Woman," *Black Panther* 2.6 (September 14, 1968): 6.

43. "Black and Beautiful," *Black Panther* 1.5 (July 20, 1967): 15, 17, 18.

44. "Black Panthers Gain Support," *Christian Science Monitor*, November 18, 1968; "Black Panthers Outline Stand," *Hartford Courant*, April 1, 1969; "Black Panther Case Courtroom Provides Contrasts," *Hartford Courant*, November 24, 1969; "'Fuzzy-Haired' Prof. Angela Davis Receives Anonymous Letters," *Los Angeles Sentinel*, October 2, 1969; "Wife, Mother, and Revolutionary," *Washington Post*, January 5, 1970.

45. Letters to the editor, "Back to the Hot Comb," *Ebony*, November 1969, 19. See also Craig, *Ain't I a Beauty Queen?*, 125.
46. "Cosmetics for Blacks Reflect Growing Pride," *Los Angeles Times*, December 27, 1970; "Civil Rights Enjoys Riches," *Chicago Daily Defender*, June 17, 1968; "The Afro and Its Meaning to the Black Beautician," *New York Amsterdam News*, July 5, 1969.
47. "Wear It Your Way," *Chicago Defender*, April 5, 1975.
48. "Report from Black America," *Newsweek*, June 30, 1969, 22.
49. See Rossinow, "Revolution Is About Our Lives."
50. Ehrenreich, *Hearts of Men*, chapter 5; Breines, "The 'Other' Fifties," 399–400.
51. Coleman, "Dressing for the Revolution," 186.
52. "The White Revolution," *New Left Notes* 2.25 (June 26, 1967): 20.
53. "The Teenage Scapegoat," *New Left Notes* 2.25 (June 26, 1967): 9.
54. Gitlin, *Sixties*, 163; Rossinow, "Revolution Is About Our Lives," 104–5.
55. Gitlin, *Sixties*, 163.
56. R. D. Myers, *Toward a History of the New Left*, 6; Rossinow, "Revolution Is About Our Lives"; Gitlin, *Whole World Is Watching*, 30–31, 131.
57. Quoted in Lieberman, *Prairie Power*, 47.
58. Quoted in Lieberman, *Prairie Power*, 152, 168.
59. Gitlin, *Whole World Is Watching*, 31.
60. "The Teenage Scapegoat," *New Left Notes* 2.25 (June 26, 1967): 9.
61. See L. Cohen, *Consumer's Republic*.
62. Gitlin, *Sixties*, 12.
63. The Port Huron Statement of Students for a Democratic Society, 1962, http://coursesa.matrix.msu.edu/~hst306/documents/huron.html.
64. "What Is a Hippie?," *Haight-Ashbury Maverick* 1.4 (1967): 1.
65. "Short Trips," *Haight-Ashbury Maverick* 1.4 (1967): 2.
66. "Hippies Voice Philosophy, Love," *Los Angeles Times*, July 23, 1967.
67. J. Rubin, *Do It!*, 96.
68. "Letter from a Beatnik," *The Illustrated Paper* (SF) no. 3 (August 1966), 7, reel 1, Underground Press Collection.
69. Hodgdon, *Manhood in the Age of Aquarius*, xli, 41; Deloria, "Countercultural Indians and the New Age," 66; "Squirrels, Beads, and the Hippie-Bead Fad Give Navajos a Lift," *New York Times*, September 7, 1968.
70. Dana Densmore, "Tarzan Had Long Hair Too," *No More Fun and Games*, no. 4 (April 1970): 70.
71. Lemke-Santangelo, *Daughters of Aquarius*, 72.
72. Coleman, "Dressing for the Revolution," 188.
73. "Notes to Tourists," *Haight-Ashbury Maverick* 1.6 (1967): 2.

74. "Hippies Say They Need Protection from Police," *San Francisco Chronicle*, October 11, 1967.

75. J. Rubin, *Do It!*, 94.

76. Hoffman, *Revolution for the Hell of It*, 71.

77. "Atlanta: The Great Hippie Hunt," *Time*, October 10, 1969, 22.

78. J. Rubin, *Do It!*, 93–95.

79. Ann Landers, "Getting Through the Hair," *Washington Post*, June 28, 1970.

80. Quoted in Lieberman, *Prairie Power*, 168.

81. Appy, *Working-Class War*, chapter 1.

82. The Port Huron Statement of Students for a Democratic Society, 1962, http://coursesa.matrix.msu.edu/~hst306/documents/huron.html.

83. The Port Huron Statement of Students for a Democratic Society, 1962, http://coursesa.matrix.msu.edu/~hst306/documents/huron.html.

84. "Hippies Voice Philosophy, Love," *Los Angeles Times*, July 23, 1967.

85. See Takaki, *Double Victory*.

86. Ehrenreich, *Hearts of Men*, 105–6. For more on the relationship between the Vietnam War and images of masculinity, see Dean, *Imperial Brotherhood*; and Jeffords, *Remasculinization of America*.

87. "What Does It Take to Be a Man?" *The Seed* (Chicago) 1.10 (November 3–24, 1967): 8–9, reel 4, Underground Press Collection.

88. "Hair Piece," *The Seed* (Chicago) 1.6 (August 11–25, 1967): 18, reel 4, Underground Press Collection.

89. Letter dated February 1967, reel 19, series 3, section 1 (correspondence 1965–70), SDS Papers.

90. Stacewicz, *Winter Soldiers*. Although some Vietnam War veterans grew their hair long and adopted hippie styles of dress, Andrew E. Hunt, in *The Turning: A History of Vietnam Veterans Against the War*, argues that members of Vietnam Veterans Against the War "rejected the countercultural fashions of the era. When they appeared at debates or interviews or on TV shows, VVAW representatives usually wore short hair and dressed in suits and ties" (21). These differences in the secondary sources might suggest debates within VVAW over dress and self-presentation in their politics.

91. "A Curse on the Men in Washington, Pentagon," *Street Raps: A Com/co Annotated Anthology* (1966–1967), box 1, folder 6, SFPL Hippie Collection.

92. Gitlin, *Whole World Is Watching*, 31, 113.

93. See "Still Something Special," *San Francisco Sunday Examiner and Chronicle*, June 2, 1968; "Haighties Move Across Bay," *San Francisco Examiner*, March 10, 1967.

94. Document NY 100–148047, reel 1, section 1, FBI file on SDS.

95. Schrecker, *Many Are the Crimes*, chapter 4.

96. Memorandum dated July 9, 1965, reel 1, section 9, and memorandum dated August 11, 1966, reel 2, section 19, FBI file on SDS.

97. Memorandum dated May 11, 1967, reel 2, section 26, FBI file on SDS.

98. Memorandum dated May 8, 1967, reel 2, section 26, FBI file on SDS.

99. "Students Aid America's Foes," *Times-Picayune*, November 7, 1965; "Leftists Meet at Clear Lake," *Des Moines Register*, August 29, 1966. These news clippings, dated after the memorandums cited in several of the preceding notes, can be found in the files that the FBI kept on SDS activities, suggesting that the FBI may have supplied these news outlets with information for the articles.

100. Memorandum dated July 9, 1965, reel 1, section 9, FBI file on SDS.

101. Miller, *Democracy Is in the Streets*, 248–49; Gitlin, *Whole World Is Watching*, 88–90; see also "Paul Booth," *Harvard Crimson*, November 2, 1965.

102. Transcript from "Off the Cuff," aired June 7, 1965, on WBKB TV Channel 7 in Chicago, reel 1, section 6, FBI file on SDS.

103. "Anatomy of a Liberal," *New Guard* 5.6 (June 1965): 11; "The Beatles Salivation Plot," *New Guard* 5.6 (June 1965): 18; "Rebellion at Berkeley," *New Guard* 5.9 (September 1965): 6.

104. "Spotlight On: State Chairmen," *New Guard* 5.6 (June 1965): 22; "Spotlight On: State Chairmen," *New Guard* 7.5 (May 1967): 19; "Spotlight On: State Chairmen," *New Guard* 7.4 (April 1967): 24; "Spotlight On: State Chairmen," *New Guard* 7.3 (March 1967): 23; "Berry's World," *New Guard* 7.6 (Summer 1967): 4.

105. Letters to the editor, *New Guard* 5.8 (August 1965): 22; Letters to the editor, *New Guard* 6.5 (May 1966): 26.

106. "Report on Civil Disorders Spurs Wallace's Growth," *Los Angeles Times*, March 13, 1968; "Wallace Hits Professors Who Support Viet Cong," *Hartford Courant*, September 15, 1968; "The Wallace Boom: Third-Party Candidate Shakes Major Parties as He Wins Followers," *Wall Street Journal*, September 17, 1968.

107. "Republicans Like Wallace on Tour," *New York Times*, November 6, 1967.

108. "Turbulence Marks Wallace's Trip along Campaign Trail," *Los Angeles Times*, October 13, 1968; "Hecklers Try Using Silence on Wallace," *Chicago Tribune*, October 23, 1968.

109. "Violence Erupts as Wallace Is Heckled at Big Rally in S.F.," *Los Angeles Times*, October 14, 1968.

110. See Sugrue, *Origins of the Urban Crisis*; Formisano, *Boston Against Busing*; Nicolaides, *My Blue Heaven*.

111. Dan Carter, *Politics of Rage*, 313.

112. "Who Inhabits 'Wallace Country'?" *Baltimore Sun*, October 3, 1968. See also Hamill, "Wallace"; and Novak, "Why Wallace?"

113. "On the Hustings with Wallace in California," *Los Angeles Times*, December 17, 1967; "'It Isn't a Mirage They're Seeing,' Says George Wallace," *New York Times*, September 22, 1968.

114. Braunstein and Doyle, *Imagine Nation*, 6.

115. Spiro Agnew, speech at Brigham Young University, May 9, 1969, in Agnew, *Collected Speeches*, 19.

116. "Mr. Agnew Takes on the Nation's Youth," *Hartford Courant*, November 27, 1969; Perlstein, *Nixonland*, 430–31. Agnew's attacks were not the first time that conservative politicians accused liberals of being effete or effeminate; similar attacks were common in the 1940s and 1950s, when conservatives accused liberals of being "soft" on communism. See Dean, *Imperial Brotherhood*; and Cuordileone, *Manhood and American Political Culture*.

117. Agnew, *Collected Speeches*, 75.

118. "On the Hustings with Wallace in California," *Los Angeles Times*, December 17, 1967.

119. See Rising, *Clean for Gene*, 67; "Be Clean For Gene," *Newsweek*, March 18, 1968, 51–52; "Students Trim for McCarthy," *Hartford Courant*, March 20, 1968; "Mr. Clean Makes It in New Hampshire," *New Republic*, March 23, 1968, 13; Stavis, *We Were the Campaign*, 16; Stout, *People*, 164.

120. "Crusade of the Ballot Children," *Time*, March 22, 1968, 13.

121. "Students Trim for McCarthy," *Hartford Courant*, March 20, 1968.

122. See "Hecklers at Boston Rally," *New Left Notes* 1.14 (April 22, 1966): 2.

123. "Four SDS Members Attacked in Apartment," *New Left Notes* 1.38 (October 7, 1966): 2.

124. See Gitlin, *Sixties*, chapter 10; "Rusk at the Fairmont—A View From One Corner," *New Left Notes* 3.3 (January 22, 1968): 3.

125. See Farber, *Chicago '68*.

126. See, for example, "Youths Dominate Capital Throng," *New York Times*, October 22, 1967; "Political Activism New Hippie 'Thing,'" *New York Times*, March 24, 1968.

127. "Police vs. Nonconformity," *New York Times*, December 2, 1968.

128. Stark, *Police Riots*, 112–13.

129. Hoffman, *Revolution for the Hell of It*, 49.

130. D. Walker, *Rights in Conflict*.

131. D. Walker, *Rights in Conflict*, viii–ix.

132. "Poll Shows 71.4% Find Police Action Justified in Chicago," *New York Times*, August 31, 1968.

133. "Only in America: More on the Convention," *Chicago Daily Defender*, September 9, 1968.

3. "NO WOMAN CAN BE FREE"

1. "Notes on Cutting My Hair," *Ain't I A Woman?* 1.11 (January 29, 1971): 2.
2. See Kreydatus, "Marketing to the 'Liberated' Woman"; Scott, *Fresh Lipstick*; Collins, *When Everything Changed*.
3. See Cobble, *Other Women's Movement*, 180; Echols, *Daring to Be Bad*, 92–101; Rosen, *World Split Open*, 160.
4. New York Radical Women, "No More Miss America," 184–85.
5. Friedan, *Feminine Mystique*; May, *Homeward Bound*, chapter 9.
6. Cobble, *Other Women's Movement*, chapter 7; Harrison, *On Account of Sex*, chapter 10; Rosen, *World Split Open*, chapter 3.
7. Jo Freeman, "How 'Sex' Got into Title VII."
8. Kessler-Harris, *In Pursuit of Equity*, chapter 6.
9. Nancy Hewitt has offered an important critique of the "wave" metaphor in describing the history of feminist activism, stressing continuities in feminist thought and action rather than dividing feminist history into distinct waves or periods. See Hewitt, *No Permanent Waves*.
10. Women, of course, did not themselves divide as neatly as these labels suggest; for example, many women were members of both their local NOW chapters and other women's liberation groups. In general, I use the terms "women's liberationist" to describe younger women who joined feminist activism based on their experiences in other leftist and radical movements of the 1960s, and "women's activist" to describe women who participated in organizations like NOW that focused on legislative and legal change.
11. See Evans, *Personal Politics*; Echols, *Daring to Be Bad*, chapters 1–2.
12. Una Stannard, "If the Shoe Pinches," *Everywoman* 2.12 (August 21, 1971); "What the Hippies Gave to Us," *San Francisco Chronicle Sunday Punch*, December 22, 1968; "Short trips," *Haight-Ashbury Maverick* 1.4 (1967): 2. See also Lemke-Santangelo, *Daughters of Aquarius*, 72.
13. "Hairy Women Protest Fairy Queen," *The Rag* 2.39 (September 23, 1968): 8.
14. Evans, *Personal Politics*; Rossinow, "Revolution Is About Our Lives."
15. Coryell, "What's in a Name?," 216.
16. "What Is the Difference? Women's Rights and Women's Liberation," reel 2, folder 12B (Position papers, n.d.), Female Liberation: A Radical Feminist Organization Records, 1968–1974 (part of Grassroots Feminist Organizations, Part I: Boston Area Second Wave Organizations, 1968–98), Gale Cengage Primary Source Microfilm Collection.
17. Maureen Davidica, "Women and the Radical Movement," *No More Fun and Games: A Journal of Female Liberation*, no.1 (1968).
18. Evans, *Personal Politics*, 192; Echols, *Daring to Be Bad*, 45.

19. Lynn Piartney, "A Letter to the Editor of *Ramparts Magazine*," *Notes from the First Year*, 1968.
20. Evans, *Personal Politics*; Echols, *Daring to Be Bad,* chapters 1–2; Rosen, *World Split Open*, chapter 4.
21. Willis, "Women and the Myth of Consumerism," 288–90. See also "'Consumerism' and Women," folder: "Early Women's Liberation SF," Sally Gearhart Papers, GLBTHS.
22. Kreydatus, "Marketing to the 'Liberated' Woman," 43–49.
23. "Truth and Beauty," *A Change Is Gonna Come* 1.4 (April 1971): 5.
24. Ellen Willis, "Whatever happened to women? NOTHING—That's the Trouble: A Report on the New Feminism," *Mademoiselle*, September 1969.
25. Una Stannard, "If the Shoe Pinches," *Everywoman* 2.12 (August 21, 1971).
26. "Make-up Slave," *A Change Is Gonna Come* 1.2 (February 1971): 2. See also Lynn O'Conner, "Male Supremacy," folder: "Early Women's Liberation SF," Sally Gearhart Papers, GLBTHS.
27. "What the Well-Dressed Dyke Will Wear," *Cowrie* 1.5 (February 1974): 21.
28. "Lesbian Feminist Declaration of 1976," reel 68, folder 06221, Lesbian Herstory Archives Subject Files (LHA), Thompson Gale Primary Source Microfilms.
29. Once again, these labels are imperfect; many lesbians were active in NOW chapters and in women's liberation organizations as well as in separate groups for lesbians. In general, I use the term "lesbian feminist" to describe women who identified as lesbians or who wrote in periodicals devoted to lesbian/feminist issues. On the growth of lesbian feminism and divisions between lesbian and straight women, see Echols, *Daring to Be Bad*, chapter 5; Jay, *Tales of the Lavender Menace*; Stein, *Sex and Sensibility*; and Gerhard, *Desiring Revolution*, chapters 3 and 5.
30. Radicalesbians, "The Woman-Identified Woman," *Come Out!* 1.4 (June/July 1970): 12–13.
31. Sally Gearhart, "Lesbianism as a Political Statement," *Sisters* 1.2 (December 1970): 1.
32. See Mead, *Male and Female*; Money, Hampson, and Hampson, "Hermaphroditism," 285. See also Meyerowitz, *How Sex Changed*, chapter 3.
33. Jo Freeman, "Women's Liberation Front," reprinted from *The Moderator*, November 1968, folder: "Early Women's Liberation SF," Sally Gearhart Papers, GLBTHS.
34. Una Stannard, "If the Shoe Pinches," *Everywoman* 2.12 (August 21, 1971); "Stamp Out High Heels," reprinted in *Dear Sisters*, 40; "Make-up Slave," *A Change Is Gonna Come* 1.2 (February 1971): 2; Lynn O'Conner, "Male Supremacy," folder: "Early Women's Liberation SF," Sally Gearhart Papers,

GLBTHS; Sharon Zecha, "Being a Real Woman," *Born a Woman*, no. 1 (Fall/ Winter 1971): 31.

35. Reid, "Coming Out in the Women's Movement," 99–100.

36. "What Every Young Girl Should Ask!" reel 68, folder 06221, LHA.

37. Una Stannard, "If the Shoe Pinches," *Everywoman* 2.12 (August 21, 1971); "Stamp Out High Heels," reprinted in *Dear Sisters*, 40; "Make-up Slave," *A Change Is Gonna Come* 1.2 (February 1971): 2; Lynn O'Conner, "Male Supremacy," folder: "Early Women's Liberation SF," Sally Gearhart Papers; Una Stannard, "Clothing and Sexuality," *Everywoman* 2.13 (Sept 10, 1971): 6.

38. "Rita Right on Radical Fashion," *Lesbian Tide* 2.7 (February 1973): 11.

39. "What the Well Dressed Dyke Will Wear," *Cowrie* 1.2 (June 1973): 5. See also "Well-Trained Hair," *Lavender Woman* 4.1 (February 1975): 8.

40. Sharon Zecha, "Being a Real Woman," *Born a Woman*, no.1 (Fall/Winter 1971): 31.

41. Cassell, *Group Called Women*, chapter 6. See also Kaminski, "From Personal to Public," 149.

42. Ellen Cantarow, "Some Autobiographical Reflections, Or: A Case In Point," *Female Liberation Newsletter* 1.1 (1969): 2.

43. "Did you know . . . ," *Sisters* 4.6 (June 1973): 18.

44. On the growing popularity of fashions in the late 1960s and early 1970s, see "If a Fashion's Good Enough for Her, It's Good Enough for Him," *New York Times*, January 6, 1968; "Uniworld of His and Hers," *Life*, June 21, 1968, 86–90.

45. Heilbrun, *Toward a Recognition of Androgyny*, ix–x.

46. Lydia Darnell, "Unisex Fashions and Equality," *Chicago Tribune*, June 13, 1972.

47. "Make a Ladder of Your Hair, Rapunzel," *Free Press Underground* 3.3 (March 1968): 4.

48. "Dyke Image," *Dykes and Gorgons* 1.1 (May-June 1973): 4.

49. Deevey, "Such a Nice Girl," 25.

50. "What the Well-Dressed Dyke Will Wear," *Cowrie* 1.2 (June 1973): 5.

51. "Finally out of Drag," *Dykes and Gorgons* 1.1 (May–June 1973): 3.

52. "Dyke Image," *Dykes and Gorgons* 1.1 (May–June 1973): 4.

53. "A Feminist Perspective: Dyke and Proud," *Advocate*, no. 171 (August 27, 1975): 32.

54. "What the Well-Dressed Dyke Will Wear," *Cowrie* 1.2 (June 1973): 6.

55. "Are Blue Jeans Mandatory?" *San Francisco Sunday Examiner and Chronicle*, May 3, 1970.

56. See, for examples, Una Stannard, "Editorial: Beauty is a Beast," *SF NOW*

Newsletter, March 1970; "Feminists View the Fashion Scene," sf now *Newsletter* 1.6 (May 15, 1970): 12, box 60, folder 13, Martin/Lyon Papers, GLBTHS.

57. Cassell, *Group Called Women*, 85.

58. Letter to Aileen Hernandez, box 47, folder 12, series XIII, now Records, Schlesinger Library, Radcliffe Institute for Advanced Study at Harvard University.

59. Scott, *Fresh Lipstick*, 285.

60. Press Release, now New York, March 29, 1967, and "Announcement of Press Conference and Request for Coverage," June 12, 1967, box 48, folder 29, series XIII, now records.

61. Friedan, *It Changed My Life*, 173. Emphasis in original. See also Rosen, *World Split Open*, 86–87; Kreydatus, "Marketing to the 'Liberated' Woman," 48.

62. Rosen, *World Split Open*, 83; Echols, *Daring to Be Bad*, chapter 5; Jay, *Tales of the Lavender Menace*.

63. See Chauncey, "From Sexual Inversion to Homosexuality," 87–117; Smith-Rosenberg's chapter, "New Woman as Androgyne: Social Disorder and the Gender Crisis, 1870–1936," in *Disorderly Conduct*; Newton, "Mythic Mannish Lesbian."

64. Echols, *Daring to Be Bad*, chapter 5; Breines, *Trouble Between Us*.

65. "Rita Right on Radical Fashion," *Lesbian Tide* 2.7 (February 1973): 11.

66. Robin Morgan, "Lesbianism and Feminism: Synonyms or Contradictions?" *Second Wave* 2.4 (1973): 19.

67. N. Williamson, "Case for Studied Ugliness," 10.

68. "The Controversy over 'Androgyny,'" *Women: A Journal of Liberation* 4.1 (Winter 1974): 58–59.

69. "Butch or Fem? The Third World Lesbian's Dilemma," *Coming Out Rage* (May 1973): 11.

70. Quoted in Enke, *Finding the Movement*, 55.

71. See Kennedy and Davis, *Boots of Leather, Slippers of Gold*.

72. Stein, *Sex and Sensibility*, 83.

73. Discussion with Marisela Chavez, Schlesinger Library Summer Seminar "Sequels to the 1960s," Radcliffe Institute for Advanced Study, Harvard University, June 2008.

74. See Wallace, "Black Feminist's Search for Sisterhood."

75. "Cosmetics for Blacks Reflect Growing Pride," *Los Angeles Times*, December 27, 1970; "Civil Rights Enjoys Riches," *Chicago Daily Defender*, June 17, 1968; "The Afro and Its Meaning to the Black Beautician," *New York Amsterdam News*, July 5, 1969.

76. "Are Blue Jeans Mandatory?" *San Francisco Sunday Examiner and Chronicle*, May 3, 1970.

77. Letters, *Cowrie* 2.1 (April 1974): 7.

78. Letters, *Cowrie* 1.5 (February 1974): 11.

79. Dori Fields, "Dyke-ism Is Dying," *Gay-Vue* 2.2 (February 1972): 2.

80. "Our Own Feelings About Androgyny," *Women: A Journal of Liberation* 4.1 (Winter 1974): 32–33.

81. See Kennedy and Davis, *Boots of Leather, Slippers of Gold*; Case, "Towards a Butch-Femme Aesthetic"; Cvetkovich, "Recasting Receptivity."

82. Boyd, *Wide Open Town*, 180, 192–93; D'Emilio, *Sexual Politics, Sexual Communities*, 106. Marcia Gallo's study of the DOB, however, found that opinions on self-presentation within the organization were much more complex than these works suggest. See Gallo, *Different Daughters*, 23–24.

83. "The Realities of Lesbianism," *Motive*, March–April 1969, reprinted in "Lesbians Speak Out" (n.d.), 4–10, folder: "Lesbians, early 1970s," Anson Reinhart Papers, GLBTHS; see also "Who is a Lesbian?" box 35, folder 14, Martin/Lyon Papers, GLBTHS; speech in Bellingham, April 6, 1973, box 40, folder 16, Martin/Lyon Papers, GLBTHS; Martin and Lyon, *Lesbian/Woman*, 12–23, 74–78.

84. Abbot and Love, "Is Women's Liberation a Lesbian Plot?," 445.

85. "Something It Means to Be a Lesbian," Gay Women's Liberation, Berkeley, December 1969, printed in "Lesbians Speak Out," folder: "Lesbians, early 1970s," Anson Reinhart Papers, GLBTHS.

86. "Gay Women's West Coast Conference," *Everywoman* 2.10 (July 9, 1971).

87. "Distinctions: The Circle Game," *Amazon Quarterly* 1.2 (February 1973): 26.

88. National Organization for Women, Statement of Purpose, 1966, http://now.org/history/purpos66.html.

89. Self, *All in the Family*, 135.

90. Self, *All in the Family*, 147.

91. Self, *All in the Family*, 329.

92. Letters, *Voice of the Women's Liberation Movement*, 1.4 (October 1968): 11.

93. "On the Yin Side: Fall Fashions for Feminists," *Second Wave* 2.2 (1972): 45.

94. *Women: A Journal of Liberation* 4.1 (Winter 1974): 24.

95. "Being a Long-haired Dyke," reel 62, folder 05720, LHA.

96. "Our Own Feelings About Androgyny," *Women: A Journal of Liberation* 4.1 (Winter 1974): 32–33.

97. "Herstory," *Lesbian Tide*, October 1971, 8.

98. "One Dyke's Declaration of Independence," *Lesbian Connection* 2.2 (May 1976): 3.

99. Image of Task Force News, July 1973 memo, box 30, folder 65, series VIII, NOW records.

100. Weisstein and Booth, "Will the Women's Movement Survive?," insert p. 2.
101. Letters, *Cowrie* 2.2 (June/July 1974): 16–17.
102. "The Movement: They Act the Part," *Boston Globe*, August 10, 1969. See also Kaminski, "From Personal to Public," 181.
103. "Blacks and Women's Lib Picket Sahl," *San Francisco Chronicle*, May 23, 1970.
104. Scott, *Fresh Lipstick*, 297–98; "Gloria Steinem's Putdown," *San Francisco Sunday Chronicle and Examiner*, February 13, 1972; "Germaine Greer," *Life*, May 7, 1971, 30.
105. Harriet Van Horne, "Militants' Mistake," *San Francisco Examiner*, August 23, 1970.
106. Morton Hunt, "Up Against the Wall, Male Chauvinist Pig!" *Playboy*, May 1970, 95, 206. See also Pitzulo, "Battle in Every Man's Bed."
107. Helen Lawrenson, "The Feminine Mistake," *Esquire*, January 1971, 83, 146–54. See also Kaminski, "From Personal to Public," 167.
108. "Question Man: Would You Join the Women's Liberation Movement?" *San Francisco Chronicle*, April 17, 1970.
109. "Harris Poll: A Look at the American Woman," *San Francisco Chronicle*, March 24, 1972; "Women Against Liberation," *San Francisco Chronicle*, May 25, 1971.
110. See Phyllis Schlafly, "What's Wrong With 'Equal Rights' for Women?"; from the *Phyllis Schlafly Report*, February 1972, and reprinted in Levy, ed., *America in the Sixties*, 221–28.
111. See Critchlow, *Phyllis Schlafly and Grassroots Conservatism*.
112. "The Pictures the Press Didn't Print," *Phyllis Schlafly Report* 9.11, section 2 (June 1976): 1; "Why the Equal Rights Amendment Should Be Rejected," *Phyllis Schlafly Report* 10.9, section 2 (April 1977): 2.
113. "Why Women Should Not Serve in Military Combat," *Phyllis Schlafly Report* 13.8, section 2 (March 1980): 1–2.
114. Critchlow, *Phyllis Schlafly and Grassroots Conservatism*, 224–25, 229, 236.
115. "At War with the Pink Ladies," *Mother Jones* 2.9 (November 1977): 21–22.
116. "Libbers Talking Their Way into Trouble," *Washington DC Evening Star and Daily News*, February 21, 1973.
117. "Pants, Suitable," *Buffalo News*, November 19, 2000; "Wearing the Pants: Envisioning a Female Commander-in-Chief," *Washington Post*, December 9, 2007; "Donatella Versace Tells Hillary Clinton to Take Her Pants Off," *StyleList*, February 8, 2007; "Slacking Hillary," *New York Sun*, June 3, 2008; "Column: Perceptions of Female Politicians Affected by Appearance," *Daily Nebraskan*, September 17, 2008; "Sarah Palin Sexism Watch: Skirt-Wearing, SexyMom Edition," Feministing.com, September 8, 2008.
118. See Baumgardner and Richards, *Manifesta*.

1. "Drag Debut," *Gay Sunshine* 1.7 (June-July 1971): 15.

2. Cole, *Don We Now Our Gay Apparel*, 88. For examples of gay activists using the term "gender fuck" to describe political drag, see "Preview With Pictures: The Queens," *Advocate*, no. 166 (June 18, 1975): 33; "The Politics of Drag," *Advocate*, no. 217 (June 15, 1977): 33.

3. This chapter will focus on gay male activism rather than lesbian or lesbian feminist activism, although women and lesbians will be included where appropriate. Lesbians were usually outnumbered by men in gay organizations, often organized separately from gay males, and oftentimes aligned themselves with the feminist movement rather than the gay liberation movement. An exception can be found in the case of Philadelphia; see Marc Stein, *City of Sisterly and Brotherly Loves*. However, particularly in the gay liberation era, women often felt excluded from predominantly gay male organizations and formed separate lesbian organizations to combat what they claimed was sexist treatment by gay males. I have therefore decided to include the lesbian and lesbian feminist politics of self-presentation in the preceding chapter on feminism. See Armstrong, *Forging Gay Identities*, 140–47; Marotta, *Politics of Homosexuality*, chapters 9 and 11; and McGarry and Wasserman, *Becoming Visible* 179–97.

4. See Hekma, "'Female Soul in a Male Body'"; Chauncey, "From Sexual Inversion to Homosexuality."

5. See Duberman, *Stonewall*; David Carter, *Stonewall*.

6. See D'Emilio, *Sexual Politics, Sexual Communities*; Bérubé, *Coming Out Under Fire*; Johnson, *Lavender Scare*.

7. D'Emilio, *Sexual Politics*, 119.

8. Johnson, *Lavender Scare*, 201; M. Stein, *City of Sisterly and Brotherly Loves*, 273; *Gay Pioneers*. On the increasing militance of some Mattachine Society chapters in the 1960s, see D'Emilio, *Sexual Politics*, chapters 9–11; on the formation of SIR, see Boyd, *Wide Open Town*, 227–31.

9. Suran, "Coming Out Against the War," 465, 470–71.

10. See Jay and Young, introduction to *Out of the Closets*, xxxiv.

11. Clipping *San Francisco Chronicle*, November 4, 1969.

12. Photograph in *Berkeley Barb*, January 2, 1970; "Gay Labor Pain," *Berkeley Times*, January 30, 1970; "'Boys in the Band' Picketed," *San Francisco Chronicle*, March 28, 1970.

13. *Gay Pioneers*.

14. Jay and Young, introduction to *Out of the Closets*, xxxiv.

15. "Dept. Store Faggot," *Gay Sunshine* 1.1 (August/September 1970): 2.

16. "Homosexual Call for Militancy," [news clip, n.d.], box 21, folder 30, Martin/Lyon Papers, GLBTHS.

17. "Sir?," *San Francisco Free Press* 1.4 (November 1–14, 1969): 7.

18. See cover, *The Insider*, November 11, 1970.

19. "Editorial: I," *Come Out!* November 1969, reprinted in *Come Out! Selections from the Radical Gay Liberation Newsletter.*

20. Third World Gay Revolution and Gay Liberation Front (Chicago), "Gay Revolution and Sex Roles," reprinted in Jay and Young, *Out of the Closets*, 252.

21. A. N. Diaman, "On Sex Roles," *Gay Flames* pamphlet no. 11, folder 5, Stephen Lowell Papers, GLBTHS.

22. Third World Gay Revolution and Gay Liberation Front (Chicago), "Gay Revolution and Sex Roles," 252.

23. Tony Diaman, "The Search for the Total Man," *Come Out!* 1.7 (December–January 1970): 22.

24. For other gay liberation critiques of gendered heterosexuality and norms of masculinity, see "Fear of Self," *Gay Sunshine* 1.1 (August-September 1970): 14; "Will You Still Need Me When I'm 64," *Gay Sunshine* 1.5 (January 1971): 9; "Gay Defense Rally at Hayward State," *Gay Sunshine* 1.6 (March 1971): 3; "Masculinity As an Oppressive Ideology," *Gay Sunshine*, no. 14 (August 1972): 5; "Random Notes," and "Gay Oppression," *People's Gay Sunshine* (n.d.): 6, 13.

25. Martha Shelley, "Gay Is Good," *Gay Flames* pamphlet no. 1, box 1, folder 43, Charles Thorpe Papers, SFPL.

26. "Fear of Self," *Gay Sunshine* 1.1 (August–September 1970): 14.

27. "Homosexuals in Revolt: The Year That One Liberation Movement Turned Militant," *Life*, December 31, 1971, 66–67.

28. On "camp" or festive appropriations of drag, see Boyd, *Wide Open Town*, chapter 1; Chauncey, *Gay New York*, chapter 11; Johnson, "Kids of Fairytown"; and Drexel, "Before Paris Burned." Drag shows and balls were a significant part of SIR's social and fundraising events in the 1960s; see "Halloween Ball," *Vector* 4.1 (December 1967): 21; "'Millie' Premiere a S.I.R. Triumph!," *Vector* 3.11 (October 1967): 5; "Sirlebrity Capades '67: A Review," *Vector* 4.2 (January–February 1968): 4–5; "This Was Halloween," *Vector* 4.12 (December 1968): 21–23; "Questions Unanswered," *Vector* 1.3 (1965): 1; "The Empress' Military Ball," *Vector* 4.3 (1968): 20. See also Luther Hillman, "'The Most Profoundly Revolutionary Act a Homosexual Can Engage In.'"

29. Guy Nassberg, "Revolutionary Love: An Introduction to Gay Liberation," *Gay Flames* pamphlet no. 11, box 1, folder 43, Charles Thorpe Papers, SFPL.

30. See "Court Okays Skag Drag, Police Demur," *Advocate*, no. 100 (December 6, 1972): 18; for other examples of gay liberationists using political drag tactics, see "R.I.P. Offs," *Gay Sunshine* 1.1 (August-September 1970): 7; "Don't Call Us We'll Call You," *Gay Sunshine* 1.3 (November 1970): 16.

31. Clendinen and Nagourney, *Out for Good*, 43.

32. See "Homosexuals in Revolt: The Year That One Liberation Movement Turned Militant," *Life*, December 31, 1971, 66–67; and the film *Question of Equality*.

33. Alinder, "Gay Liberation Meets the Shrinks," 143.

34. "Gay 'Guerilla's' Picket Drag Ball," *San Francisco Free Press* 1.4 (November 1–14, 1969): 1; "Gay? To Our Brothers and Sisters, What Are You Doing Here?," box 1, folder 13, Charles Thorpe Papers, SFPL; Berlandt, "My Soul Vanished from Sight," 54.

35. "Camp Out?," *Gay Sunshine* 1.1 (August–September 1970): 9.

36. David Bertelson, "A Comparative Approach to the Meaning of Gay Liberation," March 1971, box 22, folder 15, Martin/Lyon Papers, GLBTHS.

37. Rossinow, *Politics of Authenticity*, 298; Estes, *I Am A Man!*, chapter 7.

38. Kissack, "Freaking Fag Revolutionaries," 104–34, 111.

39. Lekus, "Queer Harvests," 57–91.

40. "Why Are We Rocking the Boat?" CHF *Newsletter*, April 29, 1969, 1.

41. "A Meaning of the States Lines Confrontation," CHF *Newsletter*, May 13, 1969, 1–2.

42. "Gay Militants Demonstrate for Rights at UC Berkeley," *Advocate* 3.11 (December 1969): 3.

43. See "Drag Queens Demonstrate," *Drag*, 1.1 (n.d.): 5; Ted Rauch, "Transvestism and Gay Liberation," *Gay Activist* 1.7 (November 1971): 5; Letter from the GAA to the *New York Times*, dated July 29, 1971, reel 7, box 17, folder 9, News and Media Relations Committee, Correspondence, GAA records; "Statement Against Transvestism," *Drag* 5.18 (1974): 36–37, 42.

44. See Meyerowitz, *How Sex Changed*, 235; Marcus, *Making History*, 192–93.

45. "The Wearing of Drag," *Vector* 3.5 (March 1967): 16–17.

46. "Statement Against Transvestism," *Drag* 5.18 (1974): 36–37, 42.

47. "Mailbag: Transsexuals & TVs: Pro & Con," *Advocate*, no. 114 (June 20, 1973): 36.

48. Arthur Evans, "Should TVs Embarrass Gay Cause?" *Advocate*, no. 112 (May 23, 1973): 37.

49. Reverend Edward J. Hansen, "The Church and the Tenderloin" (Sermon), July 17, 1966; and Edward Hansen and Fred Bird, Mark Forrester and Victor J. Des Marais Jr., "The White Ghetto: Youth and Young Adults in the Tenderloin Area of Downtown San Francisco," [paper, n.d.], Ed Hansen Papers, GLBTHS; "The Fairytale Ballad of Katy the Queen," *Vanguard*, no.

1 (1966). See also Members of the Gay and Lesbian Historical Society of Northern California, "MTF Transgender Activism," 349–72.

50. See *Vanguard*, n.d., box 21, folder 3, Martin/Lyon Papers, GLBTHS.

51. Clendinen and Nagourney, *Out for Good*, 171; *Question of Equality*.

52. Armstrong, *Forging Gay Identities*, 85–87. On the use of Marxist ideology in 1960s-era social movements, see Pulido, *Black, Brown, Yellow and Left*.

53. "Anti-Thanksgiving March Stuns Exploiters—Ends in Good Vibes at SIR," *San Francisco Free Press* 1.6 (December 7–21, 1969): 2.

54. "God Save the Queen," *Gay Sunshine* 1.3 (November 1970): 2.

55. Arthur Evans, "Should TVs Embarrass Gay Cause?" *Advocate*, no. 112 (May 23, 1973): 37.

56. Meyerowitz, *How Sex Changed*, chapters 3 and 6.

57. "Transformation," *Vector* 4.6 (May–June 1968): 17. See also "Tenderloin Transsexual," *Vanguard* 1.9 (n.d.): n.p.

58. *Screaming Queens*. See also Meyerowitz, "Sex Change and the Popular Press," 159–88.

59. "Mailbag: Transsexuals & TVs: Pro & Con," *Advocate*, no. 114 (June 20, 1973): 36.

60. "Transsexual Ban Splits DOB Unit," *Advocate*, no. 102 (January 3, 1973): 14; "Transsexual Issue Plagues Lesbians," *Advocate*, no. 111 (May 9, 1973): 4; "Lesbian Conference a Bomb," *S.F. Women's Newsletter*, May 1973, 8; "News," *Drag* 3.10 (n.d.): 6–7. See also Meyerowitz, *How Sex Changed*, 258–61.

61. "Politics of Drag," *Lavender Woman* 2.5 (August 1973): 13.

62. Randy Shilts, "Fantasy Kingdoms of Rhinestone and Royalty," *Eugene Register-Guard Sunday Magazine*, February 9, 1975, 5.

63. "Response from the Red Dyke Theater," *Lesbian Connection* 1.7 (September 1975): 11.

64. Robin Morgan, "Lesbianism and Feminism: Synonyms or Contradictions?" *Second Wave* 2.4 (1973): 18. For other examples of lesbian feminist criticisms of drag and transvestites, see "What the Well-Dressed Dyke Will Wear," *Cowrie* 1.5 (February 1974): 21–22; "My Mother the Drag Queen," *San Francisco Women's Newsletter*, August 1973, 7; "Drag: Misogyny in Disguise," *Sojourner: The Women's Forum* 2.2 (October 1976): 5.

65. "God Save the Queen," *Gay Sunshine* 1.3 (November 1970): 2.

66. Bob Kohler, "Right On!" *Come Out!* 1.3 (April–May 1970): 5.

67. "Androgyny and Male Supremacy," *The Effeminist*, no. 1 (May 1971): 1.

68. Kenneth Pitchford, "Faggot Militants: From Sexual Liberation to Revolutionary Effeminism," *Double-F: A Magazine of Effeminism*, no. 1 (1972): 8; Steven Dansky, "The Gay Enemy," *Double-F: A Magazine of Effeminism*, no.

2 (Winter/Spring 1973): 37. See also Kenneth Pitchford, "Where We Came from and Who We Are," *Flaming Faggots*, Summer 1972, 23; "Principles of Revolutionary Effeminism," *Double-F: A Magazine of Effeminism*, no. 2 (Winter/Spring 1973): 3–4; John Knoebel, "Funeral Procession," *Double-F: A Magazine of Effeminism*, no. 2 (Winter/Spring 1973): 7–8; all available in box 1, folders 1–3, Steve Dansky Papers, M.E. Grenander Department of Special Collections and Archives, State University of New York at Albany (SUNY).

69. See letter from Barbara Stephens, box 21, folder 6, Martin/Lyon Papers, GLBTHS; "T.V. Guide," *Gay Sunshine* 1.6 (March 1971): 6.

70. "Del Martin—Columnist Resigns, Blames Male Chauvinism," *Vector* 6.10 (October 1970): 35–37.

71. "Don't March! It's Part of a Sexist Plot," *Double-F: A Magazine of Effeminism*, no. 2 (Winter/Spring 1973): 11.

72. "Gay Pride Week," *Focus: A Journal for Gay Women*, July 1973, 5; "Drags and TVs Join the March," *Drag* 3.11 (1973): 4–5. See also Marotta, *Politics of Homosexuality*, 295–97; Marcus, *Making History*, 266–68; Duberman, *Stonewall*, 235–39; Clendinen and Nagourney, *Out for Good*, 169–73; Retzloff, "Eliding Trans Latino/a Queer Experience in U.S. LGBT History," 140–61; *Question of Equality*.

73. Karla Jay, "The Decline and Fall of an Idealist OR Why Ain't I Marching Anymore," *Lesbian Tide* 3.1 (August 1973): 10.

74. Eskridge, "Challenging the Apartheid of the Closet," 927–30.

75. Marotta, *Politics of Homosexuality*, chapter 8.

76. "Intro 475 May Dog Lindsay Campaign," *Advocate*, no. 78 (February 2, 1972): 1; "Commitments Fail Test: Intro 475 Defeated Again," *Advocate*, no. 92 (August 16, 1972): 1.

77. Ted Rauch, "Transvestism and Gay Liberation," *Gay Activist* 1.7 (November 1971): 5.

78. "Unruly Hearing Fails to Move Intro 475," *Advocate*, no. 74 (December 8, 1971): 3.

79. Marotta, *Politics of Homosexuality*, 222.

80. "Intro 475 Defeated," *Advocate*, no. 79 (February 16, 1972): 1.

81. "What is GAA?" reel 17, box 22, folder 2, printed ephemera, 1972, GAA records; Minutes of Gay Activists Alliance Meeting, September 24, 1970, reel 13, box 19, folder 1, Minutes—General Meetings, 1970, GAA records; Gay Activists Alliance Meeting Minutes, December 10, 1970, reel 13, box 19, folder 1, Minutes—General Meetings, 1970, GAA records.

82. Ted Rauch, "Transvestism and Gay Liberation," *Gay Activist* 1.7 (November 1971): 5.

83. "A Time and a Place," *New York Mattachine Times*, December 1971, 1.

84. Ted Rauch, "How to Save Intro 475," reel 11, box 18, folder 11, *Gay Activist* (news sheet), GAA records.

85. "Won't Be Sacrificial Lambs, Drags Vow," *Advocate*, no. 75 (December 22, 1971): 12; see also "Transvestite Rebuffs 'Straight' Gays," *Gay Activist* 1.6 (December–January 1972): 11.

86. "Intro 475—Round 3," *Gay Activist* 1.9 (February 1972): 8.

87. "Intro 475 Defeated in Third Vote," *Advocate*, no. 112 (May 23, 1973): 1; "City Council Committee Rejects Homosexual Bill," *New York Times*, April 28, 1973; "A Rights Bill for Homosexuals Rejected Again in City Council," *New York Times*, December 21, 1973.

88. "Dressing 'Rider' Under Wraps," *Advocate*, no. 132 (February 27, 1974): 6; "Homosexual Bill Gains in Council," *New York Times*, April 19, 1974; "TVs Excluded from Gay Civil Rights Bill," *Drag* 4.14 (1974): 8; "City Council's Bill on Homosexual Rights," *New York Times*, May 5, 1974.

89. See "Midwest TS's and TV's Fight for Civil Rights," *Drag* 6.23 (1975): 25; "State Laws, 1975," jour-box 1, folder 27, Randy Shilts Papers, SFPL; "'No Compromise' Gay Coalition May Sink Rights Bill," *Advocate*, no. 163 (May 7, 1975): 4; Clendinen and Nagourney, *Out for Good*, 236–38.

90. "State Laws, 1975," jour-box 1, folder 27, Randy Shilts Papers, SFPL.

91. "State Laws, 1975," jour-box 1, folder 27, Randy Shilts Papers, SFPL; "Crippled Rights Measure Passes Mass. House," *Advocate*, no. 165 (June 4, 1975): 4; "Massachusetts Senate Defeats Job Rights Bill," *Advocate*, no. 166 (June 18, 1975): 4.

92. "State Laws, 1975," jour-box 1, folder 27, Randy Shilts Papers, SFPL.

93. Unmarked news clipping dated May 25, 1978, box 7, folder: "Gay Rights 2," Harvey Milk Papers, SFPL. Bryant's campaign is also recounted in Clendinen and Nagourney, *Out for Good*, chapters 22–23.

94. "Gays' White House Visit Angers Anita," *Los Angeles Times*, March 28, 1977; "Bryant Rants . . . No Sunshine," *Lesbian Tide* 6.6 (May/June 1977): 16.

95. "Miami's Gay Rights Ordinance Repealed," *San Francisco Sunday Examiner and Chronicle*, June 12, 1977; "The Battle over Gay Rights," *Newsweek,* June 6, 1977, 16.

96. "Anita's Side Wins Easily—Miami Gays Defeated," *San Francisco Chronicle*, June 8, 1977.

97. Murray S. Edelman, "A Survey of Anti-Gay Attitudes of Dade County Voters," box 7, folder: "Gay Rights 1," Harvey Milk Papers, SFPL.

98. Clendinen and Nagourney, *Out for Good*, 191–92.

99. "'Soap' Protest," *It's Time* 3.9 (August–September 1977): 3; "Media Notes," *It's Time* 4.1 (October 1977): 2.

100. "Not All Quiet on the Gay Lib Front," *Drag* 5.17 (1974): 5; "Gay Is Not Proud ... of Queens on Parade," *Drag* 5.18 (1974): 32; "All Not Quiet on the Gay Lib Front," *Vector* 11.2 (February 1975): 30; "Gay Pride March '77," *Drag* (1977): 22.

101. "Media Accepts Gay Demands," *Lesbian Tide* 3.6 (January 1974): 4.

102. "Gay People: Your Friends, Neighbors, and Co-Workers," jour-box 8, folder 23, Randy Shilts Papers, SFPL.

103. "Questions and Answers about Homosexuality," box 7, folder: "Gay Rights 2," Harvey Milk Papers, SFPL.

104. David B. Goodstein, "Snub by Solons Points Up Law Reform Problems," *Advocate*, no. 117 (August 1, 1973): 2. See also "The Man in the Gay Flannel Suit," *Los Angeles Free Press*, July 30–August 5, 1976; Clendinen and Nagourney, *Out for Good*, 249.

105. "Homosexuals Ask for Job Equality," *San Jose Mercury*, September 11, 1974; "The Battle over Gay Rights," *Newsweek*, June 6, 1977, 16–26.

106. "The Battle over Gay Rights," *Newsweek*, June 6, 1977.

107. "In and Out of Drag," *San Francisco Examiner and Chronicle Sunday Living Magazine*, May 28, 1978, 31.

108. Harvey Milk, "It's Not a Festive Day," *San Francisco Sentinel*, June 17, 1977.

109. "250,000 Gays, Supporters in High-Spirited S.F. March" [unmarked news clipping], jour-box 5, folder 34: "Gay Parade, 1978," Randy Shilts Papers, SFPL; Clendinen and Nagourney, *Out for Good*, 320.

110. Armstrong, *Forging Gay Identities*, 107–10.

111. "Is Gay Liberation Dead? Skirting the Issue," *Vector* 12.6 (June/July 1976): 31, 35–37.

112. Armstrong, *Forging Gay Identities*, 91; Marcus, *Making History*, 257–59; McGarry and Wasserman, *Becoming Visible*, 199–219.

113. Eisenbach, *Gay Power*, 258.

114. Levine, *Gay Macho*, 7.

115. "Where Have All the Sissies Gone?," *Christopher Street* 2.9 (March 1978): 4; "The Ends of Sensitivity," *Advocate*, no. 245 (July 12, 1978): 18; "Making Too Much Mucho About Macho," *Advocate*, no. 266 (May 3, 1979): 20–21.

116. Levine, *Gay Macho*, 5.

117. "The Village People," jour-box 8, folder 15: "Village People, 1978," Randy Shilts Papers, SFPL.

118. See Cole, *Don We Now Our Gay Apparel*, 95.

5. "SEEING LONG HAIR ON MEN"

1. "San Francisco Lounge Bans All Long-Hairs—Like Stockbrokers," *Wall Street Journal*, October 15, 1971.

2. "Clift Hotel Opens Doors to Longhairs," *Los Angeles Times*, December 13, 1974.

3. Frank, *Conquest of Cool*.

4. See Frank, *Conquest of Cool*, chapter 9.

5. See Self, *American Babylon*, chapter 6; Sugrue, *Origins of the Urban Crisis*.

6. See Gitlin, *Sixties*; Farber, *Chicago '68*; Jacobs, *Ways the Wind Blew*; Berger, *Outlaws of America*.

7. "Theater: 'Hair'—It's Fresh and Frank," *New York Times*, April 30, 1968; Levy, *America in the Sixties*, 195.

8. James, "'The Movies Are a Revolution,'" 299.

9. Discussions of feminism were an exception to this formula; for example, Gloria discovers that Mike is not supportive of her feminist pursuits in season one, episode eleven.

10. Cowie, *Stayin' Alive*, 192–93.

11. Cowie, *Stayin' Alive*, 9.

12. "Ellen Peck: Haircut Hassle," *Chicago Tribune*, July 29, 1971.

13. Dear Abby, *Los Angeles Times*, August 23, 1970.

14. "Long Tresses Cost Fireman His Post," *Chicago Tribune*, March 1, 1972; "Marine Longhairs Get Aid of Pucinski," *Chicago Tribune*, April 27, 1972; "Guardsmen Sent Home to Cut Hair," *Washington Post*, April 15, 1973; "Battle over Hairstyles Raging at Fort Meade," *Washington Post*, July 6, 1973.

15. "Rumpled Generation Shapes Up," *Hartford Courant*, July 11, 1970.

16. "Men's Fashion Industry Lends an Ear to Consumer," *Los Angeles Times*, June 7, 1970.

17. "Assault on Unisex," *Chicago Tribune*, May 26, 1971.

18. "Corporate Look: Is It about to Change?" *New York Times*, October 3, 1971.

19. "Keep This under Your Hat," *Newsweek*, July 26, 1971, 30–31.

20. "Hippie Description," *Los Angeles Times*, August 25, 1971.

21. "'I Don't Have Heroes Anymore,'" *Washington Post*, August 27, 1972.

22. "Long Hair, Mod Dress, But He's a GOP Pro," *Los Angeles Times*, October 11, 1971.

23. "Rumpled Generation Shapes Up," *Hartford Courant*, July 11, 1970.

24. "Are Nation's Barbers about to Be Rescued?" *Hartford Courant*, February 23, 1972.

25. "Long-Tressed Males Facing End of Hair-Raising Adventure," *Hartford Courant*, March 16, 1972. See also "Ears See Comeback as Men's Manes Fall," *Chicago Tribune*, April 1, 1972; "Collar Clip: Longer Hair No Longer That Long," *Los Angeles Times*, April 5, 1972.

26. "Collar Clip: Longer Hair No Longer That Long," *Los Angeles Times*, April 5, 1972.

27. "Mini'Pinions," *Chicago Tribune*, July 23, 1970; see also "A Hairy Contest," *Chicago Tribune*, August 23, 1970.

28. "Mini'Pinions," *Chicago Tribune*, July 23, 1970.

29. "A Hairy Contest," *Chicago Tribune*, August 23, 1970.

30. See "It's a Man's Prerogative," *GQ* 37.2 (March 1967): 56; "Gentlemen," *GQ* 37.4 (May 1967): 43; "Introducing Six New Sensations for Your Body," *GQ* 38.7 (November 1968): 20; "Chanel for Men," *GQ* 39.2 (March 1969):11; Chanel advertisement, *GQ* 39.5 (September 1969): 1; Fabergé advertisement, *GQ* 39.5 (September 1969): 24.

31. ". . . Or You Belong to One of the Protest Groups," *New York Times*, September 25, 1970. See also "Say Goodbye to Short Skirts," *Hartford Courant*, February 1, 1970; "Dissenters Say 'POOFF' to Style World," *Los Angeles Times*, March 2, 1970; "No Shortage of Long Skirt Foes," *Los Angeles Times*, March 9, 1970; "The Battle of the Hemline," *Newsweek*, March 16, 1970, 70; "Midis Inch Toward Approval," *Los Angeles Times*, March 16, 1970; "Dead Knees Displease," *Los Angeles Times*, March 30, 1970; "Midis Bring Romance Back to Fashion's No-Man's-Land," *Los Angeles Times*, April 5, 1970; "Designers' Sales Go Up as Hem Lines Fall," *New York Times*, June 1, 1970; "Buyers," *Washington Post*, September 27, 1970; "'Slaughter on 7th Avenue,'" *Washington Post*, November 18, 1970; "The Midi Laid an Egg in 1970, But It Did Hatch Other Fashions," *New York Times*, January 1, 1971; "Leggy Look OK for Job Seekers in L.A.," *Los Angeles Times*, January 14, 1970; "Command Decisions in Favor of Pants," *Business Week*, October 31, 1970, 20.

32. "Dissenters Say 'POOFF' to Style World," *Los Angeles Times*, March 2, 1970; "The Battle of the Hemline," *Newsweek*, March 16, 1970, 70; Ann Landers, *Hartford Courant*, September 28, 1970.

33. "Designers' Sales Go Up as Hem Lines Fall," *New York Times*, June 1, 1970.

34. E. Myers, "Burning Bras," 289.

35. "Pantsuit Voted Tops for Fall," *Los Angeles Times*, September 13, 1970.

36. "Pantsuit Voted Tops for Fall," *Los Angeles Times*, September 13, 1970.

37. "Pantsuits Rescue Garment Makers," *Business Week*, January 2, 1971, 54.

38. "Long Hair Gets OK after Indian Protest," *Los Angeles Times*, November 23, 1972; *Embers 1970*, Yearbook of Amity Regional High School, Woodbridge, Connecticut.

39. "Come in Pantsuit, Change to a Skirt," *Hartford Courant*, August 8, 1970; "Pants: They're Going to Any Lengths," *New York Times*, November 26, 1975; Edith Head, "Yesterday's Vamps Are Today's Ladies," *Hartford Courant*, November 27, 1970.

40. "California Couture," *Los Angeles Times*, March 21, 1971.

41. "Pants: They're Going to Any Lengths," *New York Times*, November 26, 1975.

42. Art Seidenbaum, "Where Are the Girls?" *Los Angeles Times*, April 25, 1972. See also "Women's Wear Puzzles Investor," *Christian Science Monitor*, October 31, 1970.

43. "Women's Lib Gets Members," *Hartford Courant*, September 3, 1970; "American Image," *Los Angeles Times*, November 25, 1973; "A Few Women Sizzle but Boycott Is Fizzle," *Chicago Tribune*, October 30, 1975; "Something New in the Women's Movement," *New York Times*, December 12, 1973.

44. "Midis Inch toward Approval," *Los Angeles Times*, March 16, 1970.

45. "No Shortage of Long Skirt Foes," *Los Angeles Times*, March 9, 1970.

46. "No Shortage of Long Skirt Foes," *Los Angeles Times*, March 9, 1970.

47. "Pantique No. 2," *Los Angeles Times*, May 3, 1970.

48. "Hot Pants Worn by Engineer," *Hartford Courant*, September 1, 1971.

49. "Fashions," *Los Angeles Times*, January 28, 1971.

50. "The Uniform Look of S.F.'s Female Executives," *San Francisco Chronicle*, January 20, 1978.

51. "Accent on Fashion," *Philadelphia Tribune*, January 26, 1971.

52. "Fashions," *Los Angeles Times*, January 28, 1971.

53. "Midi-length Hemlines Showing Up for Spring," *Chicago Daily Defender*, November 11, 1970; "Fashions," *Los Angeles Times*, January 28, 1971; Edith Head, "'Tis the Season to Be Pretty," *Hartford Courant*, March 5, 1971; "Hooks' Line . . . on Fashion," *Chicago Daily Defender*, March 3, 1971; Edith Head, "Fashion Forecast Emphasizes Softness," *Hartford Courant*, April 23, 1971.

54. "Slip on a Style for All Seasons—the Pantsuit," *Chicago Tribune*, July 14, 1974.

55. "Woman Likes Her Pantsuit," *Hartford Courant*, February 5, 1973.

56. "The Afro and Its Meaning to the Black Beautician," *New York Amsterdam News*, July 5, 1969.

57. "More Men Taking to the 'Natural' Hair Style," *Norfolk New Journal and Guide*, December 16, 1967; "Looking on in Norfolk," *Norfolk New Journal and Guide*, April 20, 1968; "Negro Models Capitalize on Their African Heritage," *Los Angeles Times*, August 20, 1968; "Beyond the Afro: Baldness and Braids," *Washington Post*, August 8, 1971.

58. S. Walker, "Black Is Profitable," 254.

59. S. Walker, "Black Is Profitable," 255.

60. "Cosmetics for Blacks Reflect Growing Pride," *Los Angeles Times*, December 27, 1970.

61. "Dynamite Naturals," *Essence* 1.1 (May 1970): 38–39.

62. S. Walker, "Black Is Profitable," 255.

63. "Ironic Backlash? Afro Hairstyle: A U.S. Original, Africans Say," *Los Angeles Times*, September 22, 1970.

64. "Perki's Panacea," *Los Angeles Sentinel*, December 7, 1972.

65. "Black Cultural Nationalism," *Black Panther* 2.18 (December 21, 1968): 15. See also "Capitalism," *Black Panther* 2.24 (March 3, 1969): 13; Linda Hamilton, "On Cultural Nationalism," *Black Panther*, February 2, 1969, reprinted in Foner, *The Black Panthers Speak*.

66. C. V. Hamilton, "How Black Is Black?," 25.

67. "All Hair Is Good Hair," *New Pittsburgh Courier*, February 3, 1973.

68. "Beyond the Afro: Baldness and Braids," *Washington Post*, August 8, 1971; "Braids 'in' This Season," *Los Angeles Sentinel*, March 8, 1973; "Bushes and Braids," *Chicago Defender*, August 21, 1973; "All Hair Is Good Hair," *New Pittsburgh Courier*, February 3, 1973.

69. "Natural Afro Losing Its Frizz as Relaxed Hair Comes Back," *Los Angeles Times*, October 27, 1972.

70. "All Hair Is Good Hair," *New Pittsburgh Courier*, February 3, 1973.

71. "Natural Afro Losing Its Frizz," *Los Angeles Times*, October 27, 1972; "Wear It Your Way," *Chicago Defender*, April 5, 1975.

72. "Wear It Your Way," *Chicago Defender*, April 5, 1975.

73. See *Essence* 1.1 (May 1970) and *Essence* 1.2 (June 1970).

74. "Black Women Prefer Own Look," *Los Angeles Sentinel*, October 9, 1975.

75. "Personal Touches," *Baltimore Afro-American*, October 11, 1975.

76. "Negro Models Capitalize on Their African Heritage," *Los Angeles Times*, August 20, 1968.

77. "Black Models Reject Afro Garb, Hair," *Chicago Daily Defender*, October 12, 1968.

78. Advertisement, *Essence* 1.2 (June 1970): 2.

79. See Self, *American Babylon*.

80. Byrd and Tharps, *Hair Story*, 61.

81. "Rudi Needles Romance," *Washington Post*, January 8, 1970; Smith, *Fashionable Clothing from the Sears Catalogs*.

82. "A Boutique for Men, But It Has a Wider Appeal," *New York Times*, October 2, 1970.

83. "A Men's Boutique, But the Women Will Love It," *New York Times*, October 11, 1971.

84. "Fashion for the '70s," *Life*, January 9, 1970, 115–17; "Rudi Needles Romance," *Washington Post*, January 8, 1970; [Photo standalone—no title] *Hartford Courant*, January 11, 1970, 29A.

85. "Take Your Arm, Sir?" *Hartford Courant*, October 24, 1971; "Esterel Shows

Long Dresses for Men," *Irish Times*, January 27, 1970; "Men and the Cosmetics Game," *New York Times*, March 17, 1970; Bill Cunningham, "The Young Men Are Seen," *Chicago Tribune*, December 20, 1971; "Eye Shadow and Lipstick—For Men," *New York Times*, May 13, 1974.

86. Bill Cunningham, "The Young Men Are Seen," *Chicago Tribune*, December 20, 1971.

87. "Pasadena Rock Bill Has Alice Cooper," *Los Angeles Times*, January 20, 1970.

88. "Outrageous Behavior, Chicken Feathers and Rock," *Washington Post*, February 8, 1970. See also "Concert in Drag by Alice Cooper, a Boy and Band," *New York Times*, May 8, 1971.

89. "Iggy and Alice—The Outer Fringes," *Chicago Tribune*, April 19, 1971.

90. "Lucky Glam Rock," *Guardian*, September 2, 1972.

91. "Theatrics Sweeping Pop Music Scene," *New York Times*, September 11, 1972.

92. "Iggy and Alice—The Outer Fringes," *Chicago Tribune*, April 19, 1971; "Alice Cooper? David Bowie? Ugh! And Ugh Again!" *New York Times*, September 24, 1972.

93. "His Name Is Alice Cooper," *Chicago Tribune*, December 12, 1971.

94. "Former New York Doll Abandons Zap-Happy Genderfuck for Less Punk and More Funk," *Advocate*, no. 253 (November 1, 1978): 33.

95. "Patti Smith—A Return of Passion," *Los Angeles Times*, November 25, 1975; "Lock Up Your Sons, Moms, It's the Runaways," *Washington Post*, March 19, 1977.

96. "Gonna Be So Big, Gonna Be a Star, Watch Me Now!" *New York Times*, December 21, 1975.

97. "Female Rockers—A New Breed," *Los Angeles Times*, June 18, 1978.

98. "Runaways: Young, Female, Fun," *Los Angeles Times*, May 22, 1976.

99. "Patti Smith, Traveling Light, With Magic at the Core," *Washington Post*, January 15, 1976.

100. "Esterel Shows Long Dresses for Men," *Irish Times*, January 27, 1970.

101. "Esterel Shows Long Dresses for Men," *Irish Times*, January 27, 1970.

102. *Chicago Tribune*, December 20, 1971, B9.

103. "Polo Shirts with a New Dimension," *Chicago Tribune*, November 16, 1971.

104. "The Myriad Moods of Fashion for Fall," *Chicago Tribune*, May 24, 1972; "High Fashion Look-Alike Look," *Washington Post*, October 1, 1972.

105. Bill Cunningham, "The Young Men Are Seen," *Chicago Tribune*, March 19, 1973.

106. Herbert Brucker, "Equal Rights," *Hartford Courant*, August 24, 1974.

107. "Designers Throwing Unisex a Curve," *Los Angeles Times*, October 22, 1972.

108. "About New York: Clothes Are in Fashion Again," *New York Times*, October 23, 1974.

109. "A Whole New Thing on Campus Scene," *Los Angeles Sentinel*, September 26, 1974; "Sensible Clothes That Reflect Now," *Los Angeles Times*, November 19, 1974.

6. "NOT AN EFFORT TO ACHIEVE A UNISEX SOCIETY"

1. *City of Columbus v. Rogers*, 41 Ohio St. 2d 161 (1975); "City Cross-Dressing Ban Is Repealed, But Ohio Court Agrees to Hear Case," *Advocate*, no. 145 (August 28, 1974): 14; "Cross-Dressing Laws Fall," *Advocate*, no. 162 (April 23, 1975): 5. Columbus's cross-dressing ordinance was adopted in 1848; see Eskridge, *Gaylaw*, 27.

2. *Lanigan v. Bartlett and Company Grain*, 466 F. Supp. 1388 (1979).

3. See Whisner, "Gender-Specific Clothing Regulation"; Post, "Prejudicial Appearances"; Williamson, "Moving Past Hippies and Harassment"; Fisk, "Privacy, Power, and Humiliation at Work"; Levi, "Interplay Between Disability and Sexuality"; Levi, "Some Modest Proposals for Challenging Established Dress Code Jurisprudence"; Levi, "Misapplying Equality Theories."

4. "'Mod' Man and His Job," *Christian Science Monitor*, December 26, 1969.

5. "Shave and a Haircut for Hippie Postman," *San Francisco Shopping News*, February 22, 1968; "Post Office Bans Hippie Garb," *Washington Post*, February 1, 1968; "Hippie Hair Fashions Facing Ban in Cafes," *San Francisco Examiner*, August 4, 1967; "Long-Haired Waiters Ordered to Net It," *Washington Post*, August 5, 1967; "Brooklyn Precinct Tells Men to Shun the Hippie Look," *New York Times*, July 15, 1968.

6. "Paper Towel Packer Fired for Long Hair," *Chicago Tribune*, September 26, 1969; "Job Hunter to Job Holder: It Can Be a Tale of 2 Wardrobes," *New York Times*, January 6, 1970; "Leggy Look OK for Job Seekers in L.A.," *Los Angeles Times*, January 14, 1970; "Long Hair Costly on Job in California," *New York Times*, February 7, 1971; "The Newsmakers," *Los Angeles Times*, September 9, 1971; *Hartford Courant*, January 24, 1972, 20; "Salesman Fired for Long Hair May Sue on Sex Bias Basis," *Los Angeles Times*, February 15, 1972; "Long-Hair Ex-Employes [*sic*] Suing Stop & Shop Chain," *Hartford Courant*, August 9, 1972; "Judge Backs Safeway on Long Hair," *Washington Post*, December 5, 1972; "Grows Mustache, Loses Job," *Chicago Defender*, December 4, 1975.

7. For example, see "United Grounds Afro Styled Stewardess," *New Pittsburgh Courier*, October 11, 1969; "Long-Haired Teacher May Get Short Shrift," *Los Angeles Times*, May 24, 1970.

8. "Portia in a Pantsuit? Not in MY Courtroom," *Los Angeles Times*, February 21, 1971; "Sexist Judge Rules Out Pantsuit," *Everywoman* 1.4 (March 5, 1971): 14.

9. "Corporate Look: Is It About to Change?" *New York Times*, October 3, 1971.

10. "Office Dress: Not Quite Everything Goes," *New York Times*, December 28, 1975.

11. "Policeman Who Defied Haircut Order Is Fired," *Hartford Courant*, May 27, 1971.

12. "Lawman Reinstated in Haircut Dispute," *Hartford Courant*, June 11, 1971.

13. "Berkeley Policemen Can Let Hair Grow," *Hartford Courant*, July 9, 1971; "Police Haircuts," *Los Angeles Times*, September 21, 1971; "Papa Shouldn't Try to Dress a la Teen," *Norfolk New Journal and Guide*, February 3, 1973; "Town Council Votes to Abolish Hair Code for Police," *Hartford Courant*, April 16, 1974.

14. "Office Dress: Not Quite Everything Goes," *New York Times*, December 28, 1975. See also E. Myers, "Burning Bras," 321.

15. "Leggy Look OK for Job Seekers in L.A.," *Los Angeles Times*, January 14, 1970; "Command Decisions in Favor of Pants," *Business Week*, October 31, 1970, 20.

16. "1969: Year of Maxi-Strides for Women," *Los Angeles Times*, January 4, 1970.

17. "Nurses Herald Pantsuit Arrival in Day," *Los Angeles Times*, June 18, 1970.

18. "Nurses Herald Pantsuit Arrival in Day," *Los Angeles Times*, June 18, 1970; "Labor Letter," *Wall Street Journal*, October 6, 1970; "Fashion Shops Hold Breath as Skirt Lengths Slip Lower," *Christian Science Monitor*, October 21, 1970; "On-the-Job Fashion Lib a Fringe Benefit," *Los Angeles Times*, October 22, 1970; "Women's Wear Puzzles Investor," *Christian Science Monitor*, October 31, 1970; "Command Decisions in Favor of Pants," *Business Week*, October 31, 1970, 20; "Clotheslines: Jewelry Pulse Quickens on Heart," *Los Angeles Times*, November 8, 1970; "Pantsuit to Get OK as Attire for Office," *Los Angeles Times*, November 12, 1970.

19. "Pantsuits for Stewardesses," *Los Angeles Times*, February 12, 1973; "Stewardesses Stay on Top of Styles," *New York Amsterdam News*, July 10, 1971; Boris, "Desirable Dress."

20. "Command Decisions in Favor of Pants," *Business Week*, October 31, 1970, 20. See also E. Myers, "Burning Bras," 319.

21. "Long-Haired Teacher May Get Short Shrift," *Los Angeles Times*, May 24, 1970; "Nurses Herald Pantsuit Arrival in Day," *Los Angeles Times*, June 18, 1970.

22. "At Revlon, a Controversy over Who Wears the Pants," *New York Times*, June 7, 1972. See also E. Myers, "Burning Bras," 320.

23. "Weight Hostess''Afro' Boycott," *New Pittsburgh Courier*, October 4, 1969; "Airline Pays Up," *Chicago Daily Defender*, September 24, 1970.

24. "A Few Women Sizzle but Boycott Is Fizzle," *Chicago Tribune*, October 30, 1975.

25. "Jobs for College Graduates Dwindle for the Second Year," *Atlanta Daily World*, May 30, 1971. See also "Job Hunter to Job Holder: It Can Be a Tale of 2 Wardrobes," *New York Times*, January 6, 1970; "Two Worlds—The Long and the Short of It," *Los Angeles Times*, August 12, 1970; "Have We Met? Or, Hair Today, Gone Tomorrow," *Hartford Courant*, May 24, 1971.

26. "Paper Towel Packer Fired for Long Hair," *Chicago Tribune*, September 26, 1969; "The Newsmakers," *Los Angeles Times*, September 9, 1971; *Hartford Courant*, January 24, 1972, 20; "Salesman Fired for Long Hair May Sue on Sex Bias Basis," *Los Angeles Times*, February 15, 1972; "Long-Hair Ex-Employes [*sic*] Suing Stop & Shop Chain," *Hartford Courant*, August 9, 1972; "Judge Backs Safeway on Long Hair," *Washington Post*, December 5, 1972; "Grows Mustache, Loses Job," *Chicago Defender*, December 4, 1975.

27. See Graham, "Flaunting the Freak Flag."

28. *Ramsey v. Hopkins*, 320 F. Supp. 477 (N.D. Ala. 1970).

29. *Tinker v. Des Moines School District*, 393 U.S. 503 (1969); *Cohen v. California*, 403 U.S. 15 (1971).

30. *Hunt v. Board of Fire Commissioners*, 68 Misc. 2d 261 (1971).

31. *Dwen v. Barry*, 483 F.2d 1126 (1973).

32. *Hander v. San Jacinto Junior College*, 519 F.2d 273 (1975); the earlier case was *Lansdale v. Tyler Junior College*, 470 F.2d 659 (1972) (en banc), a case over-turning a public college's hair-grooming codes for college students.

33. *Braxton v. Board of Public Instruction of Duval County, Florida*, 303 F. Supp. 958 (M.D. Fla. 1969).

34. *Schneider v. Ohio Youth Commission*, 31 Ohio App. 2d 225 (1972).

35. *Lattanzio v. Pennsylvania Unemployment Compensation Board of Review*, 10 Pa. Commw.160 (1973).

36. On Justice Pashman, see "Morris Pashman, 87, Champion of Free Speech on New Jersey's Highest Court," *New York Times*, October 10, 1999.

37. *Akridge v. Barres*, 65 N.J. 266 (1974). The quote from Justice Douglas was cited from *Ferrell v. Dallas Independent School District*, 393 U.S. 856 (1968) (Douglas, J. dissenting from denial of certiorari). It was *Time* magazine that called Justice Douglas an "uncompromising libertarian" upon his retirement from the court in 1975 and highlighted his defense of the First Amendment in his jurisprudence. See "The Law: The Court's Uncompromising Libertarian," *Time*, November 24, 1975.

38. Klarman,"Backlash."

39. *Kelley v. Johnson*, 425 U.S. 238 (1976).

40. See "An Ideological Divide," *New York Times*, May 11, 2010.

41. *Jacobs v. Kunes*, 541 F.2d 222 (1976).

42. See Cobble, *Other Women's Movement*, chapter 6; Rosen, *World Split Open*, 71; Harrison, *On Account of Sex*; Jo Freeman, "How 'Sex' Got into Title VII."

43. EEOC Decision no. 70–920, June 22, 1970; EEOC Decision no. 71–779, December 21, 1970; EEOC Decision no. 71–1529, April 2, 1971; EEOC Decision no. 71–2444, June 10, 1971; EEOC Decision no. 71–2343, June 3, 1971; EEOC Decision no. 71–2620, June 25, 1971; EEOC Decision no. 72–0979, February 3, 1972; EEOC Decision no. 72–1380, March 17, 1972; EEOC Decision no. 72–1931, June 7, 1972. See *CCH EEOC Decisions* in the bibliography.

44. EEOC Decision no. 71–2343, June 3, 1971. See also EEOC Decision no. 70–920, June 22, 1970; EEOC Decision no. 71–1529, April 2, 1971; EEOC Decision no. 72–1380, March 17, 1972. All in *CCH EEOC* Decisions.

45. EEOC Decision no. 71–2444, June 10, 1971. See also EEOC Decision no. 72–0979, February 3, 1972. All in *CCH EEOC Decisions*.

46. *Griggs v. Duke Power Co.*, 401 U.S. 424 (1971).

47. *Roberts v. General Mills, Inc.*, 337 F. Supp. 1055 (1971).

48. See Biography of Don John Young, Jr. History of the Sixth Circuit, accessed March 22, 2010, http://www.ca6.uscourts.gov/lib_hist/Courts /district%20court/oh/ndoh/judges/djy-bio.html. Information on U.S District Court and Court of Appeals judges can be found on the online database Biographical Directory of Federal Judges, available at the Federal Judicial Center, http://www.fjc.gov/public/home.nsf/hisj.

49. *Donohue v. Shoe Corporation of America*, 337 F. Supp. 1357 (1972). On Pregerson's liberal reputation, see "Judge Harry Pregerson: Choosing Between Law and His Conscience," *Los Angeles Times*, May 3, 1992.

50. *Doyle v. Buffalo Sidewalk Cafe*, 70 Misc. 2d 212 (1972).

51. See "Warren J. Ferguson, 87, Federal Judge, Is Dead," *New York Times*, July 12, 2008.

52. *Aros v. McDonnell Douglas Corporation*, 348 F. Supp. 661 (1972).

53. See "Judge Gerhard Gesell Dies at 82; Oversaw Big Cases," *New York Times*, February 21, 1993.

54. *Boyce v. Safeway Stores*, 351 F. Supp. 402 (1972).

55. Katz, "Personal Appearance Regulations," 11.

56. Katz, "Personal Appearance Regulations," 11.

57. Judge Danaher wrote the majority opinion; he had been appointed by Eisenhower and was a former Republican senator from Connecticut. See "John Danaher Is Dead at 91; A Former U.S. Senator and Judge," *New York Times*, September 26, 1990. Judge Wilkey, joining Danaher, had been nom-

inated to the bench by Nixon in 1970 and became known for his conservative opinions. See "Malcolm Wilkey, Noted Judge, Dies at 90," *New York Times*, September 18, 2009. Judge Wright, who dissented, had been nominated by John F. Kennedy and was a known liberal. See "Judge J. Skelly Wright, Segregation Foe, Dies at 77," *New York Times*, August 8, 1988.

58. *Fagan v. National Cash Register Co.*, 481 F.2d 1115 (1973). See also Whisner, "Gender-Specific Clothing Regulation," 80.

59. Judges MacKinnon and Robb were appointed by Nixon in 1969; Judge Tamm had been nominated to the U.S. Court of Appeals by Johnson. See Biographical Directory of Federal Judges, Federal Judicial Center, http://www.fjc.gov/public/home.nsf/hisj.

60. *Dodge v. Giant Food, Inc.*, 488 F.2d 1333 (1973).

61. *Bujel v. Borman Food Stores*, 384 F. Supp. 141 (1974). Emphasis added. The judge in this case, Charles W. Joiner, had been appointed by Nixon in 1972. See Biographical Directory of Federal Judges, Federal Judicial Center, http://www.fjc.gov/public/home.nsf/hisj.

62. *Baker v. California Land Title Co.*, 507 F.2d 895 (1974). Judges Trask and Neill had been nominated by Nixon in 1972; Judge Carter had been appointed by Johnson in 1967. See Biographical Directory of Federal Judges, Federal Judicial Center, http://www.fjc.gov/public/home.nsf/hisj.

63. *Dodge v. Giant Food, Inc.*, 488 F.2d 1333 (1973).

64. *Baker v. California Land Title Co.*, 507 F.2d 895 (1974).

65. *Willingham v. Macon Telegraph Publishing Co.*, 482 F.2d 535 (1973). See also Whisner, "Gender-Specific Clothing Regulation," 95–96.

66. Brief for Rollins, Inc. as Amicus Curiae in Support of Petition for Rehearing En Banc, filed August 7, 1973, Fifth Circuit case 72–2078, Records of the U.S. Court of Appeals, Record Group 276, National Archives–Southwest Region.

67. Brief Amicus Curiae of Mercantile National Bank at Dallas, filed July 25, 1973, Fifth Circuit case 72–2078, Records of the U.S. Court of Appeals, Record Group 276, National Archives–Southwest Region.

68. See Williamson, "Moving Past Hippies."

69. *Willingham v. Macon Telegraph Publishing Co.*, 507 F.2d 1084 (1975) (en banc).

70. On Judge Wisdom, see Friedman, *Champion of Civil Rights*; on Judge Tuttle, see "Obituary: Judge Elbert Parr Tuttle," *Cornell Chronicle*, July 11, 1996; on Judge Simpson, see "A Guide to the Judge John Milton Bryan Simpson Papers, 1933–1983," University of Florida Special and Area Studies Collections, accessed March 20, 2010, http://web.uflib.ufl.edu/spec/pkyonge/simpson.htm.

71. *Hander v. San Jacinto Junior College*, 519 F.2d 273 (1975); Biographical Directory of Federal Judges, Federal Judicial Center, http://www.fjc.gov/public /home.nsf/hisj.

72. *Wamsganz v. Missouri Pacific Railroad Co.*, 391 F. Supp. 306 (1975). Judge Wangelin had been nominated by Nixon in 1970; see Biographical Directory of Federal Judges, Federal Judicial Center, http://www.fjc.gov/public /home.nsf/hisj.

73. *Jahns v. Missouri Pacific Railroad Co.*, 391 F. Supp. 761 (1975). Judge Regan was appointed by John F. Kennedy in 1962 but was considered "unsympathetic to civil rights causes" as a judge; see Guide to the John Keating Regan Papers, Western Historical Manuscript Collection, University of Missouri–St. Louis, accessed March 20, 2010, http://www.umsl.edu/~whmc /guides/whm0173.htm.

74. *Knott v. Missouri Pacific Railroad Co.*, 527 F.2d 1249 (1975). The three-judge panel in this case included two Nixon appointees (Judges Stephenson and Weber) and one Eisenhower appointee, Marion Charles Matthes. See Biographical Directory of Federal Judges, Federal Judicial Center, http://www.fjc.gov/public/home.nsf/hisj.

75. *Longo v. Carlisle Decoppet and Co.*, 537 F.2d 685 (1976). The judges in this case, who ruled unanimously, were Judge Friendly (appointed by Eisenhower), Judge Feinberg (appointed by Johnson), and Judge Van Graafeiland (appointed by Ford). See Biographical Directory of Federal Judges, Federal Judicial Center, http://www.fjc.gov/public/home.nsf/hisj.

76. *Fountain v. Safeway Stores*, 555 F.2d 753 (1977).

77. *Lanigan v. Bartlett and Company Grain*, 466 F. Supp. 1388 (1979). See also Whisner, "Gender-Specific Clothing Regulations," 86.

78. Banks, "Black Side of the Mirror," 18.

79. *Thomas v. Firestone Tire and Rubber Co.*, 392 F. Supp. 373 (1975).

80. EEOC Decision no. 72–0979, February 3, 1972.

81. *Thomas v. Firestone Tire and Rubber Co.*, 392 F. Supp. 373 (1975).

82. *Carswell v. Peachford Hospital*, 1981 U.S. Dist. LEXIS 14562 (1981).

83. *Jespersen v. Harrah's Operating Co.*, 444 F.3d 1104 (2006).

84. Pell was appointed by Nixon in 1970. See Biographical Directory of Federal Judges, Federal Judicial Center, http://www.fjc.gov/public/home.nsf/hisj.

85. *Carroll v. Talman Federal Savings and Loan Association*, 604 F.2d 1028 (1979). See also Whisner, "Gender-Specific Clothing Regulations," 84.

EPILOGUE

1. "Boy, 4, Chooses Long Locks and Is Suspended From Class," *New York Times*, January 13, 2010.

BIBLIOGRAPHY

ARCHIVES AND MANUSCRIPT MATERIALS

Bancroft Library, University of California–Berkeley
  Social Protest Collection
American Civil Liberties Union Archives. Series 3: Subject Files. Wilmington
  DE: Scholarly Resources, 2002. Microfilm Collection.
FBI File on the Students for a Democratic Society and the Weatherman
  Underground Organizations. Wilmington DE: Scholarly Resources, 1990.
  Microfilm Collection.
Female Liberation: A Radical Feminist Organization Records, 1968–1974. Gale
  Cengage Primary Source. Grassroots Feminist Organizations, Part 1: Bos-
  ton Area Second Wave Organizations, 1968–1998. Woodbridge CT: Primary
  Source Media, 2008. Microfilm Collection.
Gay Activists Alliance: From the International Gay Information Center, the
  New York Public Library. Gay Rights Movement, Series 2. Woodbridge CT:
  Research Publications, 1998. Microfilm Collection.
Gay and Lesbian Politics and Social Activism: Selected Periodicals from the
  GLBT Historical Society of Northern California. Gay Rights Movement,
  Series 8. Woodbridge CT: Primary Source Microfilm, 2004. Microfilm
  Collection.

Herstory Feminist Periodicals. Wooster OH: Bell and Howell, 1972. Microfilm Collection.

GLBT Historical Society of Northern California (GLBTHS)
    Anson Reinhart Papers
    Arthur Corbin Papers
    Del Martin/Phyllis Lyon Papers
    Ed Hansen Papers
    Sally Gearhart Papers

Lesbian Herstory Archives Subject Files. Thompson Gale Primary Source Microfilms Collection. Gay Rights Movement, Series 7. Woodbridge CT: Primary Source Microfilm, 2004.

National Archives–Southwest Region
    Records of the U.S. Court of Appeals, Record Group 276, Fifth Circuit case 72-2078

San Francisco Bay Area Gay and Lesbian Serials. Berkeley: University of California, 1991. Microfilm Collection.

San Francisco Public Library (SFPL)
    Charles Thorpe Papers
    Harvey Milk Papers
    Hippie Collection
    Randy Shilts Papers
    Stephen Lowell Papers

Schlesinger Library, Radcliffe Institute of Advanced Study, Harvard University
    Boston NOW Papers
    NOW Records

Special Collections and Archives, State University of New York at Albany (SUNY)
    Steve Dansky Papers

Sterling Memorial Library Manuscripts and Archives, Yale University
    Gay and Lesbian Liberation Collection
    Students for a Democratic Society Papers, 1958–1970. Microfilm of the original records at the State Historical Society of Wisconsin. Glen Rock NJ: Microfilming Corporation of America, 1977.

Underground Press Collection. Wooster OH: Bell and Howell, 1985. Microfilm Collection.

PUBLISHED WORKS

Abbot, Sidney, and Barbara Love. "Is Women's Liberation a Lesbian Plot?" In *Woman in Sexist Society*, edited by Vivian Gornick and Barbara Moran. New York: Basic Books, 1971.

Agnew, Spiro. *The Collected Speeches of Spiro Agnew*. New York: Audubon Books, 1971.

Alinder, Gary. "Gay Liberation Meets the Shrinks." In *Out of the Closets: Voices of Gay Liberation*, edited by Karla Jay and Allen Young, 141–45. New York: New York University Press, 1992. First published 1970.

Anderson, Terry. *The Movement and the Sixties*. New York: Oxford University Press, 1995.

Appy, Christian. *Working-Class War: American Combat Soldiers and Vietnam*. Chapel Hill: University of North Carolina Press, 1993.

Armstrong, Elizabeth. *Forging Gay Identities: Organizing Sexuality in San Francisco, 1950–1994*. Chicago: University of Chicago Press, 2002.

Bailey, Beth. *Sex in the Heartland*. Cambridge: Harvard University Press, 1999.

Banks, Taunya Lovell. "The Black Side of the Mirror: The Black Body in the Workplace." In *Sister Circle: Black Women and Work*, edited by Sharon Harley and the Black Women and Work Collective, 13–28. New Brunswick: Rutgers University Press, 2002.

Banner, Lois. *American Beauty*. New York: Knopf, 1983.

Barnard, Malcolm. *Fashion as Communication*. London: Routledge, 1996.

Baumgardner, Jennifer, and Amy Richards. *Manifesta: Young Women, Feminism, and the Future*. New York: Farrar, Straus and Giroux, 2000.

Baxandall, Rosalyn, and Linda Gordon, eds. *Dear Sisters: Dispatches from the Women's Liberation Movement*. New York: Basic Books, 2000.

Beemyn, Brett. *Creating a Place for Ourselves: Lesbian, Gay and Bisexual Community Histories*. New York: Routledge, 1997.

Behling, Laura. *The Masculine Woman in America, 1890–1935*. Urbana: University of Illinois Press, 2001.

Beigel, Hugo G. "Book Review of *The New People: Desexualization in American Life*." *Journal of Sex Research* 5.1 (February 1969): 70–71.

Berger, Dan. *Outlaws of America: The Weather Underground and the Politics of Solidarity*. Oakland CA: AK Press, 2006.

Berlandt, Konstantin. "My Soul Vanished from Sight: A California Saga of Gay Liberation." In *Out of the Closets: Voices of Gay Liberation*, edited by Karla Jay and Allen Young, 38–55. New York: New York University Press, 1992.

Bérubé, Allan. *Coming Out Under Fire: The History of Gay Men and Women in World War Two*. New York: The Free Press, 1990.

The Black Revolution: An Ebony Special Issue. Chicago: Johnson, 1970.

Blood, Robert O., Jr. "Book Review of *The New People: Desexualization in American Life*." *Social Forces* 47.3 (March 1969): 359.

Bloom, Alexander, and Winifred Breines, eds. *"Takin' It to the Streets": A Sixties Reader*. 2nd ed. New York: Oxford University Press, 2003.

Blum, John Morton. *Years of Discord: American Politics and Society, 1961–1974*. New York: W.W. Norton, 1991.

Boris, Eileen. "Desirable Dress: Rosies, Sky Girls, and the Politics of Appearance." *International Labor and Working-Class History* 69 (2006): 123–42.

Boyd, Nan Alamilla. *Wide Open Town: A History of Queer San Francisco to 1965*. Berkeley: University of California Press, 2003.

Braunstein, Peter, and Michael William Doyle, eds. *Imagine Nation: The American Counterculture of the 1960s and '70s*. New York: Routledge, 2002.

Breines, Winifred. "The 'Other' Fifties: Beats and Bad Girls." In *Not June Cleaver: Women and Gender in Postwar America, 1945–1960*, edited by Joanne Meyerowitz, 382–408. Philadelphia: Temple University Press, 1994.

———. *The Trouble Between Us: An Uneasy History of White and Black Women in the Feminist Movement*. New York: Oxford University Press, 2006.

Brown, Scot. *Fighting for us: Maulana Karenga, the us Organization, and Black Cultural Nationalism*. New York: New York University Press, 2003.

Byrd, Ayana D., and Lori L. Tharps. *Hair Story: Untangling the Roots of Black Hair in America*. Rev. ed. New York: St. Martin's Press, 2014.

Carmichael, Stokely. *Stokely Speaks: Black Power Back to Pan-Africanism*. New York: Random House, 1971. First published 1965.

Carson, Clayborne. *In Struggle: sncc and the Black Awakening of the 1960s*. Cambridge: Harvard University Press, 1981.

Carter, Dan. *The Politics of Rage: George Wallace, the Origins of the New Conservatism, and the Transformation of American Politics*. New York: Simon and Schuster, 1995.

Carter, David. *Stonewall: The Riots That Sparked the Gay Revolution*. New York: St. Martin's Press, 2004.

Case, Sue-Ellen. "Towards a Butch-Femme Aesthetic." In *The Lesbian and Gay Studies Reader*, edited by Henry Abelove, Michele Aina Barale, and David Halperin, 294–306. New York: Routledge, 1993.

Cassell, Joan. *A Group Called Women: Sisterhood and Symbolism in the Feminist Movement*. New York: David McKay, 1977.

Cavan, Sherri. *Hippies of the Haight*. St. Louis: New Critics Press, 1972.

cch eeoc Decisions, 1973: A Report of Decisions Released by the eeoc from June 20, 1968, through January 19, 1973. New York: Commerce Clearing House, 1973.

Chappell, Marissa , Jenny Hutchinson, and Brian Ward. "'Dress modestly, neatly . . . as if you were going to church!': Respectability, Class, and Gender in the Montgomery Bus Boycott and the Early Civil Rights Movement." In *Gender and the Civil Rights Movement*, edited by Peter J. Ling and Sharon Monteith, 69–100. New York: Garland, 1999.

Chauncey, George Jr. "From Sexual Inversion to Homosexuality: The Changing Medical Conceptualization of Female 'Deviance.'" In *Passion and Power: Sexuality in History*, edited by Kathy Peiss and Christina Simmons, 87–117. Philadelphia: Temple University Press, 1989.

———. *Gay New York: Gender, Urban Culture, and the Making of the Gay Male World, 1890–1940*. New York: Basic Books, 1994.

Cleaver, Eldridge. "As Crinkly As Yours." *Negro History Bulletin* 30.6 (March 1962): 127–32.

Clendinen, Dudley, and Adam Nagourney. *Out for Good: The Struggle to Build a Gay Rights Movement in America*. New York: Simon and Schuster, 1999.

Cobble, Dorothy Sue. *The Other Women's Movement: Workplace Justice and Social Rights in Modern America*. Princeton NJ: Princeton University Press, 2004.

Cohen, Lizabeth. *A Consumer's Republic: The Politics of Mass Consumption in Postwar America*. New York: Knopf, 2003.

Cohen, Robert, and Reginald E. Zelnik, eds. *The Free Speech Movement: Reflections on Berkeley in the 1960s*. Berkeley: University of California Press, 2002.

Cole, Shaun. *Don We Now Our Gay Apparel: Gay Men's Dress in the Twentieth Century*. Oxford: Berg, 2000.

Coleman, Kate. "Dressing for the Revolution." In *The Free Speech Movement: Reflections on Berkeley in the 1960s*, edited by Robert Cohen and Reginald E. Zelnik, 185–88. Berkeley: University of California Press, 2002.

Collins, Gail. *When Everything Changed: The Amazing Journey of American Women from 1960 to the Present*. New York: Little, Brown, 2009.

Come Out! Selections from the Radical Gay Liberation Newspaper. New York: Times Change Press, 1970.

Cory, Donald Webster. *The Homosexual in America: A Subjective Approach*. New York: Greenberg Press, 1951.

Coryell, Julie. "What's in a Name?" In *Dear Sisters: Dispatches from the Women's Liberation Movement*, edited by Rosalyn Baxandall and Linda Gordon, 216. New York: Basic Books, 2000. First published 1971.

Cowie, Jefferson. *Stayin' Alive: The 1970s and the Last Days of the Working Class*. New York: The New Press, 2010.

Craig, Maxine Leeds. *Ain't I a Beauty Queen? Black Women, Beauty, and the Politics of Race*. New York: Oxford University Press, 2002.

Craik, Jennifer. *The Face of Fashion: Cultural Studies in Fashion*. London: Routledge, 1994.

Crane, Diana. *Fashion and Its Social Agendas: Class, Gender, and Identity in Clothing*. Chicago: University of Chicago Press, 2000.

Critchlow, Donald. *Phyllis Schlafly and Grassroots Conservatism: A Woman's Crusade*. Princeton NJ: Princeton University Press, 2005.

Cuordileone, K. A. *Manhood and American Political Culture in the Cold War.* New York: Routledge, 2005.

Cvetkovich, Ann. "Recasting Receptivity: Femme Sexualities." In *Lesbian Erotics*, edited by Karla Jay, 125–46. New York: New York University Press, 1995.

Davis, Fred. *Fashion, Culture, and Identity.* Chicago: University of Chicago Press, 1992.

Dean, Robert. *Imperial Brotherhood: Gender and the Making of Cold War Foreign Policy.* Amherst: University of Massachusetts Press, 2001.

Deevy, Sharon. "Such a Nice Girl." In *Lesbianism and the Women's Movement*, edited by Nancy Myron and Charlotte Bunch. Baltimore: Diana Press, 1975.

D'Emilio, John. *Sexual Politics, Sexual Communities: The Making of a Homosexual Minority in the United States, 1940–1970.* Chicago: University of Chicago Press, 1983.

Deloria, Philip. "Countercultural Indians and the New Age." In *Imagine Nation: The American Counterculture of the 1960s and '70s*, edited by Peter Braunstein and Michael William Doyle, 159–88. New York: Routledge, 2002.

Dochuk, Darren. *From Bible Belt to Sunbelt: Plain-Folk Religion, Grassroots Politics, and the Rise of Evangelical Conservatism.* New York: W. W. Norton, 2012.

Drexel, Allen. "Before Paris Burned: Race, Class, and Male Homosexuality on the Chicago South Side, 1935–1960." In *Creating a Place for Ourselves: Lesbian, Gay and Bisexual Community Histories*, edited by Brett Beemyn, 119–44. New York: Routledge, 1997.

Duberman, Martin. *Stonewall.* New York: Dutton, 1993.

Echols, Alice. *Daring to Be Bad: Radical Feminism in America, 1967–1975.* Minneapolis: University of Minnesota Press, 1989.

Ehrenreich, Barbara. *The Hearts of Men: American Dreams and the Flight from Commitment.* New York: Anchor, 1983.

Eisenbach, David. *Gay Power: An American Revolution.* New York: Carroll and Graf, 2006.

Enke, Anne. *Finding the Movement: Sexuality, Contested Space, and Feminist Activism.* Durham: Duke University Press, 2007.

Entwistle, Joanne. *The Fashioned Body: Fashion, Dress, and Modern Social Theory.* Cambridge UK: Polity Press, 2000.

Eskridge, William N., Jr. "Challenging the Apartheid of the Closet: Establishing Conditions for Lesbian and Gay Intimacy, Nomos, and Citizenship, 1961–1981." *Hofstra Law Review* 25.3 (Spring 1997): 819–960.

———. *Gaylaw: Challenging the Apartheid of the Closet.* Cambridge: Harvard University Press, 1999.

Eskridge, William N., Jr., and Nan B. Hunter. *Sexuality, Gender, and the Law.* 2nd ed. New York: Foundation Press, 2004.

Estes, Steve. *I Am a Man! Race, Manhood, and the Civil Rights Movement.* Chapel Hill: University of North Carolina Press, 2005.

Evans, Sara. *Personal Politics: The Roots of Women's Liberation in the Civil Rights Movement and the New Left.* New York: Vintage Books, 1979.

Farber, David. *The Age of Great Dreams: America in the 1960s.* New York: Hill and Wang, 1994.

———. *Chicago '68.* Chicago: University of Chicago Press, 1994.

———. "The Silent Majority and Talk about Revolution." In *The Sixties: From Memory to History,* edited by David Farber, 291–316. Chapel Hill: University of North Carolina Press, 1994.

———, ed. *The Sixties: From Memory to History.* Chapel Hill: University of North Carolina Press, 1994.

Feldstein, Ruth. "'I Don't Trust You Anymore': Nina Simone, Culture, and Black Activism in the 1960s." *Journal of American History* 91.4 (March 2005): 1349–79.

Fisk, Catherine L. "Privacy, Power, and Humiliation at Work: Re-Examining Appearance Regulation as an Invasion of Privacy." *Louisiana Law Review* 66 (Summer 2006): 1111–46.

Foner, Philip S., ed. *The Black Panthers Speak.* New York: Da Capo Press, 1995. First published 1970.

Formisano, Ronald. *Boston against Busing: Race, Class, and Ethnicity in the 1960s and 1970s.* Chapel Hill: University of North Carolina Press, 1991.

Frank, Thomas. *The Conquest of Cool: Business Culture, Counterculture, and the Rise of Hip Consumerism.* Chicago: University of Chicago Press, 1997.

———. *What's the Matter With Kansas?* New York: Metropolitan Books, 2004.

Freeman, Jo. "How 'Sex' Got Into Title VII: Persistent Opportunism as a Maker of Public Policy." *Law and Inequality: A Journal of Theory and Practice* 9.2 (March 1991): 163–84.

Freeman, Joshua B. "Hardhats: Construction Workers, Manliness, and the 1970 Pro-War Demonstrations." *Journal of Social History* 26.3 (Summer 1993): 725–44.

Friedan, Betty. *The Feminine Mystique.* New York: W. W. Norton, 1963.

———. *It Changed My Life: Writings on the Women's Movement.* New York: Random House, 1976.

Friedman, Joel William. *Champion of Civil Rights: Judge John Minor Wisdom.* Baton Rouge: Louisiana State University Press, 2009.

Gallo, Marcia. *Different Daughters: A History of the Daughters of Bilitis and the Rise of the Lesbian Rights Movement.* New York: Carroll and Graf, 2006.

Gay Pioneers. DVD. Directed by Glenn Holstein. Philadelphia: Equality Forum Films, 2004.

Gerhard, Jane. *Desiring Revolution: Second-Wave Feminism and the Rewriting of American Sexual Thought, 1920 to 1982*. New York: Columbia University Press, 2001.

Gilbert, James Burkhart. *A Cycle of Outrage: America's Reaction to the Juvenile Delinquent in the 1950s*. New York: Oxford University Press, 1986.

Gitlin, Todd. *The Sixties: Years of Hope, Days of Rage*. New York: Bantam Books, 1987.

———. *The Whole World Is Watching: Mass Media in the Making and Unmaking of the New Left*. Berkeley: University of California Press, 1980.

Goodman, Mitchell, ed. *The Movement Toward a New America*. New York: Knopf, 1970.

Gornick, Vivian, and Barbara Moran, eds. *Woman in Sexist Society*. New York: Basic Books, 1971.

Gosse, Van. *Where the Boys Are: Cuba, Cold War America, and the Making of a New Left*. London: Verso, 1993.

Graham, Gael. "Flaunting the Freak Flag: *Karr v. Schmidt* and the Great Hair Debate in American High Schools, 1965–1975." *Journal of American History* 91.2 (September 2004): 522–43.

Hamill, Pete. "Wallace." In *"Takin' It to the Streets": A Sixties Reader*, edited by Alexander Bloom and Winifred Breines, 300–302. 2nd ed. New York: Oxford University Press, 2003.

Hamilton, Charles V. "How Black Is Black?" In *The Black Revolution: An Ebony Special Issue*, 23–29. Chicago: Johnson, 1970.

Hamilton, Linda. "On Cultural Nationalism." In *The Black Panthers Speak*, edited by Philip S. Foner, 151–54. New York: Da Capo Press, 1995. First published 1970.

Harrison, Cynthia. *On Account of Sex: The Politics of Women's Issues, 1945–1968*. Berkeley: University of California Press, 1988.

Hartman, Susan M. "Prescriptions for Penelope: Women's Obligations to World War II Veterans." *Women's Studies* 5 (1978): 223–40.

Heilbrun, Carolyn G. *Toward a Recognition of Androgyny*. New York: Knopf, 1973.

Hekma, Gert. "'A Female Soul in a Male Body': Sexual Inversion as Gender Inversion in Nineteenth-Century Sexology." In *Third Sex, Third Gender: Beyond Sexual Dimorphism in Culture and History*, edited by Gilbert Herdt, 213–39. New York: Zone Books, 1994.

Hewitt, Nancy A., ed. *No Permanent Waves: Recasting Histories of U.S. Feminism*. New Brunswick: Rutgers University Press, 2010.

Hodgdon, Tim. *Manhood in the Age of Aquarius: Masculinity in Two Countercultural Communities, 1965–83*. New York: Columbia University Press, 2008.

Hoffman, Abbie. *Revolution for the Hell of It*. New York: Dial Press, 1968.

Hollander, Anne. *Sex and Suits: The Evolution of Modern Dress*. New York: Knopf, 1994.

Hunt, Andrew E. *The Turning: A History of Vietnam Veterans Against the War*. New York: New York University Press, 1999.

Isserman, Maurice, and Michael Kazin. *America Divided: The Civil War of the 1960s*. New York: Oxford University Press, 2000.

Jacobs, Ron. *The Ways the Wind Blew: A History of the Weather Underground*. London: Verso, 1997.

James, David E. "'The Movies Are a Revolution': Film and the Counterculture." In *Imagine Nation: The American Counterculture of the 1960s and '70s*, edited by Peter Braunstein and Michael William Doyle, 275–303. New York: Routledge, 2002.

———. *Tales of the Lavender Menace: A Memoir of Liberation*. New York: Basic Books, 1999.

Jay, Karla, and Allen Young, eds. *Out of the Closets: Voices of Gay Liberation*. New York: New York University Press, 1992. First published 1972.

Jeffords, Susan. *The Remasculinization of America: Gender and the Vietnam War*. Bloomington: Indiana University Press, 1989.

Johnson, David K. "The Kids of Fairytown: Gay Male Culture on Chicago's Near North Side in the 1930s." In *Creating a Place for Ourselves: Lesbian, Gay and Bisexual Community Histories*, edited by Brett Beemyn, 97–118. New York: Routledge, 1997.

———. *The Lavender Scare: The Cold War Persecution of Gays and Lesbians in the Federal Government*. Chicago: University of Chicago Press, 2004.

Jones, Charles E., ed. *The Black Panther Party Reconsidered*. Baltimore: Black Classic Press, 1998.

Joseph, Peniel E., ed. *The Black Power Movement: Rethinking the Civil Rights–Black Power Era*. New York: Routledge, 2006.

Kaiser, Charles. *1968 in America: Music, Politics, Chaos, Counterculture, and the Shaping of a Generation*. New York: Weidenfeld and Nicolson, 1988.

Kaminski, Theresa. "From Personal to Public: Women's Liberation and the Print Media in the United States, 1968–1974." PhD diss., University of Illinois at Urbana–Champaign, 1992.

Katz, Lawrence Allen. "Personal Appearance Regulations in Public Contract Jobs Under Title VII of the Civil Rights Act of 1964." *Arizona State Law Journal* 1976, no. 1 (1976): 1–23.

Kelley, Robin D. G. "Nap Time: Historicizing the Afro." *Fashion Theory* 1.4 (December 1997): 339–51.

Kennedy, Elizabeth Lapovsky, and Madeline Davis. *Boots of Leather, Slippers of Gold: The History of a Lesbian Community*. New York: Routledge, 1993.

Kessler-Harris, Alice. *In Pursuit of Equity: Women, Men, and the Quest for Economic Citizenship in 20th-Century America*. New York: Oxford University Press, 2001.

Kidwell, Claudia Brush, and Valerie Steele. *Men and Women: Dressing the Part*. Washington DC: Smithsonian Institution Press, 1989.

Kissack, Terrance. "Freaking Fag Revolutionaries: New York's Gay Liberation Front, 1969–1971." *Radical History Review* 62 (1995): 104–34.

Klarman, Michael J. "Backlash." Paper presented at The Future of Sexual and Reproductive Rights, Yale Law School, New Haven CT, October 11, 2008.

———. "How Brown Changed Race Relations: The Backlash Thesis." *Journal of American History* 81.1 (June 1994): 81–118.

Kreydatus, Beth. "Marketing to the 'Liberated' Woman: Feminism, Social Change, and Beauty Culture." PhD diss., College of William and Mary, 2005.

Kruse, Kevin. *White Flight: Atlanta and the Making of Modern Conservatism*. Princeton NJ: Princeton University Press, 2007.

Larner, Jeremy. *Nobody Knows: Reflections on the McCarthy Campaign of 1968*. New York: Macmillan, 1969.

Lassiter, Matthew. *The Silent Majority: Suburban Politics in the Sunbelt South*. Princeton NJ: Princeton University Press, 2006.

Levi, Jennifer L. "The Interplay between Disability and Sexuality: Clothes Don't Make the Man (or Woman), But Gender Identity Might." *Columbia Journal of Gender and Law* 15 (2006): 90–113.

———. "Misapplying Equality Theories: Dress Codes at Work." *Yale Journal of Law and Feminism* 19 (2008): 353–90.

———. "Some Modest Proposals for Challenging Established Dress Code Jurisprudence." *Duke Journal of Gender Law and Policy* 14 (January 2007): 243–55.

Levine, Martin P. *Gay Macho: The Life and Death of the Homosexual Clone*. New York: New York University Press, 1998.

Levy, Peter B., ed. *America in the Sixties—Right, Left, and Center*. Westport CT: Greenwood Press, 1998.

Lekus, Ian. "Queer Harvests: Homosexuality, the U.S. New Left, and the Venceremos Brigades to Cuba." *Radical History Review* 89 (Spring 2004): 57–91.

Lemke-Santangelo, Gretchen. *Daughters of Aquarius: Women of the Sixties Counterculture*. Lawrence: University Press of Kansas, 2009.

Lieberman, Robbie, ed. *Prairie Power: Voices of 1960s Midwestern Student Protest*. Columbia: University of Missouri Press, 2004.

Ling, Peter J., and Sharon Monteith, eds. *Gender and the Civil Rights Movement*. New York: Garland, 1999.

Lipsitz, George. "Who'll Stop the Rain? Youth Culture, Rock 'n' Roll, and Social Crises." In *The Sixties: From Memory to History*, edited by David Farber, 206–34. Chapel Hill: University of North Carolina Press, 1994.

Luther Hillman, Betty. "'The Clothes I Wear Help Me to Know My Own Power': The Politics of Gender Presentation in the Era of Women's Liberation." *Frontiers: A Journal of Women Studies* 34.2 (2013): 155–85.

———. "'The Most Profoundly Revolutionary Act a Homosexual Can Engage In': Drag and the Politics of Gender Presentation in the San Francisco Gay Liberation Movement, 1964–1972." *Journal of the History of Sexuality* 20.1 (January 2011): 153–81.

Lytle, Mark. *America's Uncivil Wars: The Sixties from Elvis to the Fall of Richard Nixon*. New York: Oxford University Press, 2006.

Malcolm X. *The Autobiography of Malcolm X*, with the assistance of Alex Haley. New York: Grove Press, 1964.

———. "Not Just an American Problem but a World Problem." In *Malcolm X: The Last Speeches*, edited by Bruce Perry, 151–81. London: Owen, 1969.

Marcus, Eric. *Making Gay History: The Half-Century Fight for Lesbian and Gay Equal Rights*. New York: Harper Perennial, 2002.

Marotta, Toby. *The Politics of Homosexuality*. Boston: Houghton Mifflin, 1981.

Martin, Del, and Phyllis Lyon. *Lesbian/Woman*. San Francisco: Glide, 1972.

Martin, William C. *With God on Our Side: The Rise of the Religious Right in America*. New York: Broadway Books, 1996.

May, Elaine Tyler. *Homeward Bound: American Families in the Cold War Era*. New York: Basic Books, 1988.

McGarry, Molly, and Fred Wasserman. *Becoming Visible: An Illustrated History of Lesbian and Gay Life in Twentieth-Century America*. New York: New York Public Library, 1998.

McGirr, Lisa. *Suburban Warriors: The Origins of the New American Right*. Princeton NJ: Princeton University Press, 2001.

Mead, Margaret. *Male and Female: A Study of the Sexes in a Changing World*. New York: William Morrow, 1949.

Meeker, Martin. *Contacts Desired: Gay and Lesbian Communications and Community, 1940s–1970s*. Chicago: University of Chicago Press, 2006.

Melinkoff, Ellen. *What We Wore: An Offbeat Social History of Women's Clothing, 1950 to 1980*. New York: Quill, 1984.

Members of the Gay and Lesbian Historical Society of Northern California. "MTF Transgender Activism in the Tenderloin and Beyond, 1966–1975." *GLQ: A Journal of Gay and Lesbian Studies* 4.2 (1998): 349–72.

Meyerowitz, Joanne. *How Sex Changed: A History of Transsexuality in the United States*. Cambridge: Harvard University Press, 2002.

————, ed. *Not June Cleaver: Women and Gender in Postwar America, 1945–1960.* Philadelphia: Temple University Press, 1994.

————. "Sex Change and the Popular Press: Historical Notes on Transsexuality in the United States, 1930–1955." *GLQ: A Journal of Lesbian and Gay Studies* 4 (1998): 159–88.

Miller, James. *Democracy Is in the Streets: From Port Huron to the Siege of Chicago.* Cambridge: Harvard University Press, 1984.

Miller, Timothy. *The Hippies and American Values.* Knoxville: University of Tennessee Press, 1991.

Money, John, Joan G. Hampson, and John L. Hampson. "Hermaphroditism: Recommendations Concerning Assignment of Sex, Change of Sex, and Psychologic Management." *Bulletin of The Johns Hopkins Hospital* 97 (1955): 284–300.

Monterey Pop. DVD. Directed by D. A. Pennebaker. 1968. Santa Monica CA: Criterion, 2006.

Morris, Jeffrey Brandon. *Establishing Justice in Middle America: A History of the United States Court of Appeals for the Eighth Circuit.* Minneapolis: University of Minnesota Press, 2007.

Morrison, Joan, and Robert K. Morrison, eds. *From Camelot to Kent State: The Sixties Experience in the Words of Those Who Lived It.* New York: Times Books, 1987.

Myers, Elizabeth A. "Burning Bras, Long Hairs, and Dashikis: Personal Politics in American Culture, 1950–1975." PhD diss., Loyola University Chicago, 2006.

Myers, R. David, ed. *Toward A History of the New Left: Essays from within the Movement.* Brooklyn: Carlson, 1989.

Myron, Nancy, and Charlotte Bunch, eds. *Lesbianism and the Women's Movement.* Baltimore: Diana Press, 1975.

Nestle, Joan, ed. *The Persistent Desire: A Butch-Femme Reader.* Boston: Alyson, 1992.

New York Radical Women. "No More Miss America." In *Dear Sisters: Dispatches from the Women's Liberation Movement*, edited by Rosalyn Baxandall and Linda Gordon, 184–85. New York: Basic Books, 2000. First published 1968.

Newton, Esther. "The Mythic Mannish Lesbian: Radclyffe Hall and the New Woman." *Signs* 9.4 (Summer 1984): 557–75.

Nicolaides, Becky M. *My Blue Heaven: Life and Politics in the Working-Class Suburbs of Los Angeles, 1920–1965.* Chicago: University of Chicago Press, 2002.

Novak, Michael. "Why Wallace?" In *"Takin' It to the Streets": A Sixties Reader*, edited by Alexander Bloom and Winifred Breines, 302–4. 2nd ed. New York: Oxford University Press, 2003.

Odenwald, Robert P. *The Disappearing Sexes*. New York: Random House, 1965.

Ogbar, Jeffrey O. G. *Black Power: Radical Politics and African American Identity*. Baltimore: Johns Hopkins University Press, 2004.

Oropeza, Lorena. *Raza, Si! Guerra, No! Chicano Protest and Patriotism during the Viet Nam War*. Berkeley: University of California Press, 2005.

Parkins, Wendy, ed. *Fashioning the Body Politic: Dress, Gender, Citizenship*. Oxford: Berg, 2002.

Peiss, Kathy. *Hope in a Jar: The Making of America's Beauty Culture*. New York: Metropolitan Books, 1998.

Perlstein, Rick. *Before the Storm: Barry Goldwater and the Unmaking of the American Consensus*. New York: Hill and Wang, 2001.

———. *Nixonland: The Rise of a President and the Fracturing of America*. New York: Scribner, 2008.

Perry, Bruce, ed. *Malcolm X: The Last Speeches*. London: Owen, 1969.

Perry, Charles. *Haight-Ashbury: A History*. New York: Random House, 1984.

Phillips-Fein, Kim. *Invisible Hands: The Making of the Conservative Movement from the New Deal to Reagan*. New York: W. W. Norton, 2009.

Pitzulo, Carrie. "The Battle in Every Man's Bed: *Playboy* and the Fiery Feminists." *Journal of the History of Sexuality* 17.2 (May 2008): 259–89.

Post, Robert. "Prejudicial Appearances: The Logic of American Antidiscrimination Law." *California Law Review* 88 (January 2000): 1–40.

Pulido, Laura. *Black, Brown, Yellow and Left: Radical Activism in Los Angeles*. Berkeley: University of California Press, 2006.

The Question of Equality, Part 1: Out Rage '69. DVD. Directed by Arthur Dong. San Francisco: KQED Video, 1995.

Reid, Coletta. "Coming Out in the Women's Movement." In *Lesbianism and the Women's Movement*, edited by Nancy Myron and Charlotte Bunch, 91–103. Baltimore: Diana Press, 1975.

Reiter, Rayna. *Towards an Anthropology of Women*. New York and London: Monthly Review Press, 1975.

Retzloff, Tim. "Eliding Trans Latino/a Queer Experience in U.S. LGBT History: José Sarria and Sylvia Rivera Reexamined." *Centro Journal* 19.1 (Spring 2007): 140–61.

Risen, James, and Judy L. Thomas. *Wrath of Angels: The American Abortion War*. New York: Basic Books, 1998.

Rising, George. *Clean for Gene: Eugene McCarthy's 1968 Presidential Campaign*. Westport CT: Praeger, 1997.

Rosen, Ruth. *The World Split Open: How the Modern Women's Movement Changed America*. New York: Viking, 2000.

Rossinow, Doug. *The Politics of Authenticity: Liberalism, Christianity, and the New Left in America.* New York: Columbia University Press, 1998.

———. "The Revolution Is About Our Lives: The New Left's Counterculture." In *Imagine Nation: The American Counterculture of the 1960s and '70s,* edited by Peter Braunstein and Michael William Doyle, 99–124. New York: Routledge, 2002.

Rubin, Isadore. "Book Review of *The New People: Desexualization in American Life.*" *Annals of the American Academy of Political and Social Science* 380 (November 1968): 225.

Rubin, Jerry. *Do It!* New York: Simon and Schuster, 1970.

Rubinstein, Ruth. *Dress Codes: Meanings and Messages in American Culture.* Boulder: Westview Press, 1995.

Rupp, Leila, and Verta Taylor. *Survival in the Doldrums: The American Women's Rights Movement, 1945 to the 1960s.* New York: Oxford University Press, 1987.

Schlafly, Phyllis. "What's Wrong with 'Equal Rights' for Women?" In *America in the Sixties—Right, Left, and Center,* edited by Peter Levy, 221–28. Westport CT: Greenwood Press, 1998.

Schrecker, Ellen. *Many Are the Crimes: McCarthyism in America.* New York: Little, Brown, 1998.

Schulman, Bruce J. *The Seventies: The Great Shift in American Culture, Society, and Politics.* New York: Free Press, 2001.

Scranton, Phillip, ed. *Beauty and Business: Commerce, Gender, and Culture in Modern America.* New York: Routledge, 2001.

Scott, Linda M. *Fresh Lipstick: Redressing Fashion and Feminism.* New York: Palgrave Macmillan, 2005.

Screaming Queens: The Riot at Compton's Cafeteria. DVD. Directed by Victor Silverman and Susan Stryker. San Francisco: Frameline Distribution, 2005.

Self, Robert O. *All in the Family: The Realignment of American Democracy Since the 1960s.* New York: Hill and Wang, 2012.

———. *American Babylon: Race and the Struggle for Postwar Oakland.* Princeton NJ: Princeton University Press, 2003.

Shilts, Randy. *And the Band Played On: Politics, People, and the AIDS Epidemic.* New York: St. Martin's Press, 1987.

Simmons, Christina. "Companionate Marriage and the Lesbian Threat." *Frontiers* 4.3 (1979): 54–59.

Smith, Desire. *Fashionable Clothing from the Sears Catalogs: Early 1970s.* Atglen PA: Schiffer, 1998.

Smith-Rosenberg, Carroll. *Disorderly Conduct: Visions of Gender in Victorian America.* New York: Knopf, 1985.

Solinger, Rickie. *Wake Up Little Susie: Single Pregnancy and Race Before Roe v. Wade*. New York: Routledge, 1992.

Spigel, Lynn. *Make Room for TV: Television and the Family Ideal in Postwar America*. Chicago: University of Chicago Press, 1992.

Spruill, Marjorie J. "Gender and America's Right Turn." In *Rightward Bound: Making America Conservative in the 1970s*, edited by Bruce J. Schulman and Julian E. Zelizer, 71–88. Cambridge: Harvard University Press, 2008.

Stacewicz, Richard. *Winter Soldiers: An Oral History of Vietnam Veterans Against the War*. New York: Twayne, 1997.

"Stamp Out High Heels." In *Dear Sisters: Dispatches from the Women's Liberation Movement*, edited by Rosalyn Baxandall and Linda Gordon, 40. New York: Basic Books, 2000.

Stark, Rodney. *Police Riots: Collective Violence and Law Enforcement*. Belmont CA: Focus Books, 1972.

Stavis, Ben. *We Were the Campaign: New Hampshire to Chicago for McCarthy*. Boston: Beacon Press, 1969.

Steele, Valerie. *Fashion and Eroticism: Ideals of Feminine Beauty from the Victorian Era to the Jazz Age*. New York: Oxford University Press, 1985.

Stein, Arlene. *Sex and Sensibility: Stories of a Lesbian Generation*. Berkeley: University of California Press, 1997.

Stein, Marc. *City of Sisterly and Brotherly Loves: Lesbian and Gay Philadelphia, 1945–1972*. Chicago: University of Chicago Press, 2000.

Storm, Penny. *Functions of Dress: Tool of Culture and the Individual*. Englewood Cliffs NJ: Prentice Hall, 1987.

Stout, Richard T. *People*. New York: Harper and Row, 1970.

Sugrue, Thomas. *The Origins of the Urban Crisis: Race and Inequality in Postwar Detroit*. Princeton NJ: Princeton University Press, 1996.

Sullivan, James. *Jeans: A Cultural History of an American Icon*. New York: Gotham Books, 2006.

Suran, Justin. "Coming Out Against the War: Antimilitarism and the Politicization of Homosexuality in the Era of Vietnam." *American Quarterly* 53.3 (September 2001): 452–88.

Takaki, Ronald. *Double Victory: A Multicultural History of America in World War II*. Boston: Little, Brown, 2000.

Teal, Donn. *The Gay Militants*. New York: Stein and Day, 1971.

Tyson, Timothy B. *Radio Free Dixie: Robert F. Williams and the Roots of Black Power*. Chapel Hill: University of North Carolina Press, 1999.

Umansky, Lauri. *Motherhood Reconceived: Feminism and the Legacy of the Sixties*. New York: New York University Press, 1996.

Van Deburg, William L. *A New Day in Babylon: The Black Power Movement in American Culture, 1965–1975.* Chicago: University of Chicago Press, 1992.

Walker, Daniel. *Rights in Conflict: The Violent Confrontation of Demonstrators and Police in the Parks and Streets of Chicago during the Week of the Democratic National Convention of 1968.* New York: Bantam Books, 1968.

Walker, Susannah . "Black Is Profitable: The Commodification of the Afro, 1960–1975." In *Beauty and Business: Commerce, Gender, and Culture in Modern America*, edited by Phillip Scranton, 254–77. New York: Routledge, 2001.

Wallace, Michele. "A Black Feminist's Search for Sisterhood." In *All of the Women Are White, All the Blacks Are Men, But Some of Us Are Brave: Black Women's Studies*, edited by Gloria T. Hull, Patricia Bell Scott, and Barbara Smith, 5–12. Old Westbury NY: The Feminist Press, 1982.

Weiss, Jessica. *To Have and to Hold: Marriage, the Baby Boom, and Social Change.* Chicago: University of Chicago Press, 2000.

Weisstein, Naomi, and Heather Booth. "Will the Women's Movement Survive?" *Sister* 4.12 (December 1975).

Whisner, Mary. "Gender-Specific Clothing Regulation: A Study in Patriarchy." *Harvard Women's Law Journal* 5 (1982): 73–120.

Williamson, Erica. "Moving Past Hippies and Harassment: A Historical Approach to Sex, Appearance, and the Workplace." *Duke Law Journal* 56 (November 2006): 681–721.

Willis, Ellen. "Women and the Myth of Consumerism." In *Dear Sisters: Dispatches from the Women's Liberation Movement*, edited by Rosalyn Baxandall and Linda Gordon, 288–90. New York: Basic Books, 2000. First published 1969.

Wilson, Elizabeth. *Adorned in Dreams: Fashion and Modernity.* Berkeley: University of California Press, 1985.

Winick, Charles. *The New People: Desexualization in American Life.* New York: Pegasus, 1968.

Young, Ralph F., ed. *Dissent in America: The Voices That Shaped a Nation.* New York: Pearson, 2006.

INDEX

Italicized page numbers indicate illustrations.

beards (*cont.*)

image, 120; and political drag, *101*,
92, 99–102; and workplace grooming, 158–59, 161, 175, 187. *See also*
facial hair; mustaches

The Beatles, xxi, 5–7, 10

Beatty, Warren, 135. See also *Shampoo*

Beautify America: Get a Haircut, 13

bell-bottom pants, xv, 18, 21–22, 24, 155

Benton, Nick, 110. *See also* effeminists

Berkeley Gay Liberation Front. *See*
Gay Liberation Front (GLF)

Berkeley Gay Women's Liberation, 80

Berlandt, Konstantin, 100

Bertelston, David, 102

birth control pill, 3, 16, 20, 84. *See also*
sexual revolution

Black, Joe, 39. *See also* Greyhound
Corporation

Black Panther Party. *See* Black
Panthers

Black Panthers, 35, 40, 103, 145, 148

Black Power. *See* Black Power
movement

Black Power movement, xvi, xx, xxi,
32, 34–42, 47, 54, 78, 95, 102–3, 125,
145–48

Booth, Heather, 83

Booth, Paul, 53

Bowie, David, 150

Boyce v. Safeway Stores, 173, 178

Brewster, Lee, 111, 115. *See also* Queens
Liberation Front

Brien McMahon High School, 1, 3, 13

Brown, James, 155

Brown, Patrick, 95

Bryant, Anita, 93, 112, 116–17, 118, 121, 188

Bujel v. Borman Food Stores, 176

Buren, Abigail Van, 132

Burroughs, Margaret, 34

butch styles, 77, 79–80, 82, 151. *See also*
dyke uniform; lesbians

Byrd, Ayana, 148

Carmichael, Stokely, 37, 44

*Carroll v. Talman Federal Savings and
Loan Association*, 183–84

Carter, Dan, 54

Cell 16, 76, 84

Chanel, Coco, 18

CHF. *See* Committee for Homosexual
Freedom (CHF)

Chisholm, Shirley, 81

Civil Rights Act of 1964, xxiii, 65, 156,
169, 171, 172, 174, 180, 183. *See also*
Title VII of the Civil Rights Act
of 1964

civil rights movement, xvii, xx, 34–35,
37, 38, 39, 42, 43, 54, 65, 94, 125

Cleaver, Eldridge, 35. *See also* Black
Panthers

Cleaver, Kathleen, 40. *See also* Black
Panthers

Clift Hotel (San Francisco), 123–25

Clinton, Hillary, 88

Coffy, 143

Cohen v. California, 162

Cold War, xxii, 33, 49, 50–51

Committee for Homosexual Freedom
(CHF), 103, 110

Compton, Kevin, 13–14

Congress to Unite Women (1969), 76, 84

Cooper, Alice, 149–50

Cosby, Bill, 144

counterculture. *See* hippies

Country Joe and the Fish, 7

Cowan, Liza, 74

Cowie, Jefferson, 130

crew cut, xxi, 5, 6, 22, 50, 131, 132, 134,
165, 178. *See also* short hair

culture wars, xvi, xx, 2–4, 27–29, 187–89

Dansky, Steve, 110. *See also* effeminists
dashikis, 38, 159. *See also* African fashions
Daughters of Bilitis (DOB), 79, 109, 111
Dave Clark Five, 7
Davidson, Carl, 44
Davis, Angela, vii, 40–41
Davis, Sammy, Jr., 144
Dear Abby, 132
Deevey, Sharon, 73
de la Renta, Oscar, 152
Democratic National Convention, xiv, xvii, 57–59, 125
DOB. *See* Daughters of Bilitis (DOB)
Dodge v. Giant Food Company, 175–76, 178, 181
Donohue v. Shoe Corporation of America, 170–71, 177
drag queens, 82, 93, 102, 104, 105–7, 109–11, 113–14, 116–19. *See also* gender fuck; political drag; street queens; transvestism
Dunbar, Roxanne, 84. *See also* Cell 16
dyke look. *See* dyke uniform
dyke uniform, 72, 79, 80, 82. *See also* butch styles
Dykes and Gorgons, 73, 74

Easy Rider, 126–28, 131
Ed Sullivan Show, 5
EEOC. *See* Equal Employment Opportunity Commission (EEOC)
effeminists, 110–11
Ehrenreich, Barbara, 50
Elliott, Beth, 109
Equal Employment Opportunity Commission (EEOC), 65, 169–70, 182

Equal Rights Amendment (ERA), 63, 86–88, 158, 183–84
ERA. *See* Equal Rights Amendment (ERA)
Evans, Arthur, 108

facial hair, 9, 24, 46, 100, 153, 161–62, 182. *See also* beards; mustaches
Fagan v. National Cash Register Company, 174–75, 177, 178, 181
Farrow, Mia, 22
"fashion feminists," 140–41, 147
FBI. *See* Federal Bureau of Investigation (FBI)
Federal Bureau of Investigation (FBI), 51–52, 59
The Feminine Mystique, 65. *See also* Friedan, Betty
feminism: and drag, 93, 109–11; and femininity, 61–63, 66–80, 82–89; ideologies of, xviii, xx, xxii, 62–68, 70–76, 79, 80, 81, 83, 98; representations in the media, 65, 76, 83–85, 129, 139–41, 143, 153. *See also* lesbian feminism; second-wave feminist movement; women's liberation movement
feminist movement. *See* feminism
First Amendment, xxiii, 164, 225n37. *See also* freedom of expression
Fonda, Peter, 126–27. See also *Easy Rider*
Fouratt, Jim, 100, 113. *See also* Gay Liberation Front (GLF)
Frank, Thomas, 125
freedom of expression, xix, xxi, xxiii, 2, 4, 11–12, 28, 47, 134, 157–58, 161–69, 180, 185. *See also* First Amendment
Freeman, Jo, 70
Freeman, Joshua B., 32

Intro 475, 112–16

Jacobs v. Kunes, 168
Jagger, Mick, 7, 150
Jay, Karla, 97
Jefferson Airplane, 7
Jespersen v. Harrah's Operating Company, 183
Jett, Joan, 150–51
jewelry, 38, 78, 89, 149
Jim Crow laws, xvii
Johnson, Lyndon B., 48, 130, 170, 171.
    See also Great Society programs
Judeo-Christian values, xix, xx

Kameny, Frank, 95
Karenga, Maulanga, 38
Keaton, Diane, 142
Kelley, Robin D. G., 34
Kelley v. Johnson, 166–68
Kennedy, John F., 180, 227n57, 228n73
Kennedy, Robert F., xiv
Kent State, 31, 32
King, Martin Luther, Jr., xiv, xvii
Kinsey, Alfred, 16
Klein, Herbert, 132
Knoebel, John, 110. *See also* effeminists
Kohler, Bob, 110. *See also* Gay Liberation Front (GLF)
Krafft-Ebing, Richard von, 93

Lanigan, Data La Von, 156, 181
Lauren, Ralph, 152
Laurence, Leo, 110. *See also* Committee for Homosexual Freedom (CHF)
lesbian feminism, xxii, 68–70, 71–74, 82, 109, 111, 116
lesbians, xxiii, 73, 76, 77, 78, 79, 80, 93, 109, 111, 117–18
Lincoln, Abbey, 34

long hair: court cases regarding, 163–68, 170–81; on gay activists, 95, 96, 97–98; in high schools, 1–2, 3, 11–13; on male adults, 22–23, 124, 132, *133*, 134–35; on male youths, 6–11, 131; on musicians, 5–6, 7, 149–50; politicization of, 44–51; reactions to, 33, 53–59; representations in popular culture, 126–30; in the workplace, 158–59, 161
Lyon, Phyllis, 79. *See also* Daughters of Bilitis (DOB)

"macho man," 120–22, *121*
makeup: anti-ERA activists and, 87; counterculture rejection of, 46, 65; court decision regarding, 183; drag and, 100, 111, 117; feminist criticism of, xxii, 62, 67–74, 78; feminist embrace of, 75, 78, 79; male musicians and, 151; media promotion of, 20, 40, 84, 147, 149; third-wave feminism and, 89
Malcolm X, 36–37
Mamas and the Papas, 7
Martin, Del, 79, 111. *See also* Daughters of Bilitis (DOB)
Mattachine Society, 94, 95, 114, 211n8.
    See also homophile organizations
May, Elaine Tyler, 16
McCarthy, Eugene, xiii, 56
Mead, Margaret, 70
midiskirt, 136–37, *138*
Miller, Bill, 99. *See also* Gay Liberation Front (GLF)
miniskirts: criticism of, xiii, 1, 4, 15–17, 28, 54–56, 62, 66–67; embrace of, 14, 21, 74, 136–41; hippies and, 46; male musicians and, 150–51; representations in popular culture of, 129; in the workplace, 158–59

Port Huron Statement, xviii, 45, 49.
See also Students for a Democratic
Society (SDS)
Pregerson, Harry, 171, 226n49
Presley, Elvis, 5

QLF. *See* Queens Liberation Front
(QLF)
Quatro, Suzi, 150
Queen, 150
Queens Liberation Front (QLF), 105,
111, 115

Radicalesbians, 70
Ramsey v. Hopkins, 160–61
Reagan, Ronald, 55
Regan, John, 180, 228n73
Reid, Coletta, 71
Reiner, Rob, 129. See also *All in the
Family*
Rivera, Sylvia, 106–7, 111
Roberts v. General Mills, 170, 177
Roe v. Wade, 166, 167
Rogers, John Terry, 155–56
Rolling Stones, 7
Rubin, Jerry, 46, 47, 48
Runaways, 151

Sassoon, Vidal, 22
Schlafly, Phyllis, 63, 86, 87, 188
Schneider v. Ohio Youth Commission, 164
SCLC. *See* Southern Christian Leader-
ship Conference (SCLC)
SDS. *See* Students for a Democratic
Society (SDS)
second-wave feminist movement, 62,
65, 75, 81, 83, 89, 205n9. *See also*
women's liberation movement
Seidenbaum, Art, 139
Self, Robert, 81

sexual revolution, xix, xxi–xxii, 3–4, 15–
16, 33, 67, 126, 135
Shaft, 143
Shampoo, 135–36
Shelley, Martha, 99. *See also* Gay Lib-
eration Front (GLF)
short hair: and black women, 34–35,
40, 147; as feminist style, 61, 71–73,
76, 80; and male respectability, 6,
7–10, 34, 39, 43, 53, 94; as popular
women's style, 4, 13, 20, 22, 24
Silverstein, Mike, 91, 107, 110. *See also*
Gay Liberation Front (GLF)
Simone, Nina, 34
Simpson, John Milton Bryan, 177–
79, 227n70. See also *Willingham v.
Macon Telegraph Company*
SIR. *See* Society for Individual Rights (SIR)
Smith, Patti, 150–51
SNCC. *See* Student Nonviolent Coordi-
nating Committee (SNCC)
Society for Individual Rights (SIR), 94,
97, 100, 101, 105, 108, *121*
Southern Christian Leadership Con-
ference (SCLC), 38
Stanis, Bern Nadette, 146
STAR. *See* Street Transvestite Action
Revolutionaries (STAR)
Stark, Rodney, 57
Steinem, Gloria, 84
Stewart, Rod, 150
Stonewall Inn. *See* Stonewall Rebellion
Stonewall Rebellion, 94, 95, 98, 105,
106, 115
Stop the Draft Week, 56
street queens, 104–8, 110, 119. *See also*
drag queens; gender transgression;
transvestism
Street Transvestite Action Revolution-
aries (STAR), 105

CPSIA information can be obtained at www.ICGtesting.com
Printed in the USA
LVOW07*0420150915

454205LV00009B/183/P